HUGH LATIMER

HUGH LATIMER

BY

HAROLD S. DARBY

WIPF & STOCK · Eugene, Oregon

Wipf and Stock Publishers
199 W 8th Ave, Suite 3
Eugene, OR 97401

Hugh Latimer
By Darby, Harold S.
Copyright©1953 Methodist Publishing - Epworth Press
ISBN 13: 978-1-5326-4346-0
Publication date 11/15/2017
Previously published by Epworth Press, 1953

Contents

3

Foreword

I COUNT it a very real privilege to write a brief foreword to the last book by my friend Harold Darby. It is a deep regret that he did not live to see its publication, but, like all his friends, I am indeed thankful that he was spared to complete the manuscript.

He wrote this life of Hugh Latimer not just because he wanted to write something, but because he felt an urge to work at this particular book. He had an intense admiration for the man of whom he has written.

It was inevitable that, being himself a born preacher, he should speak as a preacher of a preacher. This careful book moves to its climax with steady steps. There is no false emotional hustle, no exaggerated special pleading. We are presented with a living picture of a man—not a stained-glass window saint nor a fanatical reformer, but a man of sturdy faith and passionately sincere convictions, who was, above all things, human!

This book, besides giving us a clearly-defined picture of Hugh Latimer, reveals the personality of the author as preacher, teacher and historian.

Thanks are due to Mrs Darby, who has placed her husband's books at the service of the proof-reader; to the Principal of Handsworth for giving access to the Library; to the Rev. E. Gordon Rupp for many valuable suggestions; and, in particular, to the Rev. J. Dennis Cope, who has read proofs, prepared an Index, and in many ways assisted the completion of the manuscript for publication.

LESLIE F. CHURCH

CHAPTER ONE

Birth and Education

THE PENDULUM has swung far since the days of our grandfathers when the three martyrs at Oxford were looked upon as symbols of a great deliverance wrought once for all. But if the life of Latimer is symbolic of anything, it stands with Wyclif's and Wesley's to demonstrate the power of preaching based on the Bible which touches the hearts and minds of the people.

Of all the men concerned, for selfish or unselfish reasons, with the English Reformation, none was more popular in his own time than Latimer, and none has a greater place in the affection of posterity. His forthright speech still rings from the printed page with the accent of the English countryside, so that a modern reader can feel something of the power which once dominated the court of Edward the Sixth and the vast crowds who gathered to hear him in church or in the open air at St Paul's 'in the shrouds'. Others did as much, perhaps more, to establish the religion which has become typical of English Christianity. Cranmer, in his incomparable liturgical work, has shaped the devotions and thereby the speech of our race. Parker, Latimer's younger contemporary, later ensured that middle way so characteristic of the English Church and people. But Archbishop Parker the average Englishman knows not at all, and Cranmer, apart from the *Prayer Book*, he remembers as a martyr indeed, but one who seemed to vacillate and compromise with men and principles most of the days of his life. With Latimer it is otherwise. What he did is not so apparent and concrete; but what he was endures in the memory of men. Like Queen Elizabeth the First, his greatest pride was that he was 'mere English', of this land, this people, this speech, this destiny. Insular, perhaps. He had no outlook beyond these shores, and certainly never left them. Here was his love and his strenuous life. He loved his brethren, the common people; and they in their turn did not fail to recognize his unbounded spiritual sincerity where so much about them was obviously only veneered with religion.

7   A*

No one today would contend that the English Reformation was solely the achievement of thoroughly spiritual reformers, endowed with the highest gifts and disciplined by the greatness of their responsibility to God. Nor is Henry the Eighth likely to be regarded again as the king Froude admired. Yet even Henry may not have been quite so rapacious, cruel, and completely selfish as some writers would have us think. It is arguable that a man of such unquestionable general sincerity as Latimer would not have been loyal as he was to Henry unless he saw in the king qualities which may have escaped the notice of readers of documents. And at the court of Edward the Sixth, that unhappy, faction-ridden place, no one was more definite in his protests against corruption and selfish ambition as this same preacher of the Gospel, Hugh Latimer.

It was by preaching that he won his first fame in Cambridge. It was as a preacher he did all his best work. On his last day he turned the flames that flared about him in the Town Ditch at Oxford into an unquenchable metaphor. That word about the lighting of the candle which, by God's grace, should never be put out, reveals the man. It is among our memorable sayings like Grenville's last order or Nelson's signal.

Latimer was born about 1485 in a little farmhouse at Thurcaston just outside Leicester. He was named Hugh after his father. There were older brothers, but they died in infancy or youth; and he had six sisters. He grew up familiar with the things of farm and village in that late medieval England which was soon to pass away.

The mark of the country is not in us now as it was among our fathers. It is of little use to employ in London or industrial towns figures of speech which would ring home in a village in Devon or Derbyshire. But when Latimer spoke in London he had audiences who understood all the terms of country life. The grocer and merchant then were not much farther away from the furrow than the ploughman himself. Where others might lose their accent in the clichés of schools and councils, he remained the same recognizable Hugh Latimer of Leicestershire without pretence of camouflage in the presence of kings or courtiers, and equally free from that inverted snobbery which boasts of its original lack of privilege and opportunity in the faces of those who never knew social hardship.

He said at his first preaching [1] before King Edward the Sixth,

My father was a yeoman, and had no lands of his own, only he had a farm of three or four pound by year at the uttermost, and hereupon he tilled so much as kept half a dozen men. He had walk for a hundred sheep; and my mother milked thirty kine. He was able, and did find the king a harness with himself and his horse, while he came to the place that he should receive the king's wages. I can remember that I buckled his harness when he went unto Blackheath field. He kept me to school, or else I had not been able to have preached before the king's majesty now. He married my sisters with five pound, or twenty nobles apiece; so that he brought them up in godliness and fear of God. He kept hospitality for his poor neighbours, and some alms he gave to the poor. And all this he did of the said farm, where he that now hath it payeth sixteen pound by year, or more, and is not able to do anything for his prince, for himself, nor for his children, or give a cup of drink to the poor.

The sting of that paragraph is in the tail, with its devastating comparison between life in Henry the Seventh's time and his grandson's. The picture of the yeoman's holding in the 1490's, however much the light of happy memory may have played upon it, is pleasing, definite, settled. And the preacher has kept well enough in touch with the life of his native village to be able to quote the difference in rent and costs known by his father and the less fortunate man now tilling the same land.

Until he went up to Cambridge Latimer was as much tied to his first neighbourhood as any other boy of the same station. Foxe [2] mentions his precocity and that he was at home until he was four years old when, 'seeing his ready, prompt and sharp wit', his father

purposed to train him up in erudition and knowledge of good literature; wherein he so profited in his youth at the common schools of his own country, that at the age of fourteen years, he was sent to the University of Cambridge.

It is this allusion to his age on entering the University that causes some writers—e.g. Corrie and A. J. Carlyle—to suppose the date of his birth as 1490 or thereabouts. We do not know the precise date. Some of the older writers trade too much upon the references of his contemporaries to his senior position among them. Demaus puts it at 1484–5, and that seems to accord best both with a few reputable pieces of evidence and

[1] *Sermons*, p. 101.   [2] *Acts and Monuments*, VII.437.

with the general sense of deference to him as being considerably
older than his two companions at Oxford in 1554–5. His
servant, Augustine Bernher, is the source of the remark that
in the reign of Edward the Sixth Latimer was 'above sixty-seven
years of age'.[3] If this referred to 1547, the first year of Edward's
reign, it would mean that Latimer was born not later than
1480; if it referred to the last year of his reign, it would put his
birthday not later than 1486.

In the first sermon preached before Edward the Sixth in
1549 we find Latimer calling himself an old man. 'Now in my
old age', he says, in the first paragraph of this sermon, on
8th March 1549; and in the note 'To the Reader' prefacing
the other five sermons of this series (the first seems to have been
published separately) there is the same opinion of him. 'It is
our part, therefore, to pray diligently for his continual health,
and that he may live long among us in a flourishing old age.'
But old age is always relative. Henry the Eighth spoke of
'mine old days' when he was fifty-three!

Latimer's remark that he buckled his father's harness in 1497
for his service to the King at Blackheath, the limit of the
Cornish rebels' march in their protest against Henry the
Seventh's taxation, enables us to visualize him as a boy of
twelve envying his father this adventure.

They were days of unrest, for the sea of English life remained
swollen and threatening long after Henry Tudor had gained
his victory over Richard at Bosworth. Who was to say that the
Wars of the Roses were finished once for all? The pedestrian
labours of Henry the Seventh were continued unremittingly
for upward of twenty years before his son could command
immense, accumulated wealth, and, what was infinitely more
important for the founding of a dynasty, the allegiance and a
very large measure of the affection of the whole realm. This
would be in 1509. In the meantime Latimer was growing up
and learning not only his grammar but the good habits of
military training incident to English life then.

In my time my poor father was as diligent to teach me to shoot, as
to learn me any other thing; and so I think other men did their
children: he taught me how to draw, how to lay my body in my bow,
and not to draw with strength of arms as other nations do, but with
strength of the body: I had my bows bought me, according to my

<hr>

[3] *Acts and Monuments*, p. 463.

age and strength; as I increased in them, so my bows were made bigger and bigger; for men shall never shoot well, except they be brought up in it: it is a goodly art, a wholesome kind of exercise, and much commended in physic.[4]

He never failed to draw upon these memories, and we may be sure it was one of the causes of his popularity in the pulpit.

In his early days, change of a major kind occurred so slowly that customs of grandfathers were followed by their grand-children. It would have seemed incredible to a yeoman in Leicestershire to believe that, within fifty years of the turn of the century, the bells of the great monasteries would be silent which for hundreds of years had spoken not simply of the worship of God, but of the supreme overlordship of the Church. So many who followed the plough or held lands were her vassals in things material as well as spiritual. The Lord Abbot was as great a power in the land in 1485 as any other great territorial magnate. Here in the monastery were per-petuity and unfailing succession of true heirs who would be tenacious of their rights and privileges while the old lay aristo-cracy, the descendants of the feudal lords, were doing them-selves to death as they fought for red or white rose, and oblig-ingly clearing the way for Tudor absolutism.

But the strife of kings or would-be kings touched Latimer's kind not at all. His father went to Blackheath at the call of his king far more unquestioningly than many men in our own day have gone to meet foes whose menace was to the whole civilization of the world. The defeat of his king would probably have made no difference at all to his holding of the farm at Thurcaston or to his prosperity and family happiness.

Yet there was a stir of different kind in Leicestershire, of which one can scarcely doubt that Latimer must have heard. The spiritual restlessness which had found its first voice in Wyclif a hundred years earlier was a feature of the local life. The gossip of farm-hands on the ale-bench on summer even-ings, the talk of women in the churchyard after mass, wisps of idea and doctrine, of opinion and development, verses of Scrip-ture spoken in the mother-tongue—travelled without chron-iclers being able to note their passage. Villages and farmhouses were very isolated. The countryman, tied to the unchanging cycle of the seasons and the crops, is naturally a conservative

[4] *Sermons*, p. 197.

creature. But the social restlessness of the labourers ever since the days of the Black Death had been accompanied by another sort of discontent. If it was largely inarticulate, it was none the less real. Lollardy had a power of creeping and moving, of springing up here or there. Lutterworth, where Wyclif had died in the closing days of 1384, was a dozen miles from the village where Latimer was born a hundred years later. And Leicestershire had remained in all that time one of the countries most favourable to the doctrines Wyclif had proclaimed by word of mouth and pen.

No censorship ever imposed has been able to quell effectively the talk of peasants. Folk who labour in ones and twos in the wide fields have much time for cogitation. We have learned that truth in Europe during years of bitter war and occupation by ruthless enemies who had profited by every kind of inquisition from the past, both secular and spiritual. The early years of the fifteenth century had been given up to as thorough a purging of the countryside as was possible; but it is absurd to think that Latimer could have grown up in Leicestershire with all his instincts and appetites so normal and his robust nature developing in the pursuits of the people, without acquiring some knowledge of that spiritual strife. It had divided families, and brought imprisonment and death to some. Such things cannot be kept out of the reminiscences of old men and the fancies of the young.

The effect produced on ordinary men who were no Lollards cannot, unfortunately, be determined by historical analysis. But a consideration of human nature, and more especially of the English nature, would lead to the supposition that throughout this long period there were many impressed without being convinced, or convinced without being ready to act on their conviction.[5]

But Latimer's family was orthodox. We may judge that to be so from the manner of his upbringing, education, and personal opinions until he was thirty years of age, and he never in his sermons referred to Lollard sympathies in his home. He would assuredly have done so in his passion for those who loved 'the Word of God'. But he did grow up in that countryside and very near the town where, more than anywhere else in England, Wyclif's teachings had permeated the common life of many of the people. Leicester and its neighbourhood had been the scene both of the activities of the first generation of Lollards and of those who sought their repression. Professor G. M. Trevelyan has no doubt of this extensive restlessness:

According to the Leicester monk every second man in those parts was a Lollard. This must not be treated as a statistical fact, but only as a strong expression. Half the population had perhaps been impressed more or less favourably by some of Wyclif's doctrines, but as was proved when the Archbishop visited the diocese, few were ready to break definitely with the Church authorities.[6]

This visitation of Archbishop Courtenay was made to the huge diocese of Lincoln in 1389, both Oxford and Leicestershire, lying within its bounds, the scenes of Wyclif's greatest influence and activity.

The notorious William Swynderby had preached here, and here William Smith and his companion had committed the outrage of chopping up an image of St Katherine to cook cabbages, which was too much, as Gairdner remarks, 'even for local feeling . . . in a place which had hitherto been a hotbed of Lollardy'.[7]

The similarity in name reminds one that Sir Thomas Latimer —a local knight—was a powerful sympathizer with Lollards, but no discoverable link exists between the fifteenth-century magnate and the Tudor preacher. As a boy he would hear much talk of these disputations, for they were, after all, something more than 'old, forgotten far-off things'. Agricultural unrest, to choose no higher ground for debate, was something which affected the life and conversation of every yeoman's household. There was a close connexion between the 'poor preachers' and the men who drove the plough and herded swine, as there would be again when Independency throve in the seventeenth century or when Methodism bred men like the Tolpuddle martyrs in the nineteenth.

Thus the ideas of Luther and Latimer did not come to Englishmen in all the shocking violence of novelty since here the doctrines of Lollardy had been common talk ever since 1380.[8]

When, however, we see Latimer stride on to the stage of English public life, it is as a conservative partisan, a very

[6] ibid., p. 317.   [7] *Lollardy and the Reformation in England*, I.83.
[8] Trevelyan, op cit., p. 351.

convinced, passionate partisan, as eager as his young king, Henry the Eighth, to assert the full Catholic belief.

But how much do we know, and what can we summon from our knowledge of those times to fill out the bare outline of his transition from a boyhood, happy in the tasks and pastimes of the countryside, though apparently not blessed with great physical strength, to his appearance as the clerical don, bearer of the silver cross in university processions in 1522-3?

Of his schooldays we know nothing. Foxe's remark that he 'profited in his youth at the common schools of his own country' gives us no clue beyond assuring us that he was with other boys and not under private tuition. This is what we would expect. Even the sons of the nobility were beginning to sit on the benches of the grammar schools with the sons of neighbouring yeomen, though where a private chaplain was maintained he would be the natural instructor of the youth of the big houses. Eton and Winchester had not yet fully acquired the prestige which was soon to be theirs, and the general route to the university lay through the local school.

With all its faults and disturbances, the fifteenth century was one in which local education extended its influence, and there was an increase in the number of boys who would be scholars without aspiring to the Church. Yet the obvious career for a clever boy whose father was only a yeoman would still be in her service. The son of a butcher at Ipswich would presently dazzle the eyes of even that show-loving age as he rivalled his own monarch in his newly-built Hampton Court. Wolsey was only the last of a large number of Englishmen who could never have climbed high in the social or political sphere without taking orders. When Latimer was a boy, the newer possibilities of advancement without clerical service would not be known in Leicestershire. The schools which grounded their pupils in Latin, not only the language of the Church but of diplomacy and all learned intercourse, were not so few as we have been apt to imagine. 'Grammar schools were not, as used to be thought, the result of the English Reformation: they were its cause.'[9] For it was here that an ever-increasing proportion of the English people acquired the literacy without which advance was impossible. Apparently Latimer was as

---

[9] Trevelyan, *English Social History*, p. 75, and A. F. Leach's *The Schools of Medieval England*.

much the subject of family gossip as other boys who have left a village for the larger world. He gives an amusing sidelight of it in one of his sermons.[10]

We are on surer ground regarding his time at the University. If we do not know with precision who were his friends as an undergraduate, we can at least picture the scene of his life with fair knowledge of the occupations in work and play of his contemporaries.

There is an old tradition (Fuller believed it) that he went up to Christ's College, but it cannot be substantiated. His connexion with Clare Hall, from the time of his being appointed a Fellow in February 1510, is thoroughly authenticated. He was elected with John Powel and William Pyndar, who had both taken their degrees of Bachelor of Arts, whereas Latimer was Quaestionista.[11] A quaestionista was a man who had kept his twelve full terms at Cambridge, the number then required for qualifying for the B.A. degree, and was about to proceed to the degree.

We have seen that Foxe stated he was fourteen years of age on going up to the University, and that, if he was born, as we think, in 1485, this must be inaccurate. What was the average age of freshmen in the universities at this time? It is not now held generally, as it was formerly, that all undergraduates on admission were mere boys, the counterpart in age of those we find today in the lower forms of a public school. Professor G. M. Trevelyan, writing of the late fourteenth century (and there was no appreciable change of custom between that period and the early sixteenth century) remarks of the students: 'Some were only fourteen years old, but most were of an age rather more nearly resembling that of modern undergraduates.'[12]

Migration from one college to another was not encouraged, and the point is worth making that Latimer was elected to his fellowship at Clare before he had actually taken his first degree. One could understand such an election from the junior members of the same college more readily than from a different one.

What was the average time-table of an undergraduate in these years?

The universities had declined in both the numbers of their

<hr/>

[10] *Sermons*, p. 499.   [11] *Register of Clare Hall*, 1509–10.
[12] *English Social History*, p. 54; cf. Becon's *Works*, II.424–5: 'I was sometime a poor scholar of Cambridge. . . . I was but a child of 16 years.'

undergraduates and the influence of their seniors. The heyday of learning, when the roads were thronged with poor scholars wending their way to Paris, Bologna, Oxford, had long passed. And although the number of halls was still considerable as compared with the newer and wealthier collegiate foundations, these private halls were not crowded as they were in Wyclif's Oxford. But these early years of the sixteenth century were of the utmost importance so far as the development of Cambridge was concerned. Now, for the first time, the younger University drew level with Oxford. In a few years' time Cambridge men —Cranmer, Ridley, Latimer, Parker, and many others—would take a prominent position in the affairs of the Church and nation. Oxford would fall behind, more conservative, and also perhaps more spent, for the penalties laid upon her as the mother of Wyclif brought reactions which could not be overcome in a few years. Cambridge writers have naturally taken some pride in this growth of their University. G. M. Trevelyan has said:

Though Church and State had in 1382 successfully purged the older university of Wycliffism, it was still suspect of heresy in the minds of pious parents choosing a University. Partly for this reason the number of Oxford students fell, and the number of Cambridge students rose during the next hundred years, and royal patronage was turned to the foundation of Colleges on the banks of the hitherto neglected Cam. By the end of the Century a high proportion of Bishops were Cambridge men.[13]

Was there some such pious fear in the mind of old Hugh Latimer which prompted him to send the future reformer to Cambridge? Perhaps it was a more calculating wisdom which favoured the flowing tide of fortune. Most probably it was a mere chance, that a schoolmaster from Cambridge had instructed his boy in 'the common schools', or that a local parson had once advised him. It is, to this day, such chances which affect the entry of men at one or other of the two older universities. But whatever the reason, there can be no doubt of the way in which the fortunes of Cambridge were rising. It is shown, in a very tangible way, by the fact that in the year 1500 nine out of the twenty bishoprics were occupied by men educated at the younger University.

Yet it cannot be claimed that this brisker life was due to a

---

[13] *English Social History*, p. 78.

generally more eager intellectual temper and appetite. Indeed there were signs of revival at Oxford before Cambridge had honoured herself by admitting Erasmus as a teacher. Colet had begun to deliver his epoch-making lectures on the New Testament at Oxford [14] in 1496, and would presently invite Erasmus to be responsible for the Old Testament, an invitation which did not succeed in anchoring him to Oxford since he was bent upon further pursuit of Greek on the Continent.

Latimer would be a freshman at Cambridge when, on 22nd April 1506 Henry the Seventh visited the University *en route* for Walsingham, accompanied by his mother, the Lady Margaret, Countess of Richmond, the patroness of Divinity, and recently the foundress of Christ's College. John Fisher, Bishop of Rochester, who had won her interest for learning when her confessor, was himself the Chancellor of the University.

The University and the Mayor and his bredern met him two or three mile out of the Towne. Within a quarter of a mile ther stode first all the four Ordres of Freres and other religious and ther stode all the graduatts after their degrees in all their Habits and at the end of them was the University Cross wher was a form and a Cushion as accustomed wher the King did alight and then the Bishop of Rochester, Dr Fisher then being Chancellor of the Universitie accompanied with odir Doctors sensyd [censed] the Kyng and afterwards made a little Proposition.[15]

There was much to lament concerning the state of the University, if we are to judge by the Chancellor's remarks when preaching before the King. He was puzzled by the apathy which had befallen the place. He was not sure whether to blame town or gown, but the strife between them was bitter, fever had taken its toll, and there were too few patrons who would send up promising students; but whatever the cause, 'doubtless there had stolen over wellnigh all of us a weariness of learning and of study'.[16]

In the same year Erasmus was given the degree of Doctor of Divinity at Cambridge but did not take up his permanent residence there until 1511, and then he remained for three years. We know—for he was prolific in pouring out his disappointments—that the response to his efforts to promote Greek

[14] Seebohm, *The Oxford Reformers*, p. 4.
[15] Baker's MSS, quoted in J. C. Sorley's *Kings' Daughters*, p. 238.
[16] Fisher's *English Works* (E.E.T.S.).

studies in the University was bitterly discouraging. There is no sign at all that Latimer and his immediate friends were impressed by his presence, though they must have been aware of the little Dutchman's residence in Queens'. Latimer knew no Greek, and the spirit of humanism, of which Erasmus was the embodiment, made no appeal to him in these formative years. 'It is a sign of the state of the University that he (Erasmus) found it no use to lecture on anything more advanced than grammar. The Schoolmen were still strongly entrenched.' [17]

There would presently be some troubling of these sluggish waters, and Latimer would discover the University to be for a time the right place for his energetic, awakened self. His conversion would then direct him into new channels with a power which found the days too short, human strength too little, and academic conservatism too narrow for what he must attempt or be disloyal to the grace of God which had come to him.

We can picture with some accuracy the day of an undergraduate in those last years of Henry the Seventh.[18] Men rose betimes for chapel from five to six. Lectures began at six o'clock and went on till dinner-time which was at ten. After dinner there was leisure for an hour or more, and then work was resumed until five when supper would be eaten. After supper, more work until eight or nine o'clock. This evening work commonly consisted, in part at least, of repeating what had been learned earlier in the day. One of the major differences between the life of the modern undergraduate and that of his Tudor predecessor was due to the rarity of books and the dependence upon oral teaching. If it seems impossible that young men should apply themselves diligently to study for so many hours a day, we must take into account the greater wordiness of the teaching, its more conversational and argumentative character, which would consort better with the sheer effort of memory necessary for its retention. We have learned so much to rely upon notes and text-books that we are perhaps apt to be impatient of the slower pace at which earlier generations of students worked, as well as incredulous of their feats of memory. But, lest it should seem that this time-table is impossibly rigorous, account must be taken of the fact that

[17] P. S. Allen, *The Age of Erasmus*, p. 138.
[18] Rashdall, *Medieval Universities*, Chap. 14.

there was an average of fifty holydays (which were really holidays) in the academic year.

Food in hall has always been a subject of mirthful contempt, but with far less justice today than then. Lever, preaching at Paul's Cross in 1550, described a typical dinner for Cambridge students as being only 'a penny piece of beef amongst four, with broth and oatmeal', while supper was 'not much better than their dinner'. The all-filling potato was yet to come! Artificial light—candles—was more costly than food, and it has taken war in Europe to give us some faint understanding of the continual cold to which our forefathers were subject. Lever's reminiscence [19] that scholars 'being without fire are fain to walk or run up and down half an hour to get a heat on their feet when they go to bed' rings true to the general dread of winter. And if we are to believe Erasmus, the fare of the scholar in Paris was no better than at Oxford or Cambridge. He entered the College of Montaigu at Paris [20] in the autumn of 1495 and was ill before the next summer because of the badness of the diet. The remoteness of baths from courts and quadrangles is an ancient joke which dies hard. In Latimer's time ablutions were not too thorough. Washing could be done at a trough in the hall or outside in the open: a bath was not known.

But it was a smaller, more intimate world than ours. Coulton [21] puts the number of students in all classes at Oxford in 1450 as not more than 1000; and Cambridge was smaller. During the next hundred years the tide began to flow in favour of Cambridge, but G. M. Trevelyan comments on the smallness of the University, judged by modern standards:

Elizabethan Cambridge was a small community in which all the leading characters were likely to be known to one another and to the double public of townsmen and undergraduates. In 1586 there were 6500 inhabitants of Cambridge, of whom 1500 belonged to the University. [22]

We must therefore think of Hugh Latimer as being in a community where the possibilities of wider acquaintanceship were much greater than they are in the Cambridge of today, for the University alone is now bigger than the whole population

[19] Sermon preached at Paul's Cross; ed. Arber (1870), p. 122.
[20] P. S. Allen, op. cit., p. 102.   [21] *Medieval Panorama*, p. 409.
[22] *English Social History*, p. 185.

of Town and University in his time. Probably 1200 would
represent the maximum number of University men in the years
when he was in residence from 1506–30.

Latimer was elected Fellow of Clare in February 1510. The
remuneration [23] would be 1s. 4d. a week for commons, and an
additional £1 3s. 4d. per annum. He would, as a Fellow, have
few charges to meet for his rooms and the use of the College
buildings. The graces for his degrees in Arts exist in the
University Grace Book and show that he was excused part of
the full course—possibly because of sickness—but proceeded,
as was customary, to the B.A. degree in the Lent Term of 1510.
He was ordained at Lincoln, his native diocese, but the precise
date of his taking orders is not known. It can reasonably be
assumed to have been soon after his appointment as Fellow of
Clare. He alludes to his ordination in a sermon preached at
Stamford, 9th November 1550: [24]

I never preached in Lincolnshire afore, not came here afore, save
once when I went to take orders at Lincoln, which was a good while
ago; therefore I cannot say much of Lincolnshire, for I know it not.

He took his Master's degree in 1514 and remained—presumably teaching—in the University. There is no record of
any of his pupils except Bigenden, who was his opponent in
later years.

Apparently Latimer had already shown some of his real talent
for preaching, since in the Proctor's Books his name appears in
1522 as one of twelve men licensed by the University in accordance with a special privilege to preach anywhere in England.

In this same year (1522) Latimer was appointed to carry the
silver cross borne in university processions. This appointment
shows that he was as yet under no suspicion, and that his character was pleasing to the authorities. Strype [25] transcribes from
Ralph Morice, Cranmer's secretary, this note about Latimer,
that 'for his gravity and years preferred to the keeping of the
University Cross, which no man had to do withal but such as
one as in sanctimony of life excelled other'.

He proceeded to the B.D. degree between Michaelmas 1523
and Michaelmas 1524; but there is no record in the Grace Book.
In the Proctors' Books, ending Michaelmas 1524, there is a

[23] Demaus, *Hugh Latimer*, p. 13.   [24] *Sermons*, p. 298.
[25] *Ecclesiastical Memorials*, III.1.368.

note of Latimer's not having paid his dues, but as there are seven other names with his of men proceeding B.D., it cannot have been a very serious offence. The proctors' entry is: [26]

M. latom^er	
M. stafforth	
M. rogers	
M. foberry	*nihil.*
M. cheswryght	
M. thyxtyll	
M. nycolls	
M. hale	

Now, in the height of his zeal and the full strength of his manhood, Latimer is shown as entering into the public arena in defence of the Church. His oration on becoming B.D. was against Philip Melanchthon.

But especially his popish zeal could in no case abide in those days good master Stafford, reader of the divinity lecture in Cambridge; most spitefully railing against him, and willing the youth of Cambridge in no wise to believe him.[27]

Stafford's name in the above list shows he was of similar standing in the Spring of 1524. Later they would be allies in a common cause, but at first Latimer took pleasure in going down 'into the sopham school, among the youth, there gathered together of daily custom to keep their sophams and disputations'. The Sophany School was where the Sophisters, or students who had finished their course in logic, were allowed to take part in the disputations which were then so conspicuous in the activities of the University. Ralph Morice, indeed, attributes Latimer's conversion to Stafford.

It pleased Almighty God to call Hugh Latymer unto the knowledge of God's Holy Word, by the godly lecture of divinity read by Mr George Stafford.[28]

No doubt much that he had heard, as well as Stafford's personality, may have helped to persuade Latimer, but only subconsciously, for we have his own testimony, as well as Foxe's record, that his conversion was due to a less conspicuous person, Thomas Bilney, a Fellow of Trinity Hall.

[26] Foxe, *Acts and Monuments*, Vol. VII, App., p. 768.   [27] ibid., p. 437.
[28] Strype, op. cit., III.1.368.

CHAPTER TWO

'Little Bilney'

THE THREE greatest religious movements affecting English
life during the last four centuries all began in zealous
spiritual inquiry made by groups of young divines at Oxford
or Cambridge. Whereas, however, the leaders of the Evangelical Revival—George Whitefield and the Wesleys—lived
long and laborious days in many fields, and Pusey, Newman,
and Keble saw their work prosper amazingly in Victorian
England, the most ardent soul in Cambridge who inspired
future leaders and martyrs of the English Reformation himself
died at the stake long before the issues had been made clear.

'Little Bilney' they called him—partly because of his small
physical build, but also, one feels, partly with the diminutive
which expresses affection. Without him, humanly speaking,
we would not have had Latimer, and many another whose
name is better known than his own. One cannot read far into
the annals of those days without coming upon Bilney's name
and influence. It is like tracing the branches of a delta to a
main stream, and then pushing up its course to a tiny runnel
in the mossy hill—a single, inconspicuous spring of clear water,
and, apparently, with no great destiny. Bilney was such a
source at Cambridge.

He never came to the courts of princes; no statesmen—lay
or ecclesiastical—ever sought his opinion as they would that
of his greatest convert. He was never crowned by the populace,
a king of the pulpit at Paul's Cross. Such distinctions came to
his friends, but not to him. When he came in procession to
St Paul's, it was only as a convicted prisoner, carrying the
faggot which was an emblem of the heretic's doom he had only
narrowly escaped by submission to authority.

Yet the student of English religious life would do well to
notice the reality of his influence, upon men endowed by nature
with greater gifts than he himself possessed, for bringing out
into the full life of the nation what they had begun to acquire
in his presence. He reveals the loneliness of martyrdom in the
poignancy of a spirit that trembles on the verge, withdraws

from fear, and then, at a later time, goes to death. These points may best be observed in a short account of Bilney's life. He was a Norfolk man, born about the year 1495 in Norwich or near by, and of his parentage we know next to nothing. While still a boy he went up to Trinity Hall, was a good student and became a Fellow of his college. The fact that he had proceeded to the degree of LL.B. indicates the direction of his studies. But law soon became secondary in his life, and religion the main quest. His early ardour for perfection of life reminds one very much of Paul, Luther, and Wesley. He sought the hard and narrow way of rigour with small satisfaction; but then came the miracle of joyous love when he knew Christ as his living Saviour.

We have already noticed that Erasmus's residence at Cambridge had not influenced Latimer to learn Greek, and the same is true of Bilney. There is a fitting spiritual justice that such neglect or oversight on the part of future reformers should be redressed by their introduction to 'the Word of God' through his private labours. Apart from his teaching, the chief interest of Erasmus at this time was in the Greek text of the New Testament. He mentions four Greek manuscripts in an introduction to the first edition of his Greek New Testament with Latin translation, which was published at Basle in March 1516, dedicated to the Pope with his permission (a perfect safeguard against academic fury and theological prejudice). 'One of these has been identified, the Leicester Codex written by Emmanuel of Constantinople, which . . . was with the Franciscans at Cambridge early in the sixteenth century.' [1] It was this New Testament that was the immediate means of a conversion true to the classic type. Bilney would be twenty-one years of age in this year, 1516.

Many years later, when the consequences of his conversion had been worked out in a life which was a precursor of the strict evangelical kind, Bilney wrote a series of five letters to Tunstal, the Bishop of London, before whom, with other dignitaries, he and Thomas Arthur, a Cambridge companion, appeared on trial for heresy in 1527. These letters, written in Latin, were reprinted by Foxe, who also translated them. Bilney speaks thus of his beginnings as an advocate of the Gospel way of life.

[1] P. S. Allen, *The Age of Erasmus*, p. 144.

O mighty power of the most Highest! which I also, a miserable
sinner, have often tasted and felt, who, before I could come unto
Christ, had even likewise spent all that I had upon those ignorant
physicians; that is to say, unlearned hearers of confession; so that
there was but small force of strength left in me (who of nature was
but weak), small store of money, and very little wit or understanding: for they appointed me fastings, watching, buying of
pardons, and masses; in all which things (as I now understand) they
sought rather their own gain than the salvation of my sick and
languishing soul.

But at last I heard of Jesus, even when the New Testament was
first set forth by Erasmus; which when I understood to be eloquently
done by him, being allured rather by the Latin than by the word of
God (for at that time I knew not what it meant), I bought it even
by the providence of God, as I do now well understand and perceive: and at the first reading (as I well remember) I chanced upon
this sentence of St Paul (O most sweet and comfortable sentence to
my soul!) in 1 Timothy 1: 'It is a true saying, and worthy of all men
to be embraced, that Christ Jesus came into the world to save
sinners; of whom I am the chief and principal.' This one sentence,
through God's instruction and inward working, which I did not then
perceive, did so exhilarate my heart, being before wounded with the
guilt of my sins, and being almost in despair, that . . . immediately
I . . . felt a marvellous comfort and quietness, insomuch that 'my
bruised bones leaped for joy'.

(1st letter to Cuthbert Tunstal, Bishop of London.)[2]

Foxe commented on this first epistle, consisting of the full
story of Bilney's conversion, that it 'seemeth more effectual in
the Latin than in the English'. Certainly the reader is aware
of rare spiritual exaltation and awe in the original of the second
paragraph quoted above, which opens,

Sed tandem de Jesu audiebam, nimirum tum, cum novum Testa-
mentum primum ab Erasmo aederetur,

and leads on to the famous text from 1 Timothy which is now
the third of the 'Comfortable Words' familiar to us in the
Office for Holy Communion.

In this connexion a speculation can be made. Nothing is
told more often or more insistently by an evangelist than the
story of his own conversion. In a small man it can soon become
trite and wearisome, but in a great man it loses none of its
power through being often told. Bilney, from 1520 to 1527,

[2] Foxe, *Acts and Monuments*, IV.635.

was at the centre of the most spiritual group in Cambridge. Of that group we can speak with some certainty. It included Latimer and Matthew Parker, at least three senior members of Pembroke and three from St Benet's (now Corpus), the head of a Cambridge community (Barnes, of the Augustinians), and probably Tyndale was sometimes of the company, for his friend and helper in later years, Lambert, was one of Bilney's converts. The whole of Cambridge, in a religious sense, was presently divided into friendship with or enmity against that group. All these men would surely be as well acquainted with the story of Bilney's conversion as Methodists have been with John Wesley's. Cranmer was in Cambridge—at Jesus—and very sympathetic to reform. The 'Comfortable Words' were introduced into the First Prayer Book of Edward the Sixth in 1549. They have no place in the Mass. It seems to the present writer, at least, that insistence upon this great text by Bilney, and by Bilney's friends because of him, might well have driven its comfort and exhortation deeply into the mind of the man who, more than anybody else, gave the English people their most familiar liturgical forms. Bilney himself had called the text: 'O most sweet and comfortable sentence! . . .'

Bilney was not admitted to Holy Orders till 1519, nine years after Latimer. But immediately after his evangelical experience he had come, in Foxe's words, 'unto this point, that forsaking the knowledge of man's laws, he converted his study to those things which tended more unto godliness than gainfulness'.

The picture of Bilney's strenuous days at this period is remarkably like that of the Holy Club at Oxford two hundred years later. This little man was fervent in his study of the Scriptures, preached his spiritual experience with assiduity, but also with considerable adroitness. He knew (none so well) that this matter was perilously akin to what the Church might reckon as heresy, though for him it was God's naked truth and nothing more. He visited the sick, went to the lepers' beds and drew about them the coverlets that all other folk shrank from touching. He was continually at the jail, ready to listen to a side of the story that never comes into court. There was more true asceticism in his sparse living than in ninety-nine out of a hundred of the professed religious, the monks and friars who were nearer their dissolution than they dreamed. For eighteen months at a stretch he commonly had but one meal a day, carrying the food he thus saved to prisoners and sufferers. Yet in all this service he had but one end, and would speak of Jesus that he might bring them, one and all, where he had been.

To live on the same stair in college must have been somewhat trying—for the plain truth is, that potential martyrs can be difficult neighbours for more ordinary men. A scholar at Trinity Hall, Thirlby, occupied the room below. Thirlby became a Bishop in Mary's days and with Bonner stripped Cranmer of his insignia at his degradation at Oxford. He was addicted as an undergraduate to fluting on the recorder. He reported that Bilney seldom slept more than four hours in the night and that he could 'abide no swearing and singing'. With his dread of swearing—especially in a future Bishop and his companions—few will quarrel, and the bogey of the don who lives on the same stair has survived the centuries. But it seems Bilney openly spoke to students not only about rowdy songs, but even that singing used in Church services 'was rather a mockery of God than otherwise'. Bilney, however, when perplexed by musical interruptions in nearby rooms 'would resort strait to prayer'. Men writing essays, and scarcely helped by their neighbours' gramophones and wireless sets have, in more recent days, displayed other means of showing their discomfort!

These are little, but significant items. They show a man continually zealous—a man of one idea. If he did not clearly see already that his earthly end would be an iron chain about his body and the loneliness of dying disowned by his Mother Church, it is, after all, with martyrs as with other men, they go but one step at a time.

The great glory of Bilney is that he was the human instrument of Latimer's conversion.

We have said that there was already some stir in Cambridge over new ways of religion, particularly shown in Stafford's lecturing and in the subject of Latimer's B.D. oration. But Bilney's own spiritual experience was independent of anything that was happening on the Continent. There can be no question of Luther's views being concerned for the simple reason that Bilney's conversion occurred in the same year as Luther's first public display of dissatisfaction. Of Luther, Lindsay comments:

The earliest traces of *conscious* opposition appeared about the middle of 1516, and characteristically on the practical and not on the speculative side of theology. They began in a sermon on Indulgences, preached in July 1516. Once begun, the breach widened until Luther could contrast 'our theology' (the theology taught by Luther and his colleagues at Wittenberg) with what was taught elsewhere, and notably at Erfurt. The former represented Augustine and the Holy Scriptures, and the latter was founded on Aristotle.[3]

The great day of the nailing up of the theses which made the dispute the property of all the world was fifteen months later, All Saints' Day, 1517, so that there could be, at the beginning, no question of Lutheran influence. Demaus is quite right:

It was to a copy of this New Testament, read by a single devout student, that the origin of the Reformation movement in the University may be traced.[4]

Only in the University?

There is no evidence that Bilney knew Greek. What he says himself of his purchase of Erasmus's New Testament is that, when he bought it, it was rather for the sake of the Latin than for its being the Word of God. But the exquisite skill of the great humanist was soon subservient to the matter of the Gospel in Bilney's mind.

Yet although it is plain that Bilney's conversion was independent of Continental influence, it also cannot be doubted that the doings of Luther and the beliefs of the Continental Protestants presently had a very real interest for him and his friends. Else why should Latimer be so anxious to keep Stafford's listeners in the strait ways of medieval orthodoxy, and why should he seek to confute Melanchthon? This comes out in Latimer's own account of Bilney's approach to him. Bilney was present at Latimer's public oration and afterwards sought him out privately as his confessor. Latimer's reminiscence is as follows:

Master Bilney, or rather Saint Bilney that suffered death for God's word sake; the same Bilney was the instrument whereby God called me to knowledge; for I may thank him, next to God, for that knowledge that I have in the word of God. For I was as obstinate a papist as any was in England, insomuch that when I should be made bachelor of divinity, my whole oration went against Philip Melanchthon and against his opinions. Bilney heard me at that time, and perceived that I was zealous without knowledge: and he came to me afterward in my study, and desired me, for God's sake, to hear his confession. I did so; and, to say the truth, by his confession I learned more than before in many years. So from that time forward I began to smell the word of God, and forsook the school-doctors and such fooleries.[5]

Latimer relates that this acquaintance with Bilney in 1524 led him to share in the work of visiting prisoners in Cambridge jail and the sick folk of the town, wherever he might convert them to Christ. This work went on for some years together with their personal evangelism and preaching.

The potential reformers met regularly at 'The White Horse' —an inn conveniently near Clare, Trinity Hall, and Corpus. They were probably exhilarated at the prospect of the reform they favoured, but it was not bliss to be alive when revolution was in the air. Bilney himself was past the first flush of youth— he was nearly thirty when Latimer joined him. Latimer himself was some ten years older.

There was for them more than the spice of danger that adds zest to life. Quite apart from the King's known hatred of Luther, there was the possibility of trouble from offended dignitaries. There would be no lack of charges against these men once their views were proclaimed in pulpits farther afield. Discussion in the friendly dusk 'in Germany' (so their inn was significantly nicknamed), their snug secrecy enhanced as candles were brought and the windows were shuttered, firelight leaping about, distorting the shadows of the oak settles, and turning even little Bilney into a giant gesticulating vastly across the rafters—all this was one thing, public propaganda of their private judgements another.

Erasmus, writing three years earlier, in May 1521, had stated there were many copies of Luther's works in England, and they were widely read. It would appear to be so, for on 12th May 1521 Wolsey went in glittering state to old St Paul's and, while Fisher preached against Continental doctrines inside, in the churchyard Lutheran books were tossed into a huge bonfire. It followed that at both Universities there was a ban on these pestilential books; and, naturally, they were talked about all the more and smuggled hither and thither. That is always one of the effects of strict religious censorship. But yet, although men could hazard very good guesses at the subjects of conversa-

[5] First Sermon before the Duchess of Suffolk, *Sermons*, p. 334.

tion when Latimer and Bilney walked on the slopes in Cambridge known sarcastically as 'Heretics' Hill', and something more than guesses could be made regarding the debates at 'The White Horse', there was nothing which could be openly attacked. These men were all scrupulous in formal religion, they still heard the Office, they made no public departure from set practice. There was nothing as yet incongruous in Latimer's being named as a trustee in a deed dated 28th August 1524 by which a priest was to be appointed to say Mass in the chapel of Clare Hall for the soul of John à Bolton.[6] Even in July 1525, West, the truculent and pompous Bishop of Ely, was so far satisfied with Bilney that he granted him full licence to preach anywhere in his diocese.

But at the end of this same year, 1525, West swooped unexpectedly into church when Latimer was preaching to the members of the University, fully supposing that he would catch him redhanded at the work of spreading heretical ideas. What had happened in a few months to sting the Bishop into this state of vigilant alarm?

Latimer acted magnificently, showing himself to be not only a daring preacher, but a master of dangerous situations. Instead of continuing his sermon for a single sentence, the preacher stood silent in the pulpit while the episcopal train entered the church. When the Bishop and his retinue were all seated, he remarked:

It is of congruence meet that a new auditory, namely being more honourable, requireth a new theme, being a new argument to entreat of. Therefore it behoveth me now to divert from mine intended purpose, and somewhat to entreat of the honourable state of a Bishop. Therefore let this be the theme (quoth he) *Christus existens pontifex futurorum bonorum &c.* (Hebrews 11[11]).[7]

From this new text, chosen on the spot, Latimer proceeded to describe the true office of a Bishop. West, to his credit, stuck it out, even though Morice comments that the obvious comparison between Latimer's ideals and the actuality confronting him in West's person might have made the Bishop think that he was 'of the fellowship of Caiaphas and Annas'.

Afterwards the Bishop sent for Latimer. He thanked him for his sermon in which his own duties had been so well expounded,

[6] *Dictionary of National Biography.*
[7] Morice (Strype, *Ecclesiastical Memorials*, III.1).

and said he would kiss the preacher's foot if he would preach one sermon against Martin Luther and his doctrine. Latimer's reply is direct.

My Lord, I am not acquainted with the doctrine of Luther; nor are we permitted here to read his works; and therefore it were but a vain thing for me to refute his doctrine, not understanding what he hath written, nor what opinion he holdeth. Sure I am that I have preached before you this day no man's doctrine, but only the doctrine of God out of the Scriptures. And if Luther do none otherwise than I have done, there needeth no confutation of his doctrine.

The Bishop, with understandable asperity, finished the interview by saying: 'I perceive you somewhat smell of the pan; you will repent this gear some day.'

Was Latimer lying boldly? He must either have been doing that or declaring the plain truth. The flattering or evasive ways of a timorous nature were naturally foreign to him. Boldness is in every word, every gesture of his life except in one unhappy period presently to be noticed. Bilney was weaker in temperament and bearing, though, as it turned out, he would be the first to taste the fire.

What were the opinions preached by Bilney and substantially shared by Latimer?

It was a plea for what has often been called the Gospel way of life, a religion earnest and sincere, abstemious, humble, and feeding upon the pure teaching of the Scriptures. It revolted from sacerdotalism and ritual which had been spoiled by current superstition and the abuse of priestly privilege; but it did not as yet question the central sacramental doctrine of the Mass even though it exalted the authority of the Bible. This reforming zeal was most pronounced in Bilney's attacks upon saint and relic worship (to be carried much farther later on by Latimer). Bilney denounced the popular pilgrimages to Walsingham and Canterbury; he exhorted priests to be more active in their pastoral duties, and he refused to acknowledge the mediation of the saints. At first the diocesan authorities did not interfere, and, indeed, to the very end he was orthodox in acknowledging the sacrifice of the Mass, the doctrine of transubstantiation, and the authority of the Church. Latimer asserted roundly when preaching before Edward the Sixth in 1549 that Bilney died as a martyr against the evil power of the Papacy.[8] It was safe to be as outspoken as that in 1549. Latimer was not so definite in his defence of Bilney as a martyr when writing to Sir Edward Baynton [9] within a few months of his death at the stake in 1531. It would have been impolitic to commit his impressions or opinions to paper, for the matter of Bilney's burning had received no little attention, and Sir Thomas More was a very vigilant Chancellor.

In 1525–6, when Bilney and Latimer were in the closest daily association their views had not crystallized and hardened. They were seeking, like Wyclif before them, only the reform of what was worst in their own age. But the tussle with the Bishop of Ely could not leave Cambridge unaffected, and West must obviously wield his authority against this uprising of new, alarming doctrine boldly and ably preached.

Nicholas West was a conservative, sixty-four years of age, who had received his bishopric mainly through Wolsey's influence and because of his long service in diplomacy. He now mounted the pulpit against Latimer and his friends, choosing Barnwell Abbey as his vantage-ground. He publicly denounced Latimer and formally suspended his licence to preach in the diocese or the University. But there were a few places which could not legally come under this ban, one of them being the Augustinian Friary of which Doctor Robert Barnes [10] was the Prior—a man of increasing reputation both as a scholar and preacher, but a man of peremptory impulse whose memory rarely saved him from doing the obviously foolish thing.

Barnes was the second of Bilney's important converts and had been in close association with Latimer. Like Bilney, he was a Norfolk man. He had gone out from Cambridge to Louvain, was an ardent student of the classics, and enjoyed the reputation which belongs to a man of witty, prompt rejoinder. He now invited Latimer to preach in the chapel of the Augustinians. Friars had long been the despair of Bishops, who could rarely carry their episcopal way with them. Latimer accepted the invitation, but what he preached there on Sunday, Christmas Eve, 1525, we do not know. Barnes himself carried the war into the Bishop's camp by preaching in the church of St Edward's, connected with Trinity Hall (Bilney's college, and a lawyer's stronghold), on the same day. There was very little

[8] *Sermons*, p. 222. [9] *Remains*, p. 330.
[10] See Gordon Rupp's *The English Protestant Tradition*, pp. 31 ff.

B

of peace and goodwill in his sermon, but not a little tilting at the law, the observance of special festivals, Bishops, and the Cardinal himself—a risky business at the best of times.

Barnes may have been singularly blind to the immediate consequences, but the University authorities were not, and they had no inclination to be involved.[11] Charges were brought against him by Tyrell, a Fellow of King's, in the Schools; but the inquiry was not open to the University, as Barnes would have wished. His friends were sufficiently numerous and influential, however, to make the Vice-Chancellor wary of his course. A semi-private inquiry was held and Barnes was assured of the friendliness intended toward him. He was at length presented with a recantation which, after consultation with his own friends and sympathizers, he refused to read.

By this time news had been conveyed to London, and the Cardinal's interest was aroused. Barnes had all the impulses that can betray the popular preacher into indiscretion, and it would need a very solid and convincing apologia to bring him scot-free from the clutches of Wolsey. Whatever might have been his motives, he had done Reform no signal service by tilting against the pillars and pole-axes, golden shoes and red gloves of the pageant-loving Cardinal. Moreover, rumour had been stirring for some time that at Cambridge books of Lutheran sort were filtering in from Germany. Barnes was arrested and taken to London, and two days later brought before Wolsey privately on Wednesday, 7th February 1526. Thanks to the interest of the Cardinal's secretary, Stephen Gardiner, who had been Barnes's tutor at Cambridge, and Edward Foxe, Barnes received the advantage of this private interview and was also saved from the Tower, being allowed to lodge with a former pupil, Thomas Parnell, who had been at Louvain with him.

Whatever books had been in the possession of Barnes and his friends in Cambridge were smuggled away before the sergeant-at-arms and the University authorities could seize them; that part of the intended coup had failed. But Wolsey seems not to have been eager to push things so far, probably because of Gardiner's and Foxe's interest in Barnes. Whatever might have been his willingness to wink at mild heresy, he had no

[11] Foxe, *Acts and Monuments*, VII.452.

intention of passing over Barnes's tilting at his personal prestige and habits.

What! master doctor, had you not a sufficient scope in the Scriptures to teach the people, but that my golden shoes, my pole-axes, my pillars, my golden cushions, my crosses did so sore offend you, that you must make us 'ridiculum caput' amongst the people? We were jollily that day laughed to scorn. Verily it was a sermon more fit to be preached on a stage than in a pulpit; for at the last you said, I wear a pair of red gloves (I should say bloody gloves, quoth you,) that I should not be cold in the midst of my ceremonies.[12]

Barnes must have felt this was a heavy price to pay for the interest he had aroused on Christmas Eve in St Edward's.

Wolsey was not at all impressed with Barnes, and had it not been for Gardiner's and Foxe's friendship to him he might have had short shrift.

Turning to them as they were kneeling, pleading for Barnes and promising (but did they know their man?) that he would conform, Wolsey said: 'Stand you up! for your sakes, and the University, we will be good unto him.'

When Barnes was asked whether he would acknowledge the Cardinal's legatine powers, of which he was always not a little proud, he replied: 'I thank your grace for your good will; I will stick to the holy Scripture, and to God's book, according to the simple talent that God hath lent me.'

'Well,' retorted the Cardinal, 'thou shalt have thy learning tried to the uttermost, and thou shalt have the law.'

With Gardiner and Foxe as his guarantors, he was, however, still permitted to stay at Parnell's, where he spent an uneasy night writing in preparation for his defence. He had the assistance of three Cambridge friends, Coverdale, Goodwin, and Field. The next day he was brought, together with several German Lutherans from the Steelyard, for formal trial before the Bishops of London, Rochester, Bath, and St Asaph's. With them he was committed to the Fleet until the trial was over. The charges were based on articles which, as Mr Rupp adroitly comments,[13] were not 'within a thousand miles of any central issue of the Christian truth'. Poor Barnes was now completely in the clutches of a relentless machine. There was little hope of escape and not much apparent value in any propaganda that might derive from his stand. Gardiner and Foxe once more

<hr>

[12] ibid., V.416.   [13] op. cit., p. 36.

brought pressure to bear upon him when he was confronted
with the last terrible alternative—'Abjure or burn!' He abjured.
Brought, with the Lutherans, to St Paul's, he saw the full-
coloured panoply of the Cardinal that he had so bitterly de-
rided. Rochester (Fisher) preached against Luther, baskets
full of Protestant books were burnt, and Barnes was subjected
to the penance of a self-acknowledged heretic—walking three
times about the fire before throwing into it the faggot which he
had carried from the Fleet. He knelt down to crave forgiveness
from Mother Church in the person of Wolsey, gold shoes, red
gloves and all, and to swallow the bitter lie that he openly confessed he had been better treated than he deserved. 'And so
the cardinal departed under a canopy, with all his mitred men
with him, till he came to the second gate of Paul's; and then
he took his mule, and the mitred men came back again.' [14]
The Bishop of Rochester absolved the prisoners, receiving them
back into the Church—and Barnes returned with the others to
the Fleet. He was not permitted to return to Cambridge, but
for upward of two years was commanded to remain in the
house of the Austin Friars in London. Thence he escaped
overseas.

His ill-starred attempt at daring witness had started the
hunt. Bilney, Arthur, and Latimer would now face the Cardinal. Ralph Morice, Cranmer's secretary, wrote an account
of Latimer's appearance before Wolsey soon after Barnes's
trouble.[15] Latimer and the two others escaped the peril of
public formal trial for the present. Wolsey, always quick to
sense manliness, and with a liking for forthright personalities,
was struck by Latimer's sturdy Englishness, his bold demeanour
and frank tongue. He enjoyed his cut-and-thrust exchange
with his two chaplains, Drs Capon and Marshal, whom he had
commanded to examine him on his acquaintance with the
accepted teachings of the schools. This examination seems to
have satisfied Wolsey completely concerning Latimer's learning and orthodoxy. He then questioned Latimer himself concerning his preaching, and listened to an account of the extempore sermon which had been preached to the Bishop of Ely,
though no confession was made of his sudden change of theme
on West's entrance. Wolsey was now so much convinced that
he gave him permission to preach anywhere in England. 'If

[14] Foxe, op. cit., V.418.   [15] Strype, op. cit., III.1.368.

the Bishop of Ely cannot abide such doctrine as you have here repeated, you shall have my licence, and shall preach it unto his beard, let him say what he will.' Bilney (we infer this from details which emerged at the later trial before Wolsey) was dismissed after promising that he would not disseminate Luther's doctrine. Such a promise he might very well make, for his own conviction was originally independent of Continental influence, and he would not share all Luther's views in 1526. Bilney's restlessness, in the few remaining years of his life, and his apparent vacillation, have left a problem to posterity for his friends and foes alike. In the next year, 1527, he and Arthur were again in trouble, this time seriously, and were brought before the Cardinal for full trial. With Cambridge as a base, they had wandered about preaching, chiefly in Suffolk and Norfolk. Their most notable convert was Lambert,[16] a Mass priest who later worked as a translator and was a companion of Tyndale and Frith in Antwerp.

Bilney came to the confines of London, preaching particularly against superstitious practices associated with roods and relics. He was arrested 'and carried with Arthur to Tunstal (the Bishop of London), and so to the coalhouse'—the particularly gloomy prison at Fulham Palace. From that moment Bilney was never out of danger and never completely consistent. Latimer did not join in these expeditions, though he did not waver from his new-found faith. With the Cardinal's licence in his pocket he continued his testimony and preaching at Cambridge where it stood him in good stead.

In the meantime trouble for the established order of things was becoming evident in the sister University. Wolsey, in his anxiety to obtain the best and keenest teachers for his magnificent project, Cardinal College, Oxford, had sent agents to Cambridge in 1525, and they had little difficulty in tempting away a group of men, some eight or ten in number. It is interesting, and is a sidelight upon Wolsey's character, that, provided he got the scholarship, he was not too inquisitive about their orthodoxy. Cranmer and Parker were among those who were invited, but did not exchange the fens of Cambridge for the meadows between Cherwell and Isis where St Frideswide's provided the nucleus of buildings and funds for the new College. But the men who did go were of Bilney's circle and were to

[16] Burned in 1538.

some extent influenced by him. Richard Cox, John Clarke, John Fryer, Godfrey Harman, Henry Sumner, William Betts, John Frith, Goodman, and Ridley, are names of Cambridge men incorporated at Oxford in the late autumn of 1525.

After Wyclif's outburst in the fourteenth century Lollardy had been kept crushed, if not completely killed there, and this in spite of the new interest shown in Greek by Colet and the men of Corpus when Sir Thomas More was a student in Oxford. One can imagine this little group, exiles in spite of the new comfort and riches of the Cardinal's foundation. It was a current joke that Wolsey had planned a college and had completed 'a guzzling-hall', for the hall and kitchen were finished first, to remain among the chief glories of Christ Church to this day. The ardour of that Cambridge religious life at length made its presence felt. For three years all was quiet, and then heresy burst into sudden flame in the University—of all places, first of all in the Cardinal's new college. Inquiry was instituted. Dr London, the Warden of New College, wrote to Longland, Bishop of Lincoln:

Would God my Lord's grace had never motioned to call Clarke, nor any other Cambridge man, into his most towardly college. We were clear, without blot or suspicion, till they came; and some of them long time hath had a shrewd name.

One of the most graphic stories surviving from those days is contained in the testimony of Anthony Dalaber [17] concerning his contact with the famous Thomas Garrard. It pulses with the anxiety and excitement that must have accompanied every meeting in which young men assembled to study forbidden books, and the apprehension with which they would hear a strange step on the stair or knock upon the door. It is a part of the story of the contest of religion with tyranny which has been renewed all too vehemently in our own day.

This was just before the trial of Bilney, and Wolsey was a good deal more alert to the dangers than he had been. For many years he had been more of a thorn in the flesh to dignitaries than to humble people. Froude, in one paragraph, sums up the big difference between Wolsey and his successor as Lord Chancellor, Sir Thomas More:

Under Wolsey's chancellorship the stake had been comparatively

[17] Foxe, op. cit., V.421.

idle; he possessed a remarkable power of making recantation easy; and there is, I believe, no instance in which an accused heretic was brought under his immediate cognizance, where he failed to arrange some terms by which submission was made possible. With Wolsey heresy was an error—with More it was a crime.[18]

Now, on 27th November 1527, accompanied by the Archbishop of Canterbury (Warham), seven Bishops (including London and Ely), and many dignitaries, Wolsey had Thomas Arthur and Thomas Bilney brought before him in the chapterhouse at Westminster. It is the kind of scene that holds the eye —the grey stone arches and walls matching the autumn weather, scarlet and gold in profusion, scarlet gloves and golden cushions once more for Wolsey, purple on the Bishops, ermine on the lawyers, and Bilney, standing there in sombre clothes, small of body, shrunken by prison, unimpressive in gesture and voice. Like Paul, he knew that in his presence there was little to commend his cause.

Wolsey asked Bilney whether he had knowingly taught or preached to people in private or public, opinions which were Luther's, or those of any other men condemned by the Church. He replied that he had not wittingly done so or taught anything that he believed to be contrary to the accepted teaching of the Catholic Church. Wolsey asked him whether he had not once taken oath that he would not only refuse himself to proclaim Luther's opinions, but would impugn them. On this point poor Bilney hesitated, even—is the word too strong?—equivocated; for he admitted that he had given his word, 'but not judicially'. It seems a meaningless quibble to the modern mind. He was then sworn, and promised to answer plainly the questions put to him during the inquiry. Then Wolsey turned to Bilney's friend and pointedly asked him whether he had not said to Sir Thomas More that 'in the sacrament of the altar there was not the very body of Christ'. He denied this.

Of course, this questioning by Wolsey was merely the opening gambit. Churchmen never took the trouble to stage a fulldress inquiry without the accused man's learning what it feels like to be a mouse caught by a cat. Witnesses were called— and there was no lack of them, especially among the friars, ready to say what Bilney had preached in the diocese of Norwich as well as in London. Day after day the trial went on

[18] *History of England*, 'Henry VIII', I.6.

until 7th December—eleven days and nights of unceasing harrying, for the self-interest of the orders as well as that of the seculars was in danger. They were thoroughly angry because of the denunciation of images, pilgrimages, their own interest in them and manner of life. Bilney was sensitive and naturally timid, only impelled to his course by the urge of conscience.

Thirty-four questions were put to the accused.[19] It would be wearisome and unnecessary to give them all, but some of them are very interesting because they are pointers to the Puritanism which would presently sweep undeniably on to the stage of English life. Was Christ alone to be prayed to? Were all Christians, laity as well as clerics, priests with the right of binding and loosing, if they had received the Spirit of God? Should the language of the people be used and Masses and Gospels read publicly in the vulgar tongue? Ought the whole Scripture to be translated into English? Should all organs and all manner of singing be abolished from the worship of the Church? These are a few of the questions which show, if not what Bilney really proclaimed, at least what many people thought he believed.

Three times, under pressure from Tunstal, the Bishop of London, Bilney was exhorted to recant and place himself under the merciful judgement of the Church. On the great questions which would be pressed at Latimer's trial more than twenty years later, little was said. Bilney was orthodox on the Mass, and he made no denial of the authority of the Church. Protesting against relics, pilgrimages, and prayers to the saints, advocating accessibility of the Scriptures in the vulgar tongue and urging better observances of duty upon the clergy might be serious matters, but no single one of them was sufficient to bring a man to the stake. Yet, taken all in all, this was a charge of heresy—and how terrible heresy was in the minds of men in that day, we can have little knowledge. Nothing is more difficult than to get inside the skin, as it were, of a man daring at that time to stand alone, by the right of religious conviction privately obtained and pitting it against the awful majesty and power of the Church. For a thousand years that Church had held sway over life. The common people knew that even an Emperor had once been kept waiting, in his shirt, standing barefoot in the snow for three days until a carpenter's son, but the Pope none the less, restored him to the Church. They knew

[19] Foxe prints them; IV.624.

that the murder of an Archbishop had brought the proudest and strongest of England's kings to bitter penance, and they could not, in their wildest dreams, imagine that within their own life-time carts would rumble Londonwards from Canterbury loaded with gold and precious stones rifled from Becket's shrine to fill a more daring Henry's needy coffers. Men might writhe because of injustice, petty persecution, violation of their family life, and the whispered scandals of the village alehouse might come into writing through Chaucer's and Langland's descriptions of the religious and their ways of life. Yet the Church stood as she had done for a thousand years. The peasant in the field and the rising merchant in the town, the toiling housewife and the hawking nobleman, were like Browning's Bishop and could

> *Hear the blesssed mutter of the mass,*
> *And see God made and eaten all day long,*
> *And feel the steady candle-flame, and taste*
> *Good strong thick stupefying incense-smoke!*

The Church was not only an anvil that could wear out all hammers; the Church had a hammer that suited its own anvil, and not only a man's body and goods could be taken, but his immortal soul—that most real of all realities—could be shut out from life and hope of ease for ever and for ever. Our busy lives, in this age of mechanical miracles, with their shortened views and closed horizons, have lost the dread of eternal doom, as of a funeral bell, in those words 'for ever', but to folk even at the end of the Middle Ages what they represented mattered more than anything else. Columbus was not doing so brave a thing in confronting the unknown West as Bilney was attempting, facing an eternal voyage with no blessing of the Church upon him. He was inexpressibly lonely.

Day after day he longed to remain in full communion with the Church, but was unable to deny the truth by which Christ had made him free, and sought to show his accusers what he saw so clearly—that truly he was not in error. Day after day his superiors sought to gain his recantation. They gained Arthur's surrender fairly easily, and his sentence was not heavy —a public penance, a very short detention, and after that he was not to preach till licensed by his Bishop. A time would soon come when offenders would have shorter shrift. Now, if

B*

they could gain Bilney's recantation, might not the danger of popular and widespread heresy be averted, since this man was, in Cambridge at least, 'the first framer' of such ways?

On 4th December Tunstal pleaded with Bilney to recant, and again twice on the next day. These three times the little man was unmoved. Tunstal had had good opportunities of learning the sincerity, and even the fundamental orthodoxy of his victim, for Bilney, as well as speaking before him, had written to him the five letters which give us his inward convictions and the history of his spiritual development.

Bilney pleaded for more time in which to consult with his friends. They, as well as his opponents, were counselling submission. At his fourth and last chance he broke down and abjured. He yielded, completely and miserably.

It was on 7th December that 'He answered, that now he was persuaded by Master Dancaster and others his friends, he would submit himself, trusting that they would deal gently with him, both in his abjuration and penance'. He was condemned to a prison to be named by the Cardinal and retained during his pleasure, but first must walk bareheaded before the procession into St Paul's carrying on his shoulder the faggot, with which he was to stand full in the preacher's eye during sermon time.

It is a pathetic picture—all the sadder because Bilney, like Peter, knew that only temporary weakness had caused his denial.

His public penance done, for over a year he was in the Tower, and then, set free, he returned to Cambridge broken-hearted. Latimer and his best friends gathered round him. They found him humiliated, haunted. He had saved his body, and he was ashamed of it. Latimer spoke of his inward torment when preaching before Edward the Sixth nearly twenty years later:

I knew a man myself, Bilney, little Bilney, that blessed martyr of God, what time he had borne his fagot, and was come again to Cambridge, had such conflicts within himself, beholding this image of death, that his friends were afraid to let him be alone: they were fain to be with him day and night, and comforted him as they could, but no comforts would serve. As for the comfortable places of scripture, to bring them unto him it was as though a man would run him through the heart with a sword; yet afterward, for all this, he was revived, and took his death patiently, and died well against the tyrannical see of Rome. Wo will be to that bishop that had the examination of him if he repented not! Here is a good lesson for you, my friends; if ever you come in danger, in durance, in prison for God's quarrel, and his sake, as he did for purgatory-matters, and put to bear a fagot for preaching the true word of God against pilgrimage and such like matters, I will advise you first, and above all things, to abjure all your friends, all your friendships; leave not one unabjured. It is they that shall undo you, and not your enemies. It was his very friends that brought Bilney to it.[20]

And yet some of those friends were the brightest jewels in the martyr's crown and showed in good time that they were ready to follow him where he, first of all, in spite of his recantation before Tunstal, led the way.

For a little more than two years Bilney endured his private anguish. A reference made to him by 'his scholar' at this time leads us to suppose that he had taken up academic work again. He was certainly living in college and he took up again his work among the poor and the imprisoned. But his penitence would turn him gradually to wider fields with open-eyed vision of his danger.

[20] *Sermons*, p. 222.

CHAPTER THREE

King's Preacher

WOLSEY fell from favour in the autumn of 1529, and it is not surprising that opponents of the Cambridge reformers thought, in Morice's quaint phrase, that 'Mr Latimer's licence was extincted'. From the pulpit came his answer: 'Where ye think that my licence decayeth with my lord cardinal's temporal fall, I take it nothing so. For he being, I trust, reconciled to God from his pomp and vanities, I now set more by his licence than ever I did before, when he was in his most felicity.'

The emphasis falls on the word 'temporal'. Wolsey was still Archbishop of York, and the Pope had not diminished his authority, whatever Henry had done. One may suspect a secret chuckle in the retort. Things were very different from what they were when Wolsey had rung his little bell to call him to his presence. Morice gives no date, but the Cardinal did not lay his bones among the monks at Leicester until 30th November (St Andrew's Day) 1530. By that time Latimer had come to the notice of the King.

The matter of the royal divorce would affect the lives of many people who seemed impossibly remote from the stage when the first actors—Henry, Queen Katherine and Anne Boleyn, Wolsey, the Pope and the Emperor began to play their parts. Directly or indirectly, affairs that had long been discussed by the Cambridge reformers would become possible of achievement because of the course of events as Henry became increasingly impatient of the veto exercised by Rome.

It is certain that Henry, quite apart from the divorce, wanted to possess increasing and unrivalled power in the affairs of England. He had jousted and jested, danced and wrestled, feasted and argued, as each day made its appeal to his vanity or appetite. But no one doubted, Wolsey least of all, that if he chose to set himself to a long course, he would follow it to the end. His rebukes to the Cardinal concerning his ways of raising money for his Oxford college were enough to show that he was by no means content to remain dumb in deference to Wolsey's possible influence.[1] Wolsey, in the late summer of 1528, told Du Bellay, the French Ambassador, that he wanted to retire from international politics to serve God. He would not want that so long as he could continue safely in his service to this world.

It was very evident that the law's delays were the most useful device that Papal power could employ, and that, sooner or later, Henry's impatience would explode. Wolsey was not wrong in anticipating his own catastrophe. The King himself was present in the legatine Court on 23rd July 1529, the day on which judgement was expected. Campeggio had already been in England much too long for his own liking (though he was Bishop of Salisbury among other things), but he must have been dull indeed if he thought his bland announcement that the Court would stand adjourned until October would awaken only surprise. It was obvious at court, long before October came, that Wolsey's power was doomed. On the 19th of that month he yielded up the Great Seal to Norfolk and Suffolk, who had come over for it once before from Windsor and been refused because they were without written authority. Three days later he put himself under heavy sentence by confessing to *praemunire*. He was, however, allowed to retain his archbishopric, and a pension of 1000 marks from the bishopric of Winchester, which he had been holding *in commendam* since the death of Richard Fox in 1528. In the spring of 1530 Wolsey turned northwards to begin belatedly his duties as Archbishop in his province and diocese. He was destined to spend some six months in these tasks of pacification, for there was much pastoral work to do in restoring harmonious relationships among many of the great families living north of the Trent, besides confirming children. His arrival in his proper sphere brought him popularity for spiritual reasons that he had never known when the London crowds gaped at his splendour. But he was not destined to be installed at York—a city he never entered—for his arrest came on 4th November on the charge of high treason.

It is relevant to notice, in connexion with Wolsey's fall, the apt summary of his character written by Professor Pollard: [2]

Wolsey is supposed to have conceived vast schemes of ecclesiastical reform, which time and opportunity failed him to effect. If he had

[1] Vide Pollard, *Henry the Eighth*, p. 243.   [2] ibid., p. 117.

ever seriously set about the work, the first thing to be reformed would have been his own ecclesiastical practice. He personified in himself most of the clerical abuses of his age. Not merely an 'unpreaching prelate', he rarely said mass; his *commendams* and absenteeism were alike violations of canon law. Three of the bishoprics he held he never visited at all; York, which he had obtained fifteen years before, he did not visit till the year of his death, and then through no wish of his own.

Such characteristics in prelates were precisely those which would arouse Latimer to his strength; but one feels that between him and Wolsey there was that mutual respect which declares itself so often between strong men. Wolsey served his king better than his God: Latimer would refuse to serve his king unless he could also serve his God. The growth of Latimer as a preacher and reformer dates from the autumn of 1529 when his work at Cambridge aroused once more official hostility in the University.

But in the meantime Cranmer had begun to count for something more than a quiet student with a passion for the Scriptures and a genius for good liturgy. Stephen Gardiner, secretary to the King, and Edward Foxe, his almoner, were lodged by the royal harbinger at the house of a Mr Cressy at Waltham, Essex, about August, Henry having moved to Waltham from Greenwich. Cranmer was there, apparently as a tutor in the household for a time, having accompanied Cressy's two sons from Cambridge where there was pestilence. These royal officials were both Cambridge men and contemporaries. Gardiner was Provost of King's College and Foxe Master of Trinity Hall. They drew him out on the subject of the divorce, and Cranmer mentioned the ancient practice of consulting the divines at universities on disputed points of religion and law. Surely the crux of the whole question for the King was to know whether his marriage was invalid. If it was, then he could go ahead without the Pope and marry a lady of his choice. Cranmer's learning and manner impressed the King's men, and within a few days Henry had risen to the lure of this new hope, and was all the readier for daring action because of the failure of the Legates to assist him. Cranmer was summoned to court, and Henry found in him a likely servant for the future. He was received into the friendly household of Anne Boleyn's father, the Earl of Wiltshire, to fulfil the King's request that he should write his opinion at length with a view to its submission to the learned men of the European universities. This work occupied Cranmer through the months of the late autumn of 1529 and came first to Cambridge early in the new year, where his influence and arguments were likely to win approval.

It was while these new projects were being prepared that Latimer preached his famous sermons, 'On the Cards', just before Christmas. There is no necessity to hazard the slightest connexion between his actions and the work on which Cranmer was engaged. At this time Latimer was not intimate with Cranmer, though the mere fact that he was living at Durham Place, engaged on the King's personal cause, would be well known in the University.

Preachers in those days were especially prone to indulge their fancy and gift for figurative speech at the great feasts. Latimer always had a lively sense of the topical, and it was the general association of Christmas with domestic jollity, and the fact that games of cards were then permitted in College halls for low stakes, that drew him to preach the two sermons which, to modern taste, are far-fetched and fantastic.

And whereas you are wont to celebrate Christmas in playing at cards, I intend by God's grace, to deal unto you Christ's cards, wherein you shall perceive Christ's rule. The game that we will play at shall be called the triumph, which if it be well played at, he that dealeth shall win; the players shall likewise win; and the standers and lookers upon shall do the same; insomuch that there is no man that is willing to play at this triumph with these cards, but they shall all be winners, and no losers.[3]

This seems a long way from his text, 'Who art Thou?', taken from the Gospel for the Day (4th Sunday in Advent), but the listeners in St Edward's had plenty to reward their curiosity.

Speak this question unto ourselves, 'Who art thou?' The answer is, 'I am a Christian man'. Then further we must say to ourselves, 'What requireth Christ of a Christian man?' Now turn up your trump, your heart (hearts are trumps, as I said before) and cast your trump, your heart, on this card. . . .

The style may be irritating to our more factual age; but Latimer was engaged in a twofold task—to win the whole-

[3] *Sermons*, p. 8.

hearted allegiance of young men, many of them little more than boys, to a simple faith in Christ as well as to overturn the super-stitious practices as, by this time, he was sure they were, of his opponents. The pulpit provided entertainment as well as doctrine and debate. But Latimer's note deepens as he presses the claims of personal, practical religion upon his hearers and bids them avoid trust in the merely customary observances of the day. This is the kernel of truth for him at this time:

Evermore bestow the greatest part of thy goods in works of mercy, and the less part in voluntary works. Voluntary works be called all manner of offering in the church, except your four offering-days,[4] and your tithes: setting up candles, gilding and painting, building of churches, giving of ornaments, going on pilgrimages, making of highways, and such other, be called voluntary works . . . if thou go as many pilgrimages as thy body can well suffer, and offer as great candles as oaks; if thou leave the works of mercy and the command-ments undone, these works shall nothing avail thee.

This is by no means the essence of Luther. St James would not be an 'epistle of straw' for this preacher now or at any time; but he is discriminating between things of first importance and those which, of themselves are very secondary. This teaching was typical of the Bilney group, feeling after the implications of their newly-discovered Gospel.

But the challenge to the established order was unmistakable and was immediately taken up, especially by the Friars. It is one of the grand ironies of the history of the fourteenth and six-teenth centuries in England that the Friars, whose origin was in the preaching of an evangelism, at once simple and vernacu-lar, should be the first to defend the jots and tittles of a corrupt age. But as they had been in Wyclif's time, they would be now. Latimer's first opponent was a Prior of the Black Friars, Buckenham, who followed his rival's lead by seeking to be seasonal. He strained his arguments to fit a fanciful fame with dice, '*Cinque quatre*'—the five being selected portions of the New Testament and the *quatre* the four doctors of the Church: Ambrose, Augustine, Jerome, and Gregory. Buckenham's argu-ment was directed with bitter passion against the plea for the Scriptures in English. It seems unbelievable that a learned doctor should have attached any significance to the fear that

---

[4] Normally Christmas, Easter, Whitsuntide, and the Feast of Dedication of one's church.

the injunction, 'If thine eye offend thee, pluck it out', would cause so many people to obey it literally that it 'would fill the world with beggars'.

Latimer countered almost at once and made merry, tossing the friar's solicitude for the common people like so much hay. He had a good deal of faith in the Englishman's native use of metaphor and indulged it at the expense of Buckenham, who was sitting in the church:

When they paint a fox preaching out of a friar's cowl none is so mad to take this to be a fox that preacheth, but know well enough the meaning of the matter, which is to point out unto us, what hypocrisy, craft, and subtle dissimulation, lieth hid many times in these friars' cowls, willing us thereby to beware of them.

Latimer was enjoying himself too much, and it is not surprising that trouble lay ahead. Foxe is hopelessly adrift with his sequence of events, attributing the Bishop of Ely's censure and Barnes's permission to use the friary of St Augustine to this period. In fact, Barnes was now (Christmas 1529) on the Continent. He had, by a feigned suicide, escaped from the close confinement at Northampton which was the sequel to his two years and some nine months in comparatively loose detention in London, following his trial.

Both parties were hardening for the contest. The matter of the divorce was in all men's minds, and Wolsey had been succeeded as Chancellor by the reactionary layman, Sir Thomas More. Fisher, Bishop of Rochester, had great influence in Cambridge, and the conservatives would naturally look to these two as safeguards of the old ways. The Heads of Houses were no more sympathetic to possible riot than they have ever been, and there was no doubt of the danger that might come if the clash continued unchecked. In particular, there was a group of men from St John's College who were bitterly against Latimer—Bain, Rud, Greenwood, Proctor, and Brigenden (who had formerly been one of Latimer's pupils). The first-named of these, Bain (or Baynes) presently went into exile in Edwardian days and returned to become Bishop of Coventry and Lichfield.

The Vice-Chancellor, Buckmaster, was anxious to bring peace into his community, and after Christmas, while the stir occasioned by the sermons mentioned above was still a topic of current talk, he was reminded that other eyes were watchful of the Cambridge scene. Dr. Edward Foxe, the Royal Almoner, wrote to him in a letter dated 24th January 1530 that the King's notice had been drawn to 'the shameful contentions used now of late between Mr Latimer and certain of St John's College, insomuch His Grace intendeth to set some order therein'.[5] Private malice may be the cause, but these Johnians may be incited by their Master, a friend of Fisher, and it may be 'partly for that Mr Latimer favoureth the King's cause; and I assure you it is so reported to the King'. But Latimer may very well have been more vehement than an evangelist should be, and excess of zeal may have given offence. 'Ye shall, therefore, in my opinion do well to command both of them to silence, and that neither of them from henceforth preach until you know further of the King's pleasure.'

Dr Buckmaster gave effect to this strongly expressed wish at a meeting of the Senate [6] (29th January), and forbade further dissension, if they had any regard for the King's pleasure. Under threat of excommunication all parties were forbidden to indulge in any more spectacular preaching. Greenwood and his friends were assured that Latimer had satisfactorily answered all questions addressed to him, and he, in his turn, was warned to be circumspect and discreet in his preaching.

The sign of coming royal favour is shown by the phrase that Latimer 'favoureth the King's cause'. Subsequent events bore that out very plainly; but however eager Henry was to push forward his divorce from Katherine, there was no semblance of sympathy as yet with the plea of the Cambridge reformers for an English Bible or a religion stripped of the accretions of superstition. Although Henry was grateful for the suggestion that the advice of the Universities should be sought, which had evoked from him the typical remark that Cranmer had 'the sow by the right ear', his request for a favourable verdict was accompanied by threats against those who ventured to differ from him. He could show favour to those who were bold in espousing his 'cause', but Oxford was very sharply reminded that resistance to the King would 'stir up a hornet's nest'. The English Universities were, after all, his Universities, and should be on his side. The Spanish Universities were equally on Katherine's side, since the Emperor Charles was the monarch concerned and very much, at this juncture, on the Pope's side, quite apart from being Katharine's nephew. Verdicts from abroad were encouragingly favourable. Henry's agents, no doubt, made English gold to flow into unusual channels, but two sides could play at that game, as was well known by litigants at Papal and other Courts. Paris, Orleans, Toulouse, Bourges, Bologna, Ferrara, Pavia, Padua—it is a formidable list—all would declare in 1530 that it was not in the Pope's power to dispense with divine law. A man might not marry his deceased brother's wife. Henry would have been a very different man from the king we know, if he had left the English Universities a completely free hand to discuss this high matter impartially and with academic freedom. At Cambridge the Vice-Chancellor had scarcely finished with the internal troubles, brought to a head by the Christmas preaching, before he was asked on 15th February to put the royal question to the University.

The issue might seem to have been predetermined, but in fact there was considerable opposition. Foxe and Gardiner, came prepared to smile or frown as occasion demanded, but certainly to gain a favourable verdict for their master. The University did what large deliberative conferences have done with unfailing regularity: the decision was remitted to a committee. But who should sit upon it? Such a man as Latimer, for instance, whose opinion was already proclaimed? Objection was raised on this point,[7] but Latimer was put on the committee. Cranmer was not in Cambridge at the time. He had been there earlier, at the turn of the year and in January with his written thesis and personal presence to attempt the conversion of possible opponents to the royal cause—'Which being first attempted at Cambridge, Dr Cranmer, by his authority, learning, and persuasion, brought over divers learned men in one day, of the contrary part and opinion, to be on his part.'[8] Cranmer accompanied Anne Boleyn's father, the Earl of Wiltshire, and Stokesley and Lee on their visits to the Pope and Emperor: the embassy started at the end of January or beginning of February 1530. This was before the Cambridge verdict was obtained. Even though Gardiner later 'acquainted the King with what they had done, and how Dr Cranmer had changed the minds of five of the said learned men of Cambridge,

[7] ibid., 6247.   [8] Strype, *Cranmer*, I.i.9.

and of many others beside',[9] there was considerable opposition, and Latimer's opponents were, naturally enough, averse to furthering Henry's divorce.

Latimer's first sermon before Henry the Eighth was on the second Sunday in Lent, 13th March 1530. He received a gift [10] of £5 for this service—at least £100 in our money today. There is an engaging irony in the fact that among the people at Windsor was no other than Dr Buckmaster, who had come up dutifully to present the findings of the University concerning the marriage problem which had been settled on 9th March. We have his account of his visit, dated the Monday of Holy Week (11th April), written from Cambridge [11] to Dr Edmonds, Vicar of Alborne. The King's thanks to him seem to have smacked of bare formality, and he was aware that he was not *persona grata* as Latimer was. He had arrived at the Castle in the afternoon of the Sunday on which Latimer was preaching, in time for part of the sermon, and afterwards spoke with Gardiner and Foxe. After evensong he presented the letters of the University containing their verdict, and Henry conversed with him for 'a good while'. The King, having moved to another group in the presence-chamber, made gentle game of the Vice-Chancellor. 'But by and by he greatly praised Mr Latymer's sermon, and, in so praising; said on this wise:—This displeaseth greatly Mr Vice-Chancellor yonder. Yon same, said he unto the duke of Norfolk, is Mr Vice-chancellor of Cambridge;—and so pointed unto me.'

On the next day Buckmaster was kept hanging about until dinner time. Dr Butts then brought him a reward of £6 13s. 4d. Butts told him he could go when he liked. However, Foxe would have him speak again with the King 'and brought me into a privy place where as he would have me to wait. At after dinner I came thither and he both, and by one of the clock the King entered in. It was in a gallery. There were Mr Secretary, Mr Provost (Foxe), Mr Latimer, Mr Proctor and I, and no more: the King there talked with us until five of the clock.'

But the King was not too pleased with all he had heard concerning Dr Buckmaster's University in its attitude to the great question. '*An papa possit dispensare.*' The Vice-Chancellor was not even asked to have a drink, and so, on the next day 'de-

---

[9] Strype, *Cranmer*, p. 10.
[10] *State Papers, L. & P.*, V.p.749 (Privy Purse Expenses).   [11] ibid., IV.6325.

parted from thence, thinking more than I did say, and being glad that I was out of the court'.

There is a sting in the tail of the letter—'Mr Latimer preacheth still, *quod æmuli ejus graviter ferunt.*' It is no wonder his rivals did bear it sorely, for Latimer's star was rising, and the Vice-Chancellor had seen it for himself.

Latimer must have returned to Cambridge shortly after his visit to Windsor, but the claims of the court were laid increasingly upon him, and Foxe narrates that he 'remained a certain time in the said Dr Butt's chamber, preaching then in London very often'.[12] This refers to the summer of 1530, and the kind of opportunity afforded to him would scarcely be pleasing to those prelates who feared that the old order was in danger of changing a little too rapidly. Nix, the old, blind Bishop of Norwich (he had been consecrated in 1500) wrote [13] to Warham on 14th May 1530 making a general complaint concerning the growth in circulation of heretical literature. It had been openly stated in his diocese by people who possessed or read such books that the King himself permitted this. Nix had therefore asked the Abbot of Hyde (John Capon, brother to Wolsey's chaplain, and later Bishop of Bangor and Salisbury) to lay the matter before the King, in the confident expectation that heretics might not dare to say 'that the King's pleasure is, the New Testament in English shall go forth, and men should have it and read it'. He reports that such opinions are chiefly found among merchants and those 'that have their abiding not far from the sea', but not amongst the gentry. He also states his perturbation concerning Cambridge as a source of such trouble, naming Gunnel (Gonville) Hall—the foundation of a former Bishop of Norwich. 'I hear of no clerk that hath come out lately of that college but savoureth of the frying-pan, though he speak never so holily.'

It is not surprising that, with Bilney in his clutches a little more than a year later, Nix did not hesitate to burn him.

Nix was not alone in his concern. In the same month the King requested the Universities of Oxford and Cambridge [14] to send twelve representatives to sit on a royal commission of inquiry regarding heretical literature in general and some books in particular. The commission was to meet in London on

---

[12] *Acts and Monuments*, VII.454.   [13] App. XII, Strype's *Cranmer*.
[14] *State Papers, L. & P.*, IV.6367

Tuesday evening, 10th May. Among the twelve from Cambridge was Hugh Latimer; among those from Oxford his un-
related namesake, William Latimer, the scholar and friend of
Sir Thomas More and Erasmus, and the tutor of Cardinal
Pole. Latimer's position at Cambridge now, and his growing
reputation at court, combined to ensure his nomination. Did
Buckmaster have some puckish hope that Latimer's true loyalties would involve him in such arguments that he would be in
trouble with the Chancellor, More, and the Archbishop? Certainly if Latimer had spoken out at these committee meetings
with something of the boldness and fire of his pulpit work, he
must have been involved in a serious clash with his ecclesiastical
superiors. Foxe will have no blot on the scutcheon of his hero
if he can help it, and hastens [15] to point forward to a service
on behalf of the English Bible (which he attributes to Latimer),
the famous letter to Henry the Eighth 'for restoring again the
free liberty of reading the Holy Scriptures'. He prints the
'writing of the Bishops against English books' given on 24th
May in the Old Chapel at the Palace of Westminster in the
presence of the King. Archbishop Warham, Tunstal, the
Bishop of Durham, the Chancellor, Sir Thomas More, and
Mr Secretary Gardiner, with a large company, including the
representatives of the Universities, signed the document,[16] and
Latimer's name cannot be missed. Can excuse or reason be
offered for him? The purpose of the commission was to examine
doubtful books and also to consider the desirability of publishing the Scriptures in English, since it had been alleged that the
King was in favour of it. The practical consequence was the
publication of a declaration which was to be read by preachers,
warning their people against

. . . the books called *The Obedience of a Christian Man, The Sum of
Scripture, The Revelation of Anti-Christ, The Supplication of Beggars,
Mammona Iniquitatis, The Matrimony of Tyndale, The New Testament in
English*, of the translation which is now printed, and such other books
in English, the authors whereof either dare not, ne do not put to
their names . . .

Great emphasis was laid upon the fact that members of the
commission had complete freedom to speak according to their
conscience and learning, whatever persons might be involved
and no man was under 'any necessity to agree to the more'.

[15] *Acts and Monuments*, VII.498 ff.   [16] *State Papers, L. & P.*, IV.6402.

This is all very well, but it smacks too much of totalitarian states in the twentieth century. Holbein never had to paint Henry the Eighth receiving a minority report. But ought Latimer to have agreed to such words as these?

... it was there by a whole consent, no man repugning or again-saying, determined and agreed that the books now being abroad in the English tongue contain false traditions and corrupt doctrine far discrepant from the true sense of the gospel and catholic under-standing of Scripture, only persuading pernicious heresies to the destruction of the souls of good Christian men. . . .

The commission had considered whether it was advisable to give every man open access to the Scriptures in his own tongue and decided that, though this might be done at the King's pleasure 'the having of the whole Scripture in English is not necessary to Christian men'. The King had promised that if it were advisable at any time, he would 'cause the New Testament to be by learned men faithfully and purely translated into English tongue'.

We have no detailed account of the debates that occurred between various members of the commission. Specific items were singled out in the works examined, and Tyndale came in for particularly severe treatment.[17]

It may safely be assumed that Latimer would not be silent in the conversations, and there can be no question of his belief in many of the articles condemned. It cannot, however, be maintained that he was yet prepared to go all the way with Tyndale. We cannot assess with accuracy all that Latimer did believe at this time. Bilney was much more fully in sympathy with Tyndale's whole position, though even he was compara-tively orthodox on the Mass. Latimer, if we rely at all on the Card sermons—and they are all we have of his declared doc-trine at this time—did not proclaim the abolition of ceremonies but put them into a secondary place and insisted upon the necessity of sincerity and freedom from corruption and hypo-crisy. But he did hold to 'the Word of God' as the great essen-tial to be preached and believed, and this meant access to the Bible for Englishmen in a vernacular version. He must have agreed to the verdict of the Archbishop and his fellow com-missioners only with the gravest misgiving. There are times

[17] Vide Foxe, op. cit., V.570 ff. Foxe's first edition is almost complete in its account: the second is more selective and contains his own comments.

when it is impossible to answer with a plain 'Yes' or 'No'—and Latimer was in such a dilemma now. It often happens, however, that being involved in a public decision has an effect on one's private faith. If fear entered in, as it must have done to some extent, it would come upon him again and vanquish him before his certainty grew big enough to resist everything his conscience could not approve and set his feet unfalteringly upon his way.

The findings of the commission were given full force of law by the King within a month in '*A Proclamation* . . . for dampning of erronious bokes and heresies, and probitinge the havinge of Holy Scripture translated into the vulgar tonges of englische, frenche, or duche.' All such books were to be delivered up at once without evil consequences to the owners. If the people comply, the King intends to provide for a new translation, 'if it shal then seme to his grace convenient so to be'. It has been maintained that this contains a promise; but it is hedged round with a multitude of 'if's'. Neither Bishops nor King at this time wanted the English Bible. So far as the hopes of the Cambridge men were concerned they might find as much comfort in the yellow-hammer's song of the 'little bit of bread and no che-e-ese' as in this Proclamation.

An item of £8 paid to Foxe as Almoner for the expenses of Latimer and other unnamed Cambridge men 'for their costs from Cambridge to London, and fro thens to Cambridge again' is dated 18th September.[18] This would be tardy settling of bills if it referred to the activities of May and June, but it is another shred of evidence to show how Latimer's increasing duties at court had not cut him off, as yet, completely from Cambridge.

The famous *Letter of Master Latimer written to King Henry for restoring again the free liberty of reading the holy scriptures*, is dated by Foxe, 1st December 1530.[19] Dr Gairdner says Foxe is wrong in claiming this as Latimer's and that it is apparently the work of a layman.[20] Certainly both the manuscript copies in the Public Record Office are undated and without the name of the writer; equally certainly biographers of Latimer and historians have accepted the letter as his. Are they wrong? Foxe gives it as Latimer's work. The fact that our existing manuscript copies are undated does not preclude the possibility that the

[18] *State Papers, L. & P.*, V.p751 (Privy Purse Expenses).
[19] *Remains*, pp. 297 ff. (Foxe, op. cit., VII.506 ff.).
[20] *Dictionary of National Biography*.

copy used by Foxe was dated. It was printed in the 1563 edition and has evoked the praise of many admirers of Latimer ever since as being true to the bold nature of the man. There is nothing explicit in the Letter which betrays the identity of the writer as a layman—for Latimer and others of his group held the convictions expressed in it concerning the worldliness of many prelates and the desirability of allowing the English Bible. Dr. Gairdner affirms that Tyndale's version had been 'one of the books disapproved by Latimer and his fellow commissioners'. But the Letter pleads for the principles of having an English Bible, not for a specific version. It is unfair to speak of 'Latimer and his fellow commissioners' as though he gave his whole-hearted assent to what we know must have been against the trend of his preaching and convictions. Latimer may be accused of cowardice, even of denial of his cause, by remaining silent. But the argument from his assent and silence in May is one we dare not press as binding for the future. It may disappoint the admirer of Latimer that he must admit such failure, but conscience and growing conviction could work their way with him in succeeding months. When at length he spoke openly and plainly, so that he did fall into the hands of the Bishops, it was in just such fashion as that found in the Letter.

The events of that autumn, with Sir Thomas More vigilant as Chancellor, and the Bishops active against heresy, were such as to goad him into action, and all the time his own contacts with the court and the King were making it increasingly possible for him to state his convictions. His manner from the first commended him to Henry, and we have seen how he did not hesitate to speak to the King on matters of personal pastoral interest. Is it inconceivable that he had never conversed on this very point of an English Bible with Henry?

Froude looked at those days and people with very different eyes from those of men belonging to the mid-twentieth century so full of wars, treacheries, secret police, and bitter antagonisms of ideology. We have, at least, lived dangerously in a way unknown and impossible to a Victorian, and in a time surprisingly similar in many respects to that of Tudor England. But a reading of this 'Letter to Henry the Eighth' makes one appreciate that it is 'an address of almost unexampled grandeur'.[21] It is respectful, but bold, loyal and adventurous.

[21] Froude, *History of England*, 'Henry VIII', I.vi.

Latimer pleads that he must obey his conscience—

either I must shew forth such things as I have read and learned in
scripture, or else be of that sort that provoke the wrath of God upon
them, and be traitors unto the truth: the which thing rather than it
should happen, I had rather suffer extreme punishment.

The superior clergy are compared to the Pharisees—

And especially in this your realm, they have sore blinded your
liege people and subjects with their laws, customs, ceremonies, and
Banbury glosses, and punished them with cursings, excommunica-
tions, and other corruptions (corrections, I would say). And now,
at the last, when they see that they cannot prevail against the open
truth (which the more it is persecuted, the more it increaseth by their
tyranny), they have made it treason to your noble grace to have the
scripture in English.

He reminds the King that he is called to majesty by God—

for you be here to me and to all your subjects in God's stead, to
defend, aid, and succour us in our right; and so I should tremble and
quake to speak to your grace. But again, as concerning that you be a
mortal man, in danger of sin, having in you the corrupt nature of
Adam, in the which all we be both conceived and born; so have you
no less need of the merits of Christ's passion for your salvation than
I and other of your subjects have, which be all members of the
mystical body of Christ.

The graphic touches describing our Lord's Mother and
Joseph 'in the cold frosty winter' and the plea for the virtue of
spiritual poverty have all the marks of that adroitness in address
which belonged to Latimer's preaching. The fact is, he con-
tends, that 'they whose works be naught, dare not come to this
light', and so he presses his central plea for the English Bible.

But as concerning this matter, other men have showed your grace
their minds, how necessary it is to have the scripture in English.
The which thing also your grace hath promised by your last proclamation: the which promise I pray God that your gracious highness may shortly perform, even today, before tomorrow.

The preaching of the Gospel will inevitably be accompanied
by persecution until its final victory.

But my purpose is, for the love that I have to God principally, and
the glory of his name, which is only known by his word, and for the
true allegiance that I owe unto your grace, and not to hide in the

ground of my heart the talent given me of God, but to chaffer it forth to other that it may increase to the pleasure of God, to exhort your grace to avoid and beware of these mischievous flatterers and their abominable ways and counsels.

The conclusion is all the more daring because of its allusion to the title of which Henry was always inordinately proud, with the prayer

that your grace may be found acceptable in his sight, and one of the members of his church; and, according to the office that he hath called your grace unto, you may be found a faithful minister of his gifts, and not a defender of his faith: for he will not have it defended by man or by man's power, but by his word only. . . .

The Reformation Parliament, which began to sit in November 1529 had already shown its willingness to pare away some of the income of the clergy, and Henry would presently expect to be acknowledged as 'Supreme Head of the Church', a very different rank from that suggested to him in this letter. But the Scriptures were not forthcoming. The Gospel would be preached, and persecution would increase during the next few months.

At the end of 1530 Latimer was becoming painfully aware of the cramping effect of court life. Being a royal chaplain was not fulfilling his destiny. He longed for the greater freedom of his true work, and Butts, the physician, sympathized with him, however reluctantly. Largely at his suing and Cromwell's (now striding towards power), Latimer was given the living of West Kington on the farther confines of the diocese of Salisbury. He was installed as rector there on 14th January 1531. His diocesan was no other than Campeggio himself—the personification of absenteeism, plurality, the Papal power, against all of which this new country rector would raise up his voice.

CHAPTER FOUR

Parish Priest

LATIMER was Rector of West Kington from January 1531 until September 1535. They were changeful, momentous years for England, and he shared to the full the excitements and dangerous ventures of the time. A bare enumeration of the chief matters affecting the Church in these four years and nine months is sufficient to show what an impassable gulf would be fixed between all that men had known for centuries and the flux of the future. Not that they would realize how unalterable were the consequences of actions which to them often had at first only the significance of temporary political or diplomatic moves. Threats and gestures were common enough then as now. But in fact Henry would discover enormous advantages to himself by becoming the only ruler of his realm, in matters spiritual as well as secular. His aim was still to secure his dynasty with a lawful, unquestioned successor. If Katherine had been the mother of a living prince, Henry might have enjoyed Anne Boleyn as his mistress and few people would have worried much about it—certainly not the Pope; and the royal confessor would be there to reprove and admonish and save a certain amount of spiritual face. But what might have been has no place in historic record. It would seem that Anne did set her cap at queenship, and Henry's curiously compounded nature did harbour some genuine fear that the lesser sin of lusting for possession of Anne, whose black eyes and vivacious manner seem to have been her main physical attractions, was as nothing in comparison with the enormity that had been his in crashing against the levitical code and marrying his brother's widow.

In 1531 his anger against Papal power and his continual need of money caused him to accuse the Church in England of *praemunire*. Wolsey had been the Papal legate *a latere*, superior to Warham whose status was *legatus natus*, as it had been common to Archbishops of Canterbury for four hundred years; and he had been Henry's Chancellor. To disobey Wolsey, any time before the spring of 1529, would have been likely to incur a

King's wrath as well as a Cardinal's. It was no odds to Henry now. Because the Churchmen had accepted him as Papal legate, because thereby they were creatures of the Pope, they had broken the law of his realm. They were logicians in the schools. Let them now find what logic they could in his action —but their confession of guilt he would have, and their future obedience. In the meantime they must pay. They did pay— and the amount was crippling; £100,000 from the Convocation of Canterbury and £18,840 0s. 10d. from York. As though this were not enough, Henry must be acknowledged as Supreme Head of the Church in England. Warham's permitted clause, to salve a few consciences, 'So far as the law of Christ allows' could make little compensation and no practical difference. Everyone knew the real effect of this, and in the next year, 1532, the two Convocations submitted to the condition that no new ecclesiastical law could be made without the King's assent, and the existing canon law must be revised. Warham—the last Archbishop of Canterbury of the old order—received the re- ward of timely death in August 1532, released from anxiety and responsibility a few months before action in the matter of 'the King's cause' became absolutely imperative. Cranmer must succeed him. William the Second had once thrust the staff into Anselm's unwilling hands: now Henry the Eighth would thrust staff, mitre, and pallium upon the unwilling Cranmer, the man who could best of all serve him at this juncture. No matter that he shrank from it; no matter that he had a wife. What Cranmer must have was recognition and the formal symbols of his office, in so far as the Pope had always hitherto conferred them. Cranmer was rushed into his See, and Henry's friendship for the Pope flourished suddenly so that Cranmer might have his pall and be no less an Archbishop of Canterbury than the aged Warham now gone to his rest. What inward qualifications might be in the new Archbishop's mind as he swore the customary oaths regarding his links with the Pope were neither here nor there. Cranmer's first and finest loyalty would be to his monarch: of that Henry was quite sure, and with that Cranmer was well content. As a matter of fact, before his consecration on 30th March 1533, Cranmer made that plain to witnesses. The Crown counted supremely, and the Pope very little. These two men understood each other—and it is to Henry's credit that Cranmer could tell him what no

other counsellor dared to say. The King broke other faithful
servants of his person and interests—but this man he befriended,
and at the last would clasp his hand, when speech was gone,
in token that he trusted in God through the merits of
Christ.

By the end of January 1533, Henry was secretly married to
Anne, and no one knows by whom the ceremony was per-
formed. In June she was crowned at Westminster by Cranmer,
as Archbishop. Her baby was born in September, and on the
10th of that month the new Archbishop stood godfather to the
future Queen Elizabeth. In 1534-5 a series of Acts finally
demolished the authority of the Pope in England, and Parliament passed as the law of the land what Convocation had confessed with a futile qualification in 1531—that the King was
Supreme Head of the Church.

The Rector of West Kington had withdrawn of his own will
from the court and its perils before these things had happened.
He had said that the preaching of the Gospel would inevitably
be fraught with persecution, and before his friend, Cranmer,
came to Canterbury he would learn the prophetic nature of
his own words: for the power of the Bishops and their courts
was still great.

It is well known that sympathies of a Lollard kind existed in
Gloucestershire. Ten years before Latimer came to West
Kington, Tyndale had been living in the neighbourhood as
tutor to the family of Sir John Walsh at Little Sodbury Manor
and had got himself into trouble with the local clergy by his
outspoken comments. He was a champion of the Scriptures
already, and his criticism of the conservative 'great beneficed
men' earned for him an appearance before the Chancellor of
the diocese of Worcester, which then reached down as far as
Bristol.

Men who were alert to Tyndale's menace would not be slow
in noticing Latimer's preaching [1] and his advocacy of the
English Bible. We perhaps underestimate, in these days of
rapid travel and wireless or newspaper publicity, the way in
which a man's views could be known far away from his usual
haunts. Latimer's light had not been hidden under a bushel
at Cambridge, and a preacher to the King could be sure of an
audience in the West Country. Countryman as he was, he

[1] Foxe, *Acts and Monuments*, VII.478.

would know how to win attention, and his restless energy would not respect his parish boundaries.

Foxe prints letters that show something of the feeling soon aroused among neighbouring clergy. The first [2] is from a priest, Dr Wm. Sherwood, addressed from Derham or Dirham (Glos.) close to West Kington. It is in Latin and reproves Latimer for a general attack he made on the clergy when preaching at Marshfield in the same neighbourhood. The text of the sermon was John 10 (Christ the Good Shepherd) but Latimer, so Sherwood asserted, had identified the vast majority of Popes, Bishops, rectors, and vicars with 'thieves and robbers'. There was not enough hemp in England to hang them; and as to the Church, whoever made Peter's confession was Peter's equal. Matthew 16 referred to all Christians who made that confession. Sherwood also mentioned that Latimer's teaching was Lutheran doctrine, that all Christians are priests and receive no power through ordination which they did not have before.

Sherwood's letter professed to be corrective with Christian sincerity from a priest to his brother-priest, but its tone soon became derisive. Latimer could be as blunt and outspoken [3]— in letters as in the pulpit and said that he had been insulted more than once by Sherwood when he was under the influence of drink. He replies at length that he did not attack Popes, Bishops, and clergy in general. He made the charge of being thieves only against those who 'climbed up another way'. Nor did he deny Peter's power of the keys. He had not said, or even thought, anything of the kind, and the primacy of Peter had not been mentioned. He had urged his hearers to recall that the Church was founded on a rock, not on the sand. They should not cling to a dead faith, but show their faith in good works and so obtain eternal life. 'What could be farther from the meaning of my words than that all Christians are priests as I am? But the envious are very keen-sighted in discovering their game.' Latimer remarks in passing, 'I am too much engaged by daily preaching conveniently to answer you.'

Sherwood's second letter [4] is not so confident or arrogant as the first. He climbs down without admitting he was wrong, and reproves Latimer for the tone of his letter, denying that

[2] ibid.   [3] ibid., p. 480 (original); *Remains*, p. 309 (translation).
[4] Foxe, op. cit., VII.484.

he had ever spoken bitterly or railed 'in his cups' (*inter pocula*)
against him. He had understood that Latimer had warned his
hearers against the 'Ave Maria'. However he is glad to think
he is more orthodox than was reported, and in particular that
Latimer did not deprecate Peter's power of the keys (*nihil
omnino de vi clavium locutus*).

There is an echo of Latimer's preaching in London, prior to
his coming to West Kington, in a proposition [5] made in Convocation on the 3rd March of this same year. Tunstal had
been translated from London to Durham in 1530 and his successor, Stokesley, was not slow in beginning his efforts to bring
the Cambridge preachers to account. Crome, Latimer, and
Bilney were named together and the matter came up for consideration on 18th March and was again deferred. Of the three
men named, Latimer and Bilney were out of his grasp at present,
though Bilney that spring would begin his last itinerant preaching. Crome had been one of the habitués of the 'White Horse'
in his Cambridge days, and there can be no doubt of the
genuineness of his Protestant sympathies. He would, however,
save himself several times by recantations and survive to die
naturally in 1562, though many of his friends came to the stake
or suffered severely in prison. Crome at this time held the
rectory of St Antholin's in the City, and a year before this
citation in March 1531, had appeared before his Bishop, Henry
the Eighth also being present. He had succumbed before this
double authority and professed his general orthodoxy of belief,
and in purgatory and the necessity of fasting. Because of
Crome's recent public confession (which, however, his evangelical friends refused to believe represented his true convictions) matters were not pressed against him at Convocation in
1531.

Latimer remained in his parish at West Kington until the
summer, when he turned once more towards London. It is
surmised that influential friends, Cromwell and Butts, for
example, may have pressed him [6] to come: but he does not
mention their names in his letters to Sir Edward Baynton,
written later in the year on his return. Is it possible that he
was hoping to meet Bilney? What seems absurd is that Latimer
should have gone to London deliberately to preach in open

[5] Wilkins, *Concilia*, III.725. (Foxe, op. cit., VII, App., p. 774.)
[6] Demaus, *Hugh Latimer*, p. 117.

defiance of Stokesley, unless he completely misjudged the consequences of such action and his own possible failure to withstand the pressure of a trial if he should be arrested.

In fact, that summer saw much activity in London against potential heresy. Sir Thomas More was devoted to the old order and would do all he could to help any efforts Stokesley and his colleagues might make to prevent Lutheran, or any other, infiltration. There was considerable traffic in banned books. In 1530 Hitton, an agent helping to bring Tyndale's New Testament into England, was taken and tried: he was burned at Maidstone. Hitton, like Bilney, was from Norfolk.

There is a sombre fitness in the fact that the next man to be burned should be Bilney, the first of the Cambridge men to suffer the extreme penalty, though two others,[7] Thomas Dusgate at Exeter, and Richard Bayfield at Smithfield, would come to the stake in the same year, 1531. These all were directly or indirectly connected with the traffic in Tyndale's works; but the story of Bilney is of special importance because of his close connexion with Latimer.

One night in the spring of 1531, about ten o'clock, Bilney had called his friends together in his rooms at Trinity Hall where he bade them a solemn farewell, 'For I must needs go up to Jerusalem.' He left Cambridge and wandered about the countryside of Norfolk, distributing copies of Tyndale's New Testament, preaching in religious households in private, and openly in the fields. It would seem that he went as far as London, for he was seen at Greenwich six weeks before his arrest in Norwich, where he had given an anchoress,[8] probably Dame Agnes Edrugge, an English New Testament and *The Obedience of a Christian Man*. In this determined and open-eyed offering of himself, Bilney everywhere proclaimed his sorrow at his previous weakness, said that the doctrine he had preached before his recantation was the truth, and wished men to be warned by him 'never to trust to their fleshly friends in causes of religion'.

He came now into the grip of Nix, the blind Bishop of Norwich. Foxe reports that when Nix sent for a writ to burn Bilney, Sir Thomas More, the Lord Chancellor remarked to

---

[7] Gordon Rupp, *The English Protestant Tradition*, pp. 197 f.
[8] ibid., p. 29 n., and Blomefield, *History of Norfolk*, IV.82.

C

the messengers: 'Go your ways and burn him first; and then afterwards come to me for a bill of my hand.'

While Bilney lay in prison the Friars were diligent to obtain another recantation. They had no success. Nor was the trial lengthy. Bilney was a relapsed heretic; he had been caught in the act of disseminating heretical literature. He was examined, condemned, and degraded. The night before he went to the stake he sat quietly talking with friends, who were allowed to see him. He was of cheerful heart (and this calm joy is reflected in a fragment of a letter written to his father and mother). He said that, on the next day, though the fire might be of great heat to his body, God's Spirit would cool it. Then little Bilney, who had endured the fires of remorse, put his hand into the candle-flame and held it there, steady and unflinching. 'What do you, Master Bilney?' said the doctor who was with him. 'Nothing, but trying my flesh by God's grace, and burning one joint, when tomorrow God's rods shall burn the whole body in the fire.'

The next day, Saturday, 19th August 1531, he came, degraded and wearing a layman's gown, to the stake in Lollards' Pit in his native Norwich. He exhorted the bystanders to be true in faith and life, and forgave his enemies; but there was no recantation. After the flames had tortured him cruelly, for the dry reeds flared up swiftly and were blown backwards and forwards about him by a strong wind before the wood caught, the little body sank into nothingness.

More, in his writing against Tyndale, sought later on to establish that Bilney again recanted and read a bill of abjuration. Latimer, as we have seen, asserted that he died 'against the tyrannical see of Rome', but that was a verdict made twenty years later in a very different atmosphere from that of 1531. The reports concerning what happened at the stake [9] contain much that is confused and indefinite. If More had contented himself with pointing out that Bilney was orthodox on the Mass he would have been on surer ground. That he died without the consolation of the Sacrament and the blessing of the Church is undoubted. There was one man present at his burning who, though no martyr, was of undoubted probity—Matthew Parker; and he breathed no word of Bilney's faltering. The evidence

---

[9] Printed by Townshend in Appendix to Vol. IV, Foxe's *Acts and Monuments*.

has been carefully sifted by Mr Gordon Rupp in 'The "Recantation" of Thomas Bilney'.[10] Mr Rupp says:

Sir Thomas More, who had a large faculty for believing what he wanted to believe, chose to think that Bilney had made a complete retraction, yet he had no more evidence to go upon than that which is available to us. That evidence shows a consistency in the character of Thomas Bilney, the same hesitancy of a man of conscience, the same willingness to do all that could be granted for the avoidance of a public scandal. It fits the proceedings of his earlier trial and the last letters he penned on the very eve of his death. He loved the catholic church and treasured her sacraments. But there is no reason whatever to suppose that he renounced the gospel of the grace and glory of God which had constrained him to preach unletted by human jurisdiction. None the less, the authorities partly succeeded. They had blurred the issue. Bilney was no Lollard, but a considerable figure with a not undistinguished following in the Universities. The trumpet had sounded an uncertain note. 'Remember Bilney' warned Tyndale as he wrote to his brother John Frith as he too came near to the fiery furnace. The death of Bilney marks a stage. Hitherto in England the Lollards had provided most of the materials for trials of heresy. Like other medieval sects these underground movements existed by building a mask of subterfuge and masquerade. Now the stage was set for a more courageous witness. There was enough truth in Sir Thomas More's sneer at the perfidy of heretics to make it sting.

Among the treasures Parker later bequeathed to his college, Corpus Christi, were letters of Bilney and his Bible, much annotated in his own hand and very heavily marked at the words in Isaiah 43, 'Cum ambulaveris in igne, non combureris' (When thou walkest in the fire thou shalt not be burned).

It is plain that, before the end of the year Latimer, now back in his parish, was apprehensive of trouble. Our main source for his movements and contentions is the correspondence which passed between him and Sir Edward Baynton,[11] a local magnate whose seat at Bromham (near Devizes) was only a few miles away. Baynton was related to Cardinal Pole and well liked by the King. He had previously written to Latimer evidently acquainting him both with complaints that had been made against him and advising what he should do if summoned to appear on any charge. The first [12] of the three letters Foxe

[10] *London Quarterly and Holborn Review*, April 1942.
[11] Foxe, op. cit., VII, App., p. 776.   [12] ibid., pp. 484–97; and *Remains*, p. 322.

has printed is Latimer's reply. From it we gather that the Chancellor of the diocese, Dr Richard Hilley, had already informed Latimer that the Bishop of London had been requesting that he should be sent up for examination. Hilley was Latimer's ordinary for all practical purposes since Cardinal Campeggio was the absentee Bishop of Salisbury, but it is not surprising that, as Chancellor, he was not so strong in resisting Stokesley's claim as an English Bishop would have been if his own territory were invaded. Latimer was not in good health, 'not only exercised with my disease in my head and side', probably catarrhal and pleural complaints, 'but also with new, both the cholic and the stone'. It is 'deep winter'. From the end of the letter we see that the time is the latter end of December—'If I be not prevented shortly, I intend to make merry with my parishioners this Christmas, for all the sorrow, lest perchance I never return to them.'

He speaks of his activities in the previous summer. He had preached in the church of St Mary Abchurch, and in Kent (presumably this would be in Fisher's diocese of Rochester) and Latimer had heard of no protest to the curate from his Bishop: he is therefore all the more surprised that Stokesley is accusing him of disregarding his authority. London merchants had pressed him to preach. For their sakes he is glad he does not even know their names, and the incumbent (Thomas Clark) and his curate had surely had no idea of infringing the Bishop's rights or they would not have received him with the customary courtesies. As a matter of fact Latimer sought to excuse himself, 'but they showed not only themselves, but also many other, to be very desirous to hear me, pretending great hunger and thirst of the word of God and ghostly doctrine'. He had pointed out that his only licence was that from his University and he was not certain then that St Mary Abchurch was 'in his diocese or no, intending nothing less than to condemn his authority'. The dodge—it can be called nothing less—of preaching in a church, attached to a monastery or friary or otherwise not subject to complete episcopal authority though geographically within a diocese, had been used previously at Cambridge, as we have seen, by both Barnes and Latimer to flout the Bishop of Ely's orders. None the less, it seems strange that Latimer did not make sure, and double sure, that he was safe in preaching there. Perhaps he hoped that, if the worst came to the worst, there might be royal deliverance for him—as, indeed, there was Henry's protection at last to keep him from the full consequences of Stokesley's resentment.

The impulsiveness which often helped to bring greatness into Latimer's preaching broke out in his letters, but with unfortunate results. He explains to Baynton that he had, indeed, in his recent preaching attempted to

monish judges and ordinaries to use charitable equity in their judgments towards such as be accused, namely of such accusers which be as like to hear and bewray, as others be to say amiss; and to take men's words in the meaning thereof, and not to wrest them in another sense than they were spoken in.

He expands this with great prolixity, inferring that St Paul himself might have been the victim of wrong accusation, 'then Good St Paul [13] must have borne a fagot at Paul's Cross, my lord of London being his judge. Oh! it had been a goodly sight, to have seen St Paul with a fagot on his back, even at Paul's Cross, my lord of London, bishop of the same, sitting under the cross.'

He refers to the need of preaching with special reference to Stokesley. That prelates should be preachers was consistently his theme, and when he became a Bishop himself he was as good in performance as he had been in advice. He skirmishes around the Bishop of London's reputation: [14]

Me seemeth it were more comely for my lord (if it were comely for me to say so) to be a preacher himself, having so great a cure as he hath, than to be a disquieter and a troubler of preachers, and to preach nothing at all himself. If it would please his lordship to take so great a labour and pain at any time, as to come to preach in my little bishopric at West-Kington, whether I were present or absent myself, I would thank his lordship heartily, and think myself greatly bounden to him, that he of his charitable goodness would go so far to help to discharge me in my cure, or else I were more unnatural than a beast unreasonable; nor yet I would dispute, contend or demand by what authority, or where he had authority so to do, as long as his predication were fruitful and to the edification of my parishioners.

This matter of authority was a continual source of trouble. Latimer relied upon his being authorized by the University of Cambridge as a passport anywhere in the realm. His name

[13] Foxe, op. cit., VII, p. 486.　　　　[14] ibid., p. 487.

appears as early as 1522–3 [15] as one of twelve preachers appointed and he speaks specifically of what he deems this to imply in his first letter to Baynton: [16]

For the university of Cambridge hath authority apostolic to admit twelve yearly, of the which I am one: and the king's highness (God save his grace!) did decree that all admitted of universities should preach throughout all his realm so long as they preached well, without distrain of any man, my lord of Canterbury, my lord of Durham, with such other not a few, standing by, and hearing the decree, nothing gainsaying it, but consenting to the same.

Latimer has also heard that the Bishop of London has been informed, and conveyed the information to the King that in his sermons he has been defending Bilney and complaining about his trial. He disclaims any recent connexion with Bilney, but he does insert this testimony of character:

I have known Bilney a great while, I think much better than ever did my lord of London; for I have been his ghostly father many a time. And to tell you the truth what I have thought always in him, I have known hitherto few such, so prompt and ready to do every man good after his power. . . .

Latimer cannot approve wilful disobedience to his proper authorities by Bilney or any other man, and he will not meddle with the matter of his judgement.

As to his own preaching, Latimer claims he has taught nothing out of accord with Scripture, the fathers, and long-established interpretation. He believes the three Creeds, but there are some things about which he is not so sure as he once was—and here he gives a peep into his mind and preaching. He once was sure that the Pope was Lord of all things on earth, 'so that if he should have deprived the king of his crown or you of the lordship of Bromeham, it had been enough; for he could do no wrong'. Similarly, concerning pluralism, absenteeism, and indulgences. The dread of death, so conspicuous in Luther's young manhood, was evidently well known to Latimer.

I have thought in times past that if I had been a friar and in a cowl, I could not have been damned nor afraid of death; and by occasion of the same, I have been minded many times to have been a friar,

[15] Foxe, op. cit., VII, App., p. 776, quoting Proctors' Accounts.
[16] ibid., p. 487.

namely when I was sore sick and diseased; now I abhor my superstitious foolishness &c.

As to images of saints, of special help for various ailments, he
knows now that one is as good as another. Prayer, study of
the Scriptures, and the counsel of men who had right judgement have been his means of deliverance. And surely a man
may change his views on some points, for the Bishop of London
himself now favoured the King's cause of divorce—it might
have brought him to the fire in Pope Julius the Second's time.
As to the Bishop, 'it is a rare thing for a preacher to have
favour at his hand, which is no preacher himself, and yet
ought to be'.

Some of this was dangerous stuff, if it should ever come into
the hands of his enemies: and however much Latimer is to be
admired for boldness, his remarks about Stokesley were rash
and impudent.

Baynton replied shortly to him. He has communicated to
his friends the substance [17] of Latimer's letters (there were,
presumably, letters written earlier in the autumn as well as
the long one we have considered). For himself, he is an un-
skilled layman and his view will be that of the majority.

It is not difficult to visualize this important landowner listening to the views of conservative priests, and, if Sherwood was
typical of those in the neighbourhood, being persuaded of the
imminence of danger. Radicalism in religion has always, in
England, been associated with social agitation, in Wyclif's time
as in the days of the Tolpuddle martyrs. In fact, Latimer was
no upsetter of established rank and order. But Baynton professed friendship to him and conveyed the opinion of his friends
that Latimer should reform himself to prevent any dissension
or disunity.

Latimer's second letter [18] is more cautious and is chiefly concerned with his plea that a man should only preach that of
which he is sure. But it does not follow that points on which
men differ need cause deep dissension. For example, is it God's
word or man's judgement that a man should not marry his
brother's wife? Latimer's opinion is that it is God's, and so no
man may annul it. What is the view of Baynton's friends? It
is a rhetorical question, but it serves as a reminder that on this

[17] ibid., pp. 490–1. [18] *Remains*, pp. 334–51.

point the King's divorce will be effected or not, and Latimer is on the King's side. Only towards the end of the letter does he touch upon the topics which loom largely in the first letter. He abandons the fulsome and academic treatment of what is, or is not fatal dissension, and does not ring true to his general concreteness of style. What we possess is only a draft of what he intended to revise carefully before sending it to Sir Edward Baynton. But when he was 'beginning to write it again more truly and more distinctly, and to correct it' a man came from Sir [19] Walter Hungerford's at Farley Hungerford, a few miles from Bath, with a summons that Latimer was to appear before the Bishop of London to answer for what he had done in the summer. 'Jesu mercy, what a world is this, that I shall be put to so great labour and pains, besides great costs above my power, for preaching of a poor simple sermon.'

And so what he dreaded must happen and the journey be made in 'deep winter'. The official citation, made by Dr Richard Hilley,[20] Chancellor of Salisbury, is dated 10th January 1532. Latimer is to appear before the Bishop of London's consistory at St Paul's on 29th January between 9 and 11 a.m.

He had pleaded ill-health as a reason for not being sent to the inquiry in London, but he must also have been deeply perturbed in mind. Latimer's later profession was so sure, and his single-mindedness so evident, that his admirers are baffled by his submission to the authorities in the spring of 1532. It will serve us best, in trying to understand his failure—for he did fail to stand—if we follow the events as well as they can be ascertained.

Foxe is always loth to admit wavering by his heroes, but even he cannot make out a convincing case for Latimer's subscription to articles presented to him, and to suggest that he did not yield is flying in the face of facts.

Latimer made his journey at the worst time of the year, but we do not hear of him in London until he appears before Convocation.[21] This in itself is a little surprising, for it was at Stokesley's insistence that he had been compelled to go after his protest to his own diocesan authorities that they, and not the Bishop of London, were his immediate superiors. He was passed on from Stokesley to Convocation and appeared before

---

[19] Wordsworth, *Ecclesiastical Biography*, III.516, note.
[20] Foxe, op. cit., VIII.455.　　　　　　　　[21] ibid., VII.3, App. VI.

Warham, Stokesley, and several other prelates six weeks later, on 11th March. To clear himself of the charge that he was 'noted and suspected of his faith and erroneous preachings', he was required to show his agreement to the following articles: [22]

1. Inprimis, that there is a place of purgation for souls after this life.
2. That souls in purgatory are holpen by masses, prayer, and alms-deed.
3. That the holy apostles and martyrs of Christ, being dead, are in heaven.
4. That the same saints, as mediators, pray for us in heaven.
5. That the said saints are to be honoured in heaven.
6. That pilgrimages and oblations are meritorious for the sepulchres and relics of saints.
7. That whosoever hath vowed chastity may not marry, nor break their vow, without dispensation of the high bishop.
8. That the keys of binding and loosing, given unto Peter, doth remain to his successors bishops, although they live evil; and they were never given for any cause to laymen.
9. That it is profitable for christian men to invocate saints, that they, as mediators, may pray unto God for us.
10. That men by alms-deed, prayer and other good works, may merit at God's hands.
11. That men forbidden of the bishops, by reason of suspicion, ought not to preach till such time as they had purged themselves to them or their superiors, and be lawfully restored.
12. That the Lent, and their fasting-days, commanded by the canons, and used with the Christians, are to be kept, except necessity require otherwise.
13. That God, by the merits of Christ's passion, doth give his grace in all the whole seven sacraments to the lawful receiver.
14. That the consecrations, sanctifications, and benedictions, received in the Christian Church, are laudable and profitable.
15. That [it] is laudable and profitable, that the images of the crucifix and saints are to be had in the church, in memory, honour, and worship of Jesus Christ and his saints.
16. That it is laudable and profitable for the saints to be decked and trimmed; and to set candles burning before them, in the honour of the said saints.

Latimer was asked three times to show his penitence by subscribing to these articles. He refused. Warham accordingly pronounced him to be contumacious and, in punishment,

[22] *Remains*, p. 218.

c*

excommunicated him, decreeing that he must now remain in custody in his manor of Lambeth.

We have no record from Latimer's own words that he had been as yet strictly confined, but in a sermon preached eighteen years later at Stamford, he referred to an incident which must have belonged to this winter.

I was once in examination before five or six bishops, where I had much turmoiling. Every week thrice I came to examinations, and many snares and traps were laid to get something. Now God knoweth I was ignorant of the law; but that God gave me answer and wisdom how I should speak. It was God, indeed, for else I had never escaped them. At the last I was brought forth to be examined into a chamber hanged with arras, where I was wont before to be examined, but now at this time the chamber was somewhat altered: for whereas before there was wont ever to be a fire in the chimney, now the fire was taken away, and an arras hanging hanged over the chimney, and the table stood near the chimney's end; so that I stood between the table and the chimney's end. There was among these bishops that examined me, one with whom I have been very familiar, and took him for my great friend, an aged man, and he sat next the table end. Then among all other questions, he put forth one, a very subtle and crafty one; and such one indeed as I could not think so great danger in. And when I should make answer; 'I pray you, Master Latimer,' said he, 'speak out; I am very thick of hearing, and here be many that sit far off.' I marvelled at this, that I was bidden to speak out, and began to misdeem, and gave an ear to the chimney. And, Sir, there I heard a pen walking in the chimney behind the cloth. They had appointed one there to write all mine answers: for they made sure work that I should not start from them; there was no starting from them. God was my good Lord, and gave me answer. I could never else have escaped it. The question was this: 'Master Latimer, do you not think on your conscience, that you have been suspected of heresy?' A subtle question, a very subtle question. There was no holding of peace would serve. To hold my peace had been to grant myself faulty. To answer it was every way full of danger. But God, which alway hath given me answer, helped me, or else I could never have escaped it; and delivered me from their hands.[23]

Unfortunately, at that point, having made his personal experience serve his turn as an illustration (and Latimer was a genius at holding people's attention when they were beginning

[23] *Sermons*, pp. 294–5.

to flag) he did not go on to satisfy them or us. We do not know what he said; but the incident is sufficient to make us aware that for several months he must have been on edge, never knowing when he might be called to further examination, or what might be the charges.

Yet the early months of 1532 were not propitious for Bishops who sought to stand on the old order. The Commons were ready to pass with noticeable zest the Petition (18th March) complaining against abuses concerning mortuaries and fees, the excessive number of holidays, vexatious examination and imprisonment by Church Courts, and the presentation of infants to livings. The life and ways of the late Cardinal afforded innumerable examples of abuses. The matter of the divorce was being pursued actively, and Cranmer was conspicuously employed. Henry cherished the belief he was still completely orthodox, though the Boleyns were openly spoken of as Lutheran. But however much Henry might be in love with Anne, it would make no difference to his fundamental conceptions of the Christian faith. It is difficult for a modern Englishman to conceive that a king of Henry's appetites and ambitions could be genuinely interested in religion. Today religion affects the whole of one's life or none of it: it is supremely important or is altogether outside one's concern. Henry the Eighth was a religious man, even though he was sometimes lustful and always arrogant. The old religion in which he had been brought up was what he really loved: the power of the Papacy obstructing what he wanted turned him into a rebel against its presumption and interference. These facts enabled men of reforming mind to take advantage of certain moods or circumstances in his life in the decade between the fall of Wolsey and the passing of the Six Articles (1529–39). Often such opportunity was not unconnected with his marriages. But in 1532 the time had not yet come when even a favourite preacher like Latimer could take liberties with the accepted ceremonies or beliefs of the Church. And yet there was the uncertainty always harassing the minds of the hierarchy that though their courts spiritual still functioned, the King might interfere with them.

The articles which were presented to Latimer reflect the general charges made against men suspected of heresy at this time rather than specific instances of named sermons Latimer had preached. Indeed, his mind was not yet completely made

up as to the essentials and the non-essentials of religion. Purgatory, the mediation of the saints, pilgrimages, and images were
usages which Latimer had declared bred great abuses, and he
had certainly taken no steps to show that they were essential.
There was, as yet, no challenge concerning the Mass. They
were matters, however, of sufficient gravity to bring him into
real peril, and he had much to weigh in the balance during
the days of his excommunication.

Even now he does not appear to have been badly treated in
confinement and makes no complaint on that score. Perhaps
he would have been worse treated if he had not been so definitely the King's man regarding the divorce, besides being an
acceptable preacher.

During these days he expressed his anxieties in a long letter [24]
addressed to Warham, bitterly complaining of this hindrance
to his ministry and also that his health has deteriorated. He
speaks candidly of the subjects contained in the articles.

Latimer pleads his inability to go to the palace because of
sickness ('My head is so out of frame, and my whole body so
weak'). He complains continually of pain in the head during
this winter of 1531-2. He had originally been summoned 'to
appear only before the bishop of London; and yet the whole
process is carried on before you, my lord of Canterbury, occasionally surrounded by many other reverend fathers'. When he
was first sent up it looked as though there were some precision
and limit, but now he is continually questioned by various
people, and he cannot see the relevance of it all.

The middle of the letter is in the nature of a short apologia.

If any man has any fault to object against my preaching, as being
obscure or incautiously uttered, I am ready to explain my doctrine
by further discourse: for I have never preached anything contrary
to the truth, nor contrary to the decrees of the fathers, nor as far as
I know, contrary to the catholic faith; all which I can prove to be true
by the testimonies of my enemies and calumniators. I have desired,
I own, and do desire, a reformation in the judgment of the vulgar.

He then passes to more precise matters which have evidently
been under debate with his judges.

It is lawful, I own, to make use of images; to go on pilgrimage; it is
lawful to pray to saints; it is lawful to be mindful of souls abiding in

purgatory: but these things, which are voluntary, are so to be
moderated, that God's commandments of necessary obligation,
which bring eternal life to those that keep them, and eternal death
to those who neglect them, be not deprived of their just value. . . .

Having made this bare admission, Latimer proceeds to
develop his real theme. Some things are necessary to salvation
and involve complete obedience to God's commands. There
are others—and he is obviously alluding to those customs just
named—which have been invented by men and may not be
harmful in themselves. God, regarding human infirmity, allows
these, and to some extent approves them. But what if these
lesser things of human interest or devising should obstruct the
knowledge or performance of the essential commandments?

I therefore hitherto stand fixed on the side of the commandments of
God; so aiming, not at my own gain, but that of God: and as long
as life shall be permitted to me, I will not cease thus to continue,
imitating herein all true preachers of the word, that have hitherto
lived in the world.

He proceeds to ask why a preacher should be expected to
recommend works which could be dropped altogether without
loss. If the abuse of them is proclaimed, the use of them will
diminish. The abuses are manifest, 'And when will they be
removed, if the use be ever extolled in preaching, and the
abuse passed over in silence?' With one accord let the doctrines
of God be preached: the need is for 'true ministers of the Word'.

May God therefore provide a remedy, that, in these evil days, they
whose duty it is rather to preach themselves (for as Peter says, he
gave us commandment to preach) do not hinder those that are
willing and able to exhort. . . .

This is a glancing blow at Stokesley and all other prelates who
do not preach, and it would presently become a favourite
theme with Latimer.

He concludes that he dare not subscribe to the propositions
required since he is unwilling 'to be the author of any longer
continuance of the superstition of the people' or of his own
damnation. It is not from pride that he withholds or from
disobedience to his fathers in God, but the leaders should take
care concerning their commandments, 'since there are occasions
in which we must obey God rather than man'.

On 21st March [25] the court sat at Westminster with Stokesley as deputy for the Archbishop, so that Latimer would come face to face with his real antagonist in judgement of greater weight than that of an ordinary diocesan tribunal. Articles substantially the same as those used at the earlier session were presented for his subscription. Before he was called his judges debated the case. They would know the admissions he had made in the letter to the Archbishop and decided that if he would subscribe to Articles XI and XIV he should be released from the sentence of excommunication. These articles acknowledged the right of Bishops to bar suspect preachers and confessed belief in the Church's consecrations.

When he was summoned Latimer did reverence to the Bishop of London as the President and made his submission, beseeching forgiveness and acknowledging that he had erred in preaching against these articles. The words he uttered must have been bitter, indeed, to his taste.

My Lords, I do confess that I have misordered myself very farre, in that I have so presumptuously and boldly preached, reproving certain things by which the people that were infirm hath taken occasion of ill. Wherefore I ask foregiveness of my misbehaviour; I will be glad to make amends; and I have spoken indiscreetly in vehemence of speaking, and have erred in some things, and in manner have been in a wrong way (as thus) lacking discretion in many things.

He then prayed humbly to be absolved from the sentence of excommunication. Later in his life, when his views were much more definite, this sentence would not trouble him greatly, but at this stage of his development to be excommunicated was terrible indeed. The Bishop of London postponed the taking of the oath and subscription to the articles until 10th April when Latimer must appear again before the Archbishop (or his deputy) and the following prelates, being the judges acting for Convocation—the Archbishop of York (Edward Lee), the Bishops of Winchester (Stephen Gardiner), Rochester (John Fisher), and Exeter (John Voysey). Dr Richard Wolman, Richard Sampson (Dean of the Chapel), and Edward Foxe are also named as members of the court.

Latimer duly subscribed on the appointed day to articles XI and XIV as required, and was restored from excommunica-

[25] Foxe, op. cit., VII, App., Document VI.

tion. But this was not the end. He was to come before them again on 15th April for further proceedings.

It seems to us as though there was more than a little of the law's delays as well as proud men's contumely in these drawn-out proceedings; but it is well to recall that the days were critical for the hierarchy. Attendance upon Latimer's trial could not have been the first claim upon the time of the Bishops. There were more serious matters afoot. Parliament was sitting. It had been adjourned for Easter until 10th April—the day also of Latimer's subscription. The Bishop of Winchester [26] was busy on Monday the 15th April (another of the days of Latimer's trial) in reading to the Upper House of Convocation drafts of the reply to be made by the Bishops to the complaints of the Commons.

The tense atmosphere of these days, so decisive for the future of Church and State, may have been felt by Latimer even in spite of his personal dangers, and given him occasional spurts of hope that the present power of the hierarchy might soon be ended. The clergy had submitted to the King, and he had a few friends at court. But whatever may have been his alternations of hope and despair; whatever may have been his waverings between loyalty to the old order, with all its abuses and superstitions, and a new way of trust in God's Word which was not yet clear and commanding, Latimer's submission is baffling. He was naturally a bold man, and not a prevaricator. Physical weakness and continual cross-examination can weaken strong, determined men, as events in Europe have made plain to us in our own time. But Latimer's temperament was somewhat akin to Peter's. He might deny, but he could repent of momentary weakness. It is, however, to be noticed in his letter to Warham that he did not as yet whole-heartedly sever himself from current Church practices.

But then he did a rash, an unaccountable thing. He wrote a letter [27] to William Greenwood, his contemporary at Cambridge and of the same standing, one of the St John's men who had vigorously opposed his first evangelical preaching. This letter, if written to an old comrade might have been dangerous. Written to a man of Greenwood's kind it was bound to bring trouble. Apparently Latimer had heard that his old adversary

[26] Gairdner, *History of the English Church in the Sixteenth Century*, p. 117.
[27] *Remains*, p. 356.

was crowing over the submission he had made. If Greenwood had been acting on his own or others' behalf in attempting to draw Latimer into speaking his secret thoughts, he could scarcely have expected such success. These rash words occur:

As to the people, though I will have more respect to their capacity, yet as to my old preaching, I will not change the verity; and I will with all diligence according to my promise in my *scriptis*, do all that is in me to reprove their infirmity. There is no wretch living had more need to say with David than I, *Redime, Domine, a calumniis hominum ut custodiam mandata tua*. Of this foolish scribbling ye may know my meaning. *Vale. Tuus Latimerus*.

Latimer's words must have been communicated at once to the authorities, for when he appeared for what he expected to be the final judgement, on Monday 15th April [28] at the 98th session of Convocation, he was charged concerning letters to Greenwood and commanded to appear again on the Friday of that week (the 19th) to hear the will of the Archbishop; but when Friday came yet once more there was postponement until the following Monday. At this Latimer replied that he appealed to the King. Not many weeks had passed since the submission of the clergy. Chapnys, the Emperor's ambassador, summed up his impressions of the clergy's submission to the King that in effect 'they had declared him Pope of England'.[29]

On the Monday Stokesley was again acting for Warham and, on coming to the matter of Latimer's appeal, the Bishop of Winchester stated that it was the royal pleasure that it should be remitted to the Archbishop and Convocation. This left the legal process almost the same as before and Latimer could be called immediately. There was this significant difference, that the King was interested. Much may pass between members of courts of inquiry which cannot be preserved in bare surviving memoranda, and Stokesley now knew he would not have his desire with Latimer. It is very possible that Henry interviewed Latimer himself. The fresh confession made on 22nd April, went deeper than his earlier acknowledgement.[30]

That where he had aforetime confessed that he hath heretofore erred and that he meaned them that it was onely error of discretion, he hath sythens better seen of his own acts, and searched them more

[28] Foxe, op. cit., VII, App., Document VII.
[29] *State Papers, L. & P.*, V.105.
[30] Foxe, op. cit., VII, App., Document VIII.

deeply, and doth knowledge, that he hath not erred only in discretion, but also in doctrine; and said that he was not called afore the said lords, but upon good and just ground, and hath been by them charitably and favourably in treated. And when he had aforetime misreported of the lords, he knowledgeth, that he hath done yll in it, and desired them humbly on his knees to forgive him; and where he is not of ability to make them recompense, he said, he would pray for them.

This, taken with his apologia in the letter to the Archbishop and his earlier submission, was as full and complete a surrender as could be made. He had not come before his judges as a relapsed heretic. But he was now made aware that future misdemeanours would carry penalties increased by his present admissions. The King had made a special request now for his restoration and so the Lord Bishop of London, acting for the Archbishop of Canterbury, absolved him and restored him to the sacraments of the Church. We may be sure Stokesley did not play his part with cordial sincerity. And Latimer?

He had scarcely been freed before he was asked, of all things possible, to visit a condemned heretic, James Bainham, in Newgate on the eve of his execution.[31] The request came from three friends of the accused man and of Latimer. One was Edward Isaac of Well, Kent, and the other two the brothers, William and Ralph Morice, the latter being well-known later as Archbishop Cranmer's secretary. These three were anxious to know from Bainham's own lips the cause of his condemnation.

The course of Bainham's trial had run almost parallel with that of Latimer's, but in Stokesley's own courts. He was the son of a Gloucestershire knight, a lawyer of the Middle Temple, and he had married the widow of the famous Simon Fish, author of the *Supplication of Beggars*. This in itself would draw attention to him. Foxe, who tells his story at length,[32] remarks on his being 'an earnest reader of Scriptures, a great maintainer of the godly, a visitor of the prisoners, liberal to scholars, very merciful to his clients'. He had been taken from the Middle Temple and sent to the Tower. In spite of being racked he would not expose his friends or show where his books were. Neither would his wife. She was sent to the Fleet, and their goods were confiscated.

At Bainham's trial before Stokesley on 15th December 1531,

[31] *Remains*, p. 221.   [32] Foxe, op. cit., IV.697 ff.

he was asked what he meant by asserting that the Scripture had been preached better in the last six years than in any of the previous eight hundred. He answered:

To say plainly, he knew no man to have preached the word of God sincerely and purely, and after the rein of Scripture, except Master Crome and Master Latimer.

He also showed his approval of Tyndale's work; but the next day he made a partial submission, pleading ignorance, and was sent to prison until February when he abjured all his errors, after considerable hesitation. He was fined £20 and made to stand, carrying a faggot through sermon-time at Paul's Cross. He was free on 17th February but almost at once began to bewail his failure. Especially to a little congregation meeting in a warehouse in Bow Lane he confessed the torture of his mind, and on a Sunday in St Austin's Church he stood up holding Tyndale's New Testament and *Obedience of a Christian Man*, calling out that he had denied God, and there could be no hell-fire worse than that he was now enduring. His demonstration had the desired effect: he was arrested. Presented with questions again, he denied transubstantiation and also the power of the keys. This was on the very day Latimer made his complete submission before Stokesley, acting for Warham. Bainham was before Stokesley's Vicar-General, Foxford, at All Saints of Barking. On the 26th he was handed over by the Bishop's authority to the Lord Mayor for execution.

It amazes the modern reader that a man who had crumpled at his own trial should enter the condemned cell of one who had stood firm. Certainly Latimer had affirmed nothing before his judges deeply contrary to the articles presented to him, and was at this period of his life sound on the Mass. But his wavering at the beginning of his trial showed that at least he was in some doubt concerning such matters as purgatory, while he had openly been a champion of the Word. One would have supposed that the mere association with Bainham might have caused suspicion—but it is possible the visit was carried out with secrecy.

Latimer went with the two Morices and Edward Isaac on the 29th April and found Bainham in a dark dungeon seated on straw, with a book and a wax candle in his hand. It was Latimer's intention to comfort him as well as to inquire the reasons for his suffering, 'I, for my part, am desirous to understand the cause of your death; assuring you that I do not allow that any man should consent to his own death, unless he had a right cause to die in.' The matter that touched Latimer most nearly was Bainham's protests 'against purgatory, that there was no such thing; but that it picked men's purses; and against satisfactory masses; which (assertions of mine) I defended by the authority of the scriptures'.

It must have heaped coals of remorse on Latimer's conscience to hear these words from a man due to be burned on the morrow, and he 'did animate him to take his death quietly and patiently'. Then Bainham exhorted his ghostly mentor to stand to the defence of the truth 'for you that shall be left behind had need of comfort also, the world being so dangerous as it is'. But he broke down completely when asked about his wife. Latimer developed confidence as he reproved the condemned man for lack of faith—ready as he was to die, but not, apparently to trust that his wife would be well cared for by the goodness of God. Latimer's celibacy, or his oratory, must have got the better of him to assert 'that within these two years—peradventure in one year—she shall be better provided for, as touching the felicity of this world, than you with all your policy could for yourself, if you were presently here'. But the words must have rung with a spiritual conviction not easily apparent to us at four hundred years' remove. Bainham devoutly thanked Latimer, and especially for his words of comfort regarding his wife. The next afternoon (30th April) he died bravely at the stake in Smithfield.

Latimer went home from the crowded streets, and courtier friends that might be helpful or dangerous, to the quiet West Country. But he could have had little joy in the May time or the thrushes' song.

CHAPTER FIVE

More Trouble in the West

THAT summer Warham died. He had been a loyal servant of the King, even though his loyalty must have been strained to its limits by the arrogance of his brother of York who, as Cardinal and Legate, effaced his senior for so many years. Then came the clear signs that Henry's own policy and ambition would not be satisfied with a second place in high matters of Church order. Warham's passing made it possible to speed 'the King's cause'. Latimer, at his parish work among the farms of West Kington, must have ruminated on strange possibilities. Before Easter the primacy would be held by his friend, Cranmer. It is not therefore surprising that he ventured upon fresh proclamation of his views in a more important centre than that of his own village pulpit.

A letter of complaint was written by Richard Brown, a priest, who dates it, 'Worcester, March 18th', to Dr Baggard, Chancellor of Worcester. Brown reports that Latimer had preached at Bristol to the effect that the Virgin was a sinner, and neither she nor any other saint should be worshipped. He had also decried pilgrimages and infected the townspeople with his views. There was urgent need that definite prohibition should be sent to the Dean there, for he purposed to preach again on the Wednesday of Easter Week.

The good catholicke people in the seyde town do abhorre all soche hys prechyng. The felowe dwellyth with in the diocese of Bath [!]; and certen tymys commyth in to my lords diocese of Worcetter, thus doyng moch hurtt. I ame requiryd to certify your mastershype of thys wretchyd being in his abusyons, and that ye wolde wrytte un to the deane of Bristowe to forbede and deny the seyde Latemer to preche ther or with in ony parte of my seyde lord's diocese. Itt ys reported that he ys commandyd nott to preche with in the diocese of Bathe. Thys ye knowe now what ys to be done, as it shalbe your pleasure; and owr Lord God send you good spede in the Convocacion, and send you mery home to Worcetter.[1]

Richard Brown was quick on the mark even if he was not

---

[1] *State Papers, L. & P.*, VI.246.

accurate with regard to Latimer's cure and diocese. In Westminster the reaction was swift and definite. On 26th March Convocation [2] took formal notice of the news that Latimer was reported to have been preaching at Bristol on purgatory, the saints, and pilgrimage, matters specifically mentioned in his previous submission and the articles to which he had assented. It was decided that the details of this submission should be widely circulated to all worthy and learned men in the neighbourhoods where Latimer was said to have preached or where he might come. Moreover, Brown's suggestion was acted upon, and Latimer was suspended from any further preaching, although the Mayor had appointed him as preacher at Easter.

Latimer had, in fact, preached three sermons, the first on the morning of Sunday, 9th March, at St Nicholas's Church, the second in the afternoon at the church of the Black Friars, and the third next day at St Thomas's. The hubbub they created lasted for more than three months. The town was divided into two camps, and at length a commission had to be set up by Cromwell for the final assessment of what had, or had not, been said. His opponents staged a full-scale counter-attack, and brought in the heaviest pulpit artillery they could muster. Probably the biggest draw among these defenders of the *status quo* was an eccentric popular preacher called Hubberdin. Foxe takes great delight in narrating how, later on, he owed his death to extravagance of gesture, his dancing about in a pulpit causing it to collapse. He broke his leg and never recovered. The churchwardens, on being charged with the pulpit's being insecure, retorted that 'they had made their pulpit for preaching, and not for dancing'.[3]

Hubberdin could be counted upon to provide that kind of excitement which always stirs popular interest: it was an art of which Latimer himself was a master, though he was never a sensationalist. Apart from the local Goodryche, the Prior of St James, and Dr. John Hilsey, Prior of the Dominicans at Bristol, there were also Dr Edward Powell of Salisbury, and Dr Nicholas Wilson, the King's Chaplain, sometime of Cambridge, who had been of the minority in Convocation in asserting the Pope's power to grant dispensations for the marriage of a deceased brother's widow. Wilson was an advocate of the Papal party in Yorkshire, Lancashire, and Cheshire, and joined

[2] Foxe, *Acts and Monuments*, VII, App., Document IX.   [3] ibid., VII.478.

Latimer's opponents in Bristol. A friend of Sir Thomas More, he was at this stage a strong champion of Papal claims, though ultimately he would bow to the strong necessity of the King's will. Edward Powell,[4] like Hubberdin, an Oxford man, was Welsh and a prebendary of Salisbury. He remained consistent in his opposition to the new ways, denied the royal supremacy, refused to take the oath of succession, and was at last executed for treason at Smithfield on 30th July 1540. These all preached against Latimer 'approving purgatory, pilgrimages, the worshipping of the saints and images; also approving, that faith without good works is but dead; and that our lady, being full of grace, is and was without the spot of sin'.

Of these preachers Hubberdin was the most wildly enthusiastic and Powell the most adamant, but their general position can be gathered from the various reports. Thus, on Palm Sunday, 6th April, Hubberdin preached that the Pope was supreme over all, upheld the doctrine of Purgatory, that the Church knows what Christ preached and did, unrecorded in Scripture, and that it was not necessary for Scripture to be written. Other items in the deposition state that Hubberdin asserted that Christ's death was not in itself sufficient without the blood of martyrs, that if 'all the kings in the world do the uttermost that they can, and yet shall they never destroy our holy father the pope nor Rome'. He was opposed to the Gospel in English; it would breed heresy. But neither the Pope nor the Archbishop of Canterbury could override the authority of the local diocesan so far as licences to preach were concerned.

Whatever allowance is made for the extravagance or the orthodoxy of this preacher, and the bias of his reporters, there was matter here which would scarcely be pleasing to the King.

Powell preached on St Mark's Day, Friday 25th April and on Sunday, 27th April at St. Augustine's Green 'very sediciously'. Adultery, especially in kings, and putting away wives without the assent or dispensation of the Church must corrupt the people. He made pointed references to King David 'which his saying sounded to the hearers to the reproof of the King their governor'. All kings are subject to priests and prelates. Powell asserted that people going on pilgrimage—so long as they were away from home—had fulfilled Christ's word concerning the leaving of father, mother, and home for His sake.

<hr>

[4] *Remains*, p. 225.

'Therefore put in the box what he will, he shall have a hundred times as much here in this world, and at the last everlasting life'. The crudity of this equals that of Tetzel, Luther's *bête noire*. But Dr Powell was not only liable to take a very fanciful line in expounding the Gospels; he was toying with dangerous themes.

News of the troubles had reached London and Cromwell's ears. Baggard, the Chancellor of the diocese, showed his anxiety very plainly in an apologetic letter [5] to Cromwell at the end of April. He attempted to explain his action; he had been fearful of even more rumour and upset than there had been, but he had not thought that inhibiting Latimer would have been contrary to Cromwell's wishes, and he has unwittingly aroused displeasure. Apparently Baggard must have lifted the ban on Latimer at once, for he reports that he had preached very well at Bristol at Rogationtide. Hubbardin had been insistent in claiming permission to preach, but this he would not grant 'and will not renew it until it shall please God, the King and yourself'.

Latimer was very possibly privy to the reports that reached Cromwell; but he was not passive himself against his opponents, and referred to the charges made in three long statements. The first of these consists of 'Articles untruly, unjustly, falsely, uncharitably imputed to me, [Hugh Latimer,] by Dr Powell of Salisbury', [6] and undoubtedly belongs to the weeks (May 1533) immediately subsequent to Powell's sermons. The next is a letter remonstrating with Hubberdin: it is dated Sunday, 25th May. [7] The third is to his friend, Ralph Morice, with whom he had visited Bainham twelve months previously, and may be dated May—June 1533. [8]

These writings give the most detailed first-hand account of what he refuted as being false, and what he believed at this stage. In the letter to Morice especially he was writing to a friend who was in close sympathy with reform. Since these are not formal documents presented in a court of law, they possess some of the sting and verve which were features of his preaching and speech. Indeed, there is a good deal in the reply to Powell which suggests that we have here the written account of a spoken reply. Such words as these echo the direct speech of a

[5] *State Papers, L. & P.*, VI.411.   [6] *Remains*, p. 225.
[7] ibid., p. 317.   [8] ibid., p. 357.

preacher: 'The cross can neither hear nor speak again, no more than this pulpit: therefore we do salut it, not properly pray to it.' [9] They are words which would be accompanied by a forth-right gesture, as well, possibly, as by a reverence to the Cross.

If an estimate of Latimer's convictions at this time is sought, some examination should be made of these articles attributed to Latimer by Dr Powell, and his reply. The following selection deals with the matters given most prominence by both sides in the controversy.[10]

I. *That 'Our Lady was a sinner'*

Latimer. Forasmuch as now it is universally and constantly received and applied that she was no sinner, it becometh every man to stand and agree to the same; 'and so will I', quoth I, 'nor any man that wise is will [to] the contrary. But to my purpose, it is neither to nor from, to prove neither this nor that; for I will have her saved, and Christ her Saviour.'

His expressed intention is not to decry Mary, but to exalt Christ.

I will give as little to her as I can (doing her no wrong), rather than Christ her Son and Saviour shall lack any parcel of his glory: and I am sure that our lady will not be displeased with me for so doing. . . . It should not availed her to salvation to have been his natural mother, if she had not done the will of his heavenly Father.

Our Lady is to be honoured, and he did not deny that the *Ave Maria* is a heavenly salutation, 'not properly a prayer as the *Pater Noster* is'. Each can be said separately. Whether twenty *Aves* equals one *Pater Noster* he leaves to great clerks to determine.

For we fantasy as though the very work and labour of flummering the *Ave Maria* is very acceptable to our lady; and the more, the more acceptable: not passing how they be said, but that they be said.

Christ said, 'When you pray, say, *Pater Noster*': he said not, 'When you pray, say *Ave Maria*'. I ween Christ could teach to pray, as well as Dr Powell and master Hubberdin . . . I can prove my saying by scripture; so cannot he his. . . . Here I neither say, that our lady was a sinner, nor yet I deny the *Ave Maria*.

[9] *Remains*, p. 231.   [10] ibid., pp. 225 ff.

II. *Saints are not to be honoured*

I said this word 'saints' is diversely taken of the vulgar people: images of saints are called saints, and inhabiters of heaven are called saints. . . . Dead images are not to be prayed unto; for they have neither ears to hear withal, nor tongue to speak withal, nor heart to think withal &c. They can neither help me nor mine ox; neither my head nor my tooth; nor work any miracle for me, one no more than another: and yet I showed the good use of them to be laymen's books, as they be called; reverently to look upon them, to remember the things that are signified by them, &c. And yet I would not have them so costly and curiously gilded and decked, that the quick image of God (for whom Christ shed his blood and to whom whatsoever is done, Christ reputeth it done to himself) lack necessaries, and be unprovided for, by that occasion; for then the layman doth abuse his book.

Pilgrimages. All idolatry, superstition, error, false faith, and hope in the images, must be pared away, before they can be well done; household looked upon, poor christian folk provided for, restitutions made, all ordinances of God discharged, or ever they can be well done: and when they be at best, before they be vowed, they need not to be done. They shall never be required of us, though they be never done.

Christ's sole sufficiency. The blood of the martyrs has no effect upon the way of redemption. We may desire the prayers of the saints in heaven, but they are not necessary—

we may pray to God ourselves without making suit first to them, and obtain of him whatsoever we need, if we continue in prayer.

The saints were not saints by praying to saints, but by believing in him that made them saints . . . And yet I deny not but we may pray to saints; but rather to him, which can make us saints.

III. *'There is no fire in hell'*

Certainly there is, but of what precise sort, no one of the fathers can tell. He quotes Augustine approvingly, 'that there is no fire in hell; but what manner of fire, or in what part of the world, no man can tell, but he that is of God's privy council' (a typical Latimerian gloss upon *'hominem scire arbitror neminem, nisi forte cui Spiritus divinus ostendit'*).[11]

[11] *De Civit. Dei*, xix.16.

Latimer's own opinion is, briefly, 'I would advise every man to be more careful to keep out of hell, than trust he shall find no fire in hell.'

IV. *No purgatory after this life*

He did not deny purgatory but sought to show the 'state and condition of them that be in purgatory'. 'They be members of the mystical body of Christ as we be, and in more surety than we be.'

He gives a much more reassuring account of purgatory than the picture commonly found in his people's minds:

They need not cry loud to God: they be in Christ, and Christ in them: they be with Christ, and Christ with them. They joy in their Lord Christ alway, taking thankfully whatsoever God doth with them; ever giving thanks to their Lord God &c.

The direction of all this is very plain. The Church would have received very little money for Masses for the departed if Latimer's view had been anything other than a very new and reassuring one. He says he would 'rather be in purgatory than in the Bishop of London's prison', and if he had a thousand pounds to give, the claims of repairing dangerous roads, or poor men's unmarried daughters, or the unemployed and the sick would all come higher up the list than the need of souls in purgatory.

He rises to the full vigour of pulpit declamation, and if he had no audience to move, he was surely visualizing one—'though our soul-priests sing till they be blear-eyed, say till they have worn their tongues to the stumps, neither their singings nor their sayings shall bring us out of hell: whither we shall go for contemning of God's forbiddings'.

If there is pain in purgatory, it will not break their charity or separate them from God, though it does not follow that there is no pain at all.

An interesting letter from Dr John Hilsey,[12] prior of the Black Friars at Bristol, was addressed on 2nd May to Dr Baggard. Hilsey was originally one of Latimer's opponents, but the letter shows a change of attitude. He had already written that Latimer's preaching on pilgrimages, worshipping saints, worshipping images, purgatory &c. had caused great division

[12] *State Papers, L. & P.*, VI.433.iii.

among the citizens. But Hilsey had opposed the advocates of a counterblast of preaching against Latimer since more preaching might easily make matters worse—which is just what had happened. Hilsey then says he did himself preach against what he had supposed Latimer had proclaimed, together with 'Dr Powell, Master Goodryche, Master Hubbardyne, and the Prior of St James'. Then comes his change of line:

ffor sens I have communyd with master Lattymer, and I have harde hyme preache, and have yntytled hys sermon sentens for sentens, and I have percevyd that hys mynd ys much more agenst the abusynge off thynges than agenst the thynge hytt selfe.

Latimer appears to have won over Hilsey completely,[13] for he proceeds to say that in his opinion, if Latimer were now licensed to preach again in Bristol, he would satisfy the people and the Town Council, and moreover, if anything uncatholic were said, there would be plenty of witnesses to take note of it.

The letter,[14] which Strype confidently affirms to be Latimer's, rings true in every line to his style: it was addressed to Hubberdin immediately after his preaching in Bristol on Ascension Day and the following Sunday, 25th May 1533, though Baggard had said his licence was suspended.[15] And yet there are some curious small discrepancies or inconsistencies. In all the other accounts the chief matters of dispute centre around common practices and beliefs of the time, particularly regarding the Virgin Mary, purgatory, pilgrimages, the saying of *Aves* &c. But this letter from Latimer centres upon the dispute regarding the Old and the New Learning—with Latimer upholding the Gospel which Hubberdin had tilted at. Latimer takes pains to say that Scripture cannot be new learning—it goes much farther back than the doctors—not merely Duns Scotus and Aquinas, but even Augustine and Jerome.

But ye will saye ye condempne not the Scripture but Tyndals translacion: there in ye show your selfe contrary unto your words, for ye have condemned it in all other comen tongues, where in they be approved in other contraies; so that it is playne that it is the Scripture, and not the translacion, that ye barke against, calling it new lernyng.

Hubberdin has also said it is not the truth nor of God but

---

[13] Hilsey succeeded Fisher as Bishop of Rochester and helped Cranmer in forwarding reform.
[14] *Remains*, p. 317 ff.   [15] *State Papers, L. & P.*, VI.411.

lies and of the devil. Latimer brushes this aside with scorn: Hubberdin himself wrests Scripture absurdly from its true meaning to say that 'before the cominge of antichrist there shalbe a departynge from the pope: when at the text sayeth plainly Antichrist was come already'.

As for the persecution of priests by the teachers of the Word, can he point to one that has ever been in prison? He then says,

Need ye that I bring forth examples? Remember ye not the honest priest that the last year was martyred by you in Kent? Do you not hold Nicholson, Smyth, Patmore and Philips, with many other, in prison yet at this hour? . . .

Unfortunately for the later reader, the letter at that important point is broken off. But if the 'honest priest' is Thomas Hitton, one of Tyndale's agents for importing English New Testaments, he was burned at Maidstone on 23rd February 1530, which was not 'the last year'. The other names all occur in the lists of men summoned before the diocesan courts of London on various charges connected with heresy. Patmore was the parson of Much Hadham, Herts., who not only was charged with heretical beliefs, but with marrying his curate, Simon Smith, to Joan Bennore, for which both parson and curate paid a heavy price. Patmore was in prison, first in Stokesley's palace, and afterwards in the Lollards' Tower for over two years. Thomas Philips was a citizen of London who had been arrested by Stokesley, excommunicated, and imprisoned in the Tower, from which he only escaped by a successful appeal to the Commons in 1534 after the abolishment of the famous Heresy Act of Henry the Fourth (A.D. 1401) by which bishops could *ex officio* commit suspected heretics to prison. Sigar Nicholson, a stationer of Cambridge, had been charged with harbouring Lutheran literature. Smith, Patmore, and Phillips all figured in the round-up of heresy which had touched Latimer himself so nearly in 1532. It is presumably these references which account for the assumption that this letter belongs to 1531 rather than 1533. But we know nothing of any connexion with Hubberdin prior to the Bristol disturbances, and the specific reference to Hubberdin's 'blasphemies which ye uttered here on the Ascension Day' seems to peg down the letter to May 1533. Both Patmore and Phillips were certainly in ward in the spring of 1533.

Hubberdin had preached in Bristol on Palm Sunday, 6th April, Ascension Day, and the following Sunday, 25th May. It was in the week after that a memorial was presented by the citizens of Bristol to their Mayor and Town Council concerning the sermons and the man. Protest was made that, as the spiritual authorities will not look into the matter, the burgesses and commons must turn to the King's representatives for help to heal the discord that has been created in their midst. Instead of Hubberdin's sticking to his proper task he 'wente to his accustumed Roylynge and slaunderynge of other men'.[16] He is charged with extravagant and wild statements, particularly regarding the *Ave Maria* ('he willed the people to sey not onely ten, but ten and ten agenste oon *Pater Noster* yn twenty folde; and yet christe preferred ye and commaunded the *Pater Noster* specially and above all prayer singulerly').

Other closely-related matters are Hubberdin's affirming 'that it is a great presumpcion that a synner shulde make pety-cyon or prayer to almightie God'. The illustrations and analo-gies used by Hubberdin are extremely grotesque and some positively blasphemous—or so they are represented.

Even when one has made large allowance for the far-fetched metaphors of the preaching of the later Middle Ages which were by no means exhausted yet (and Latimer's own Sermons on the Cards are reminiscent of them), Hubberdin was obviously a freak, but a passionate and eloquent man, none the less, able to draw and hold a crowd. The petition to the Mayor is, of course, from people who were on Latimer's side, though he is not named by them.

A mutilated letter from Latimer to one, G. M., at this time vindicates himself.[17] It has the tone of a man who has been pulled forcibly out of a fight in which he would like to have remained. 'Yf I might have preached in Bristowe in Easter was [week?]. . . . I wulde have made another maner a Christe, & another maner a kynge then myn adversaries & sclaunderers did. . . .' He refers scornfully to Hubberdin and Powell, who 'doth alle thinge by information', and the Dean as the informer. They all had plenty of time and opportunity to malign him, but when he would have hauled them out to face him, they had neither time nor place for it. He acknowledges the change of

[16] Foxe, op. cit., VII, App., Document IX.
[17] ibid.

attitude already noticed in Hilsey of the Black Friars and sums
up in a telling sentence:

But I know the waspe that doth stynge them, and make them to
swelle. When purgatory ys purged, and pylgrimage pylled away
from theire abuses, profettes must nedes falle awey.

Latimer's most open and natural account of these events is
contained in the letter which he wrote (May/June 1533) to
Ralph Morice,[18] who could be relied upon to represent his point
of view to Cranmer. Morice had written to Latimer 'to my
great comfort among all these my troubles'.

Master Morice, you would wonder to know how I have been
entreated at Bristol, I mean of some of the priests, which first
desired me, welcomed me, made me cheer, heard what I said, and
allowed my saying in all things whiles I was with them. When I was
gone home to my benefice, perceiving that the people favoured me
so greatly, and that the mayor had appointed me to preach at
Easter, privily they procured an inhibition for all them that had not
the bishop's licence, which they knew well enough I have not, and
so craftily defeated master mayor's appointment, pretending that
they were sorry for it; procuring also certain preachers to blatter
against me, as Hubberdin and Powell, with other more, whom
when I had brought before the mayor and the wise council of the
town to know what they could lay to my charge, wherefore they so
declaimed against me, they said they spake of information: howbeit
no man could be brought forth that would abide by anything. So
that they had place and time to belie me shamefully; but they had
no place nor time to lay to my charge, when I was present and
ready to make them answer.

He then goes over the now familiar ground, but less formally
then in the reply to Powell, and more briefly. He had not called
Our Lady a sinner but

did reason after this manner: that either she was a sinner or no
sinner. If a sinner, then she was delivered from sin by Christ.

As to saints, he differentiated between the two common
usages.

First, images of saints are called saints, and so they are not to be
worshipped: take worshipping of them for praying to them; for
they are neither mediators by way of redemption, nor yet by way of
intercession.

[18] *Remains*, pp. 357 ff.

Yet they can be well used as laymen's books to remind them of heavenly things. But he never denied worshipping of the true saints, that is, praying to them for their intercession as our mediators. Even so Christ is the supremely necessary Mediator both for them and us. Pilgrimage he never denied, but he did object to neglect of common obligations because of it. As to the *Ave Maria*, he was simply against superstitious use of it and preference of it to the *Pater Noster*. Even our Lord's Prayer should not be used superstitiously. He is more expansive concerning purgatory, and more pungent than in his reply to Powell, especially in his terse sentences stating why he would rather be in purgatory than in the Lollards' Tower. He must have known Morice's sympathies and Cranmer's to say of the Bishop of London's prison:

In this my lord and his chaplains might manacle me by night: in that [Purgatory] they could not.

In this they might strangle me, and say that I hanged myself [an allusion to the death of Richard Hunne, who was found hanging in his cell]: in that they could not.

Ergo, I had rather to be there than here. For though the fire be called never so hot, yet if the bishop's two fingers can shake away a piece, a friar's cowl another part and *scala cœli* altogether, I will never found abbey, college, nor chantry for that purpose.

He then comes to what would increasingly be a theme of his reformation preaching—the connexion between money and purgatory, pilgrimages being necessarily involved in it, with their promise of benefits hereafter.

Consider, Master Morice, whether provision for purgatory hath not brought thousands to hell. Debts have not been paid; restitution of evil-gotten lands and goods hath not been made; Christian people (whose necessities we see . . .) are neglected and suffered to perish. . . . And verily the abuse of them cannot be taken away, but great lucre and vantage shall fall away from them, which had rather have profit with abuse, than lack the same with use; and that is the wasp that doth sting them, and maketh them to swell.

We see the development of an increasing Protestantism in his sidelong glance at the supposed special authority of the Pope in relation to the after-life.

I cannot understand what they mean by the pope's pardoning of purgatory, but by way of suffrage; and as for suffrage, unless he do

his duty, and seek not his own but Christ's glory, I had rather have
the suffrage of Jack of the scullery, which in his calling doth exercise
both faith and charity, but for his mass: and that is as good of
another simpler priest as of him. For, as for authority of keys, it is to
loose from guiltiness of sin, and eternal pain due to the same,
according to Christ's word, and not to his own private will. And as
for pilgrimage, you would wonder what juggling there is to get
money withal. I dwell within half a mile of the Fossway, and you
would wonder to see how they come by flocks out of the west
country to many images, but chiefly to the blood of Hales. And they
believe verily that it is the very blood that was in Christ's body, shed
upon the mount of Calvary for our salvation, and that the sight of it
with their bodily eye doth certify them, and putteth them out of
doubt, that they be in clean life, and in state of salvation without
spot of sin, which doth bolden them to many things.

Latimer's first mention of the great text which is the base of
the doctrine of justification by faith occurs here.

I read in scripture of two certifications: one to the Romans,
Justificati ex fide, pacem habemus; 'We, being justified by faith, have
peace with God'. If I see the blood of Christ with the eye of my
soul, that is true faith that his blood was shed for me. Another in
the Epistle of John: *Nos scimus quod translati sumus de morte ad vitam,
quoniam diligimus fratres;* 'We know that we are translated from
death to life because we love the brethren'. But I read not that I
have peace with God, or that I am translated from death to life,
because I see with my bodily eye the blood of Hales.

It would become one of the little ironies of his episcopate that,
three and a half years later, he would be critically examining
the relic at Hailes Abbey and reporting to Cromwell on it.
Latimer had obviously been enjoying himself in this letter:

Lo, sir, how I run at riot beyond measure. When I began, I was
minded to have written but half a dozen lines; but thus I forget
myself ever when I write to a trusty friend, which will take in worth
my folly, and keep it from mine enemy, &c.

He then in three short paragraphs speaks of his chief opponents. 'As for Dr Wilson I wot not what I should say; but God
endue him with charity.' He hears Wilson has gone north and
will make a tour through Yorkshire, Lancashire, and Cheshire
before reaching Bristol. This information was correct, and
Nicholas Wilson presently arrived to preach three times and

speak his mind about Latimer and to continue his championship of the Papal cause.[19]

As for Hubberdin, no doubt he is a man of no great learning, nor yet of stable wit. He is here *servus hominum*; for he will preach whatsoever the bishops will bid him preach. Verily, in my mind they are more to be blamed than he. He doth magnify the pope more than enough. . . . As touching Dr Powell, how highly he took upon him in Bristol, and how little he regarded the sword, which representeth the king's person, many can tell you.

Latimer concludes this letter with the fervent wish that he could preach before the King for every Sunday of a whole year. It would then be seen very plainly that his opponents had been belittling and belying his preaching.

The conservative views of Latimer's enemies extended dangerously towards criticism of the royal doings, even while complete loyalty to Henry was professed. A mutilated memorandum [20] addressed to Baggard as Chancellor of the diocese suggests the need for the intervention of the King's authority, and the first reason adduced is that the Dean of Bristol has forbidden the clergy to pray for the King and Queen.

Memorandum, that the deane of Bristowe hath commanded all the Curates nigh to Bristowe, that they shall not in the pulpetts pray for the kings grace, nor for the Quene's grace; and when the same deane was asked of the Maire of Bristowe why the Kings grace and the Quenes grace were not prayed for, the deane answered, that the Chauncellor of Wurcester had sent hym a commaundement so to doo: the Maire desired to see the commaundement, but the deane wuld none shewe to hym. And amongs other the same deane comaunded the Curate of henbury, that he in the pulpett shulde not pray for the kings grace nor for the Quenes, and thereof be diverse honest men witnesses.

This report then continues that Dr Nicholas Wilson has preached three times in Bristol and 'there fortified the preaching of Doctor Powell and Huberdyne &c'. Wilson had also stated publicly [21] that when Latimer was on trial before the Bishops in London in the previous year, he had appealed to the King. His Majesty had acknowledged his learning, but warned him that if he now received the King's help in his trouble with

---

[19] Memo. to Dr Baggard, Foxe, op. cit., VII, App., Document IX.
[20] ibid.   [21] *State Papers, L. & P.*, VI.433.vi.

D

the Bishops and submitted to their ruling, but later abjured, all he might expect to receive in the future would be a faggot.

But times had greatly changed in the past twelve months. If doctrine had not been substantially tampered with, practical considerations were now of chief weight. The country was excited in May 1533 by the hurried proceedings of Cranmer on the King's behalf. Anne Boleyn's condition was plain to courtiers, and no news travels faster. The Archbishop had summoned Queen Katherine to his court at Dunstable, and, on her very understandable refusal to recognize his right to assess a matter which was, at the Pope's express bidding, to be determined at Rome, she was pronounced contumacious. The annulment of Henry's marriage with Katherine was pronounced on 23rd May, and on the 28th his marriage to Anne was publicly declared. The new consort's coronation came on Whitsunday, 1st June, at Westminster.

John Floke, the Dean of Bristol, was rash indeed to give instructions, however secret, that forbade prayers for Henry. The memorandum of evidence taken by Thos. Smyth, coroner of Bristol, is dated 10th May, and records that Robert Feyllond (or Feylonde), a farmer of Henbury and parish clerk there, had said that the Dean had told the Curate of Henbury secretly 'not to reherse our soverayne lorde the kynge nor quene in his pulpytte to be prayed for, but only the spiritualtye, the temporaltie and for theym in the peynes of purgatory'. The coroner and other 'true subjects thoughte that the said commaundement of the said deane was not doone like no true feithful subject of the kyng, but by our estimacion it sounded agenst his highnes'. He had interviewed Feyllond in the presence of several witnesses, whose names he gives. Feyllond affirmed that he felt there should be no secrecy about the matter. As a loyal subject he would publish it abroad 'yn somoche that it came to the said deane's eare that his secretnesse was opyned. Whereupon he hath byn with diverse of them that yt was opynned unto, and desired them to speke noo more of the mater.'

Latimer's own relations with the supreme ecclesiastical authority now were such that his former adversaries among the Bishops could not hope for success. The letter he had written to Morice was quite sufficient, apart from anything the civic powers at Bristol might do, to bring these disturbances to the ears of Cromwell. In point of fact, a commission was set up and met at Bristol from 6th to 11th July. John Bartholomew, a local collector of customs, summed up the proceedings,[22] apparently to Cromwell, for he acknowledges receiving a commission in the King's name at six o'clock on the evening of Saturday, 5th July. He was to choose a few men to help him in thorough investigation regarding the behaviour and preached opinions of Latimer and Hubberdin, especially anything said by the latter concerning the King.

He lost no time about it, for on the afternoon of the next day, Sunday, he sat with three ex-mayors of Bristol, John Cabull (or Calle), Thomas Broke, and Richd. Tunell (or Tenall), the Lord Abbot of St Augustine's, William Burton, and a gentleman called Thomas à Bowen. They summoned before them clergy and citizens and made a careful inquiry. Latimer had preached 'dyvers sysmatyke and yronous opinions', which are those Latimer names as articles imputed to him by Powell. As a result of his preaching many have been infected of all sorts and degrees of people. The disturbances have not died down. Hubberdin had preached sharply against Latimer, seeking to prove his contentions were erroneous and schismatic. It had been bad enough during Lent, but after Easter it became worse, the supporters of Latimer's new way of preaching and Hubberdin's numerous following being in continual dispute. Witnesses attested particularly that Hubberdin proclaimed the Pope's supremacy, that Bishops were no longer chosen as formerly, and there were twenty or thirty heretics of the inhabitants of Bristol. In the Commissioners' judgement the trouble will not be lessened unless the King will provide a remedy.

The King's remedy was jail for those who were not his certain friends. There was a priest called William Heberdyn in jail at Bristol on 4th July 1533, which makes it probable that Latimer's opponent had been arrested before the Commission began to sit. The list of prisoners, which ends on 6th July 1535, also includes Dr Nicholas Wilson (10th April 1534) and Dr Edward Powell (10th June 1534).[23]

The setback of Latimer's adversaries in Bristol was severe. But Wilson was removed to Lambeth, and on 13th April 1534, when Sir Thomas More was called to subscribe to the Succession Act, he was conducted to the Tower. By Cranmer's persuasion, however, Wilson recanted and saved his life, though he did fall

[22] ibid., VI.796, 799, 873; VIII.1001.   [23] Foxe, op. cit., VII, App., p. 775.

into trouble again. Powell was of sterner stuff. It is to his credit that, with two other priests, Thos. Abell and Richd. Feather-stone, who had also been imprisoned in Bristol in 1533-4, he paid the penalty to the full. He perished at Smithfield as a traitor on 30th July 1540, having consistently refused the oath of succession and denied the royal supremacy.

The Boleynite tide was in full flow in the summer of 1533, and the immediate result was not only the removal of some of Latimer's enemies, but his being granted licence by Cranmer to preach anywhere in his Province.[24]

A Venetian correspondent, writing home on 23rd August, mentions the attention being given to the affairs of the two English bishoprics held by Italians:

The revenues of Cardinal Campeggio's bishopric of Salisbury, amounting to upwards of 5,000 ducats annual revenue, have been sequestered; and the auditor of his [Ghinucci's] bishopric of Worcester—one Latimer, heretofore accused of Lutheranism—seems to be preaching publicly against the Pope and the Papal power, so that things against the Pope are done here daily.[25]

West Kington saw the parson of the parish in residence and busy at his cure of souls during the rest of the summer, but he went up to London in the autumn. Armed with Cranmer's favour, as he had earlier been by Wolsey's, Latimer preached in the church of the Augustinian friars in October, the prior, George Brown, being friendly towards him. Latimer must have taken some delight in this, for on 24th April of the same year (1533), when the Bristol troubles were increasing, the Bishop of London had inhibited him from preaching in his diocese,[26] and warned all his clergy and the religious of whatever kind, ex-empted or not exempted from his normal powers of rule and visitation, that no one was to preach who was not specifically licensed by him. In spite of this Dr George Brown [27] (he was a strong partisan of the Boleyn interests and would later be-come Archbishop of Dublin) allowed Latimer to preach on 3rd October. This immediately opened the Bishop's vials of wrath for his and Latimer's benefit, and he repeated his in-hibition on 4th October.[28] Latimer was spreading his pernicious

[24] Vide Letter to Dean of Chapel Royal, Cranmer's *Remains*, II.309.
[25] *State Papers, C.S.P. (Venetian)*, IV.971.   [26] ibid., *L. & P.*, VI.1214.
[27] Foxe, op. cit., VII, App., Document VIII.
[28] *State Papers, L. & P.*, VI.1214.ii.

errors once more near the heart of his diocese. No doubt he would like to have given Latimer the opportunity of a practical comparison between his longing for purgatory and present discontents in Lollards' Tower. But Cromwell and Cranmer were in favour, and Stokesley's power was not what it had been in Warham's time. Chapuys, writing to the Emperor,[29] commented that Latimer disseminated more errors than Luther, and all the Bishops applied to the King to punish him except Cranmer; but the King would not hear them.

Cranmer and Cromwell were putting the finishing touches to their inquiries concerning Elizabeth Barton, the Maid of Kent. She and her close companions were exposed on a scaffold at St. Paul's while the story of her deceptions was recounted: this was on 23rd November. The unfortunate girl, afflicted with what appears to have been epilepsy, had for several years enjoyed a growing reputation as a voice from God; and it was unfortunate for her, as well as for more famous people (like Fisher, Bishop of Rochester, and Sir Thomas More), that she ever became the dupe of her confessor, a Canterbury monk, Dr. Edward Bockyng. This man's bitter opposition to the King, his projects matrimonial and doctrinal, caused her to venture upon dangerous prophecies that Henry would not hold his realm for a month after he had married Anne, and that within six months a terrible plague would strike the country, in which the King would be destroyed. The months passed, and however discontented some people might be regarding the King's consort, she and her child, with the King himself, were in rude health. Latimer was employed, as were many others, in the final inquiry, though the Maid did not come to her doom as a traitor until the following spring, when on 20th April, with her chief associates she was hanged at Tyburn, following attainder by Parliament. Cranmer, who had examined her first in the summer, believed [30] 'that she did marvellously stop the going forward of the king's marriage by the reason of her visions, which she said was of God, persuading them that came unto her how highly God was displeased therewith'.

Latimer was now fairly caught in the web of events, and he was not an unwilling victim; for some of the projects increasingly dear to him seemed possible of attainment. He returned to West Kington, but only for the mid-winter season. His

standing with Cranmer and Cromwell scarcely needed the
broad hint that he had dropped to Morice; and if he was not to
preach for a whole year to Henry the Eighth, at least he could
have the royal presence in his congregation during Lent. It
was an arrangement not made without some heart-burning on
the part of Richard Sampson, Dean of the Chapel Royal, which
was also vicarious for a more orthodox preacher (unknown to
us) who had to be jockeyed aside to make room for Latimer as
the Lenten preacher.

Cranmer wrote to the Dean as follows:[31]

Master dean, in my right hearty wise I commend me unto you.
And whereas master Latymer, a man of singular learning, virtuous
example of living, and sincere preaching the word of God, hath
lately been endangered and suffered great obloquy and also I myself,
for justly licensing him to preach within the precincts and limits of
my province, have been likewise misreported; I intending evermore
the furtherance of the truth and the pure dispensation of the word
of God, in consideration of my discharge, declaration of master
Latymer, and satisfaction of such misreporters, have most humbly
desired and sued unto the king's highness, to grant unto the said
master Latymer licence to preach before his grace all the Wednesdays of this next Lent ensuing. Therefore these shall be to desire
and require you, upon the king's pleasure thus known, for to discharge the assignment already appointed, or hereafter to be, to any
person in that behalf, and require him (if any such be) to be contented with the same; for I, upon the king's pleasure thus willing,
have already admonished the said master Latymer to provide
therefore.

Furthermore, these shall be heartily to desire you also, that my
old acquainted friend, master Shaxton, the queen's grace's almoner,
may be assigned likewise to preach the third Sunday in Lent before
the king's grace; and that you will forthwith, upon the sight hereof,
ascertain me in your letters by this bearer, accordingly to the king's
grace's said pleasure and my request. For thus doing you shall
have me ready to accomplish condignly your requests, and shew
unto you like pleasure from time to time. At Otford, the ixth day
of July [January].

The date given is manifestly wrong and should be 9th *January*.
While the references to Latimer's recent troubles, plus the fact
that we know he had written to Morice in May or June 1533,
are all relevant to a midsummer date, there is an urgency about

[31] Cranmer's *Remains*, p. 309.

the letter, anticipating it will probably conflict with arrangements already made. Moreover, the bearer of the letter is to take back Sampson's reply,[32] and this is dated 10th January. It has all the air of a man not wanting to do what he must; he has to explain the circumstances to one preacher, and the other is not personally acceptable to him.

There is one appointed for the Wednesdays in Lent, notwithstanding, if it be the King's pleasure that Latimer shall supply the same, I shall be obedient to his pleasure. And to say liberally to your Grace of that man, by my troth, I favour him in my mind for his learning; I pray God it may be moderate (the signs are not most pleasant), since that his teaching moveth no little dissension among the people wheresoever he cometh, the which is either a token of new doctrine, or else negligence in not expressing of his mind more clearly to the people. . . . It is not unknown to your Grace that he was much suspect for his preaching before all the Convocation, of the which (though it be one of the least) I was and am a poor member. Wherefore your Grace shall be author of this matter, and I no minister, except the King shall so command me.

That the Archbishop himself was not unaware of the risks run by letting his friend preach before the King is evident from the instructions he gives, in a letter which came down to West Kington parsonage in the first few days of the new year. Latimer's blood must have coursed more quickly as he visualized the opportunity now given him; and he could not lightly disregard the serious tone Cranmer adopted. How far could this fervent extempore preacher move the King in the new direction? To some extent it might depend upon the permanence of his affections for Anne and the continuance of Cromwell's sagacity.[33]

I commend me unto you &c. These be to certify you to the king's pleasure, how that his grace is contented that ye shall be admitted to preach on all the Wednesdays of this next Lent before him. Whereupon I thought it very expedient, for divers considerations reasonably me moving thereto, to admonish you of certain things in no ways to be neglect and omitted on your behalf in time of your preaching; which to observe and follow according to mine advice hereafter to you prescribed, shall at the length redound to your no little laud and praise. First, therefore take this order (if ye will), reading over the book ye take for your purpose some processes of

[32] *State Papers, L. & P.,* VII.32.   [33] Cranmer's *Remains,* p. 308.

scripture, the gospel, pistill, or any other part of scripture in the bible, and the same to expound and declare according to the pure sense and meaning thereof: wherein, above all things, it will be most convenient, that ye do not at all persuade for the defence of your own causes and matters lately in controversy; but that ye rather do seem utterly (to pass over) those your accusations, than now in that place any sparkle or suspicion of grudge should appear to remain in you for the same. This done, that likewise ye be very circumspect to overpass and omit all manner speech, either apertly or suspiciously sounding against any special man's facts, acts, manners or sayings, to the intent your audience have none occasion thereby namely to slander your adversaries; which would seem to many that you were void of charity, and so much the more unworthy to occupy that room. Nevertheless, if such occasion be given by the word of God, let none offence or superstition be unreprehended, specially if it be generally spoken, without affection.

Furthermore, I would ye should so study to comprehend your matters, that in any condition you stand no longer in the pulpit than an hour, or an hour and a half at the most; for by long expense of time the king and queen shall peradventure wax so weary at the beginning that they shall have small delight to continue throughout with you to the end. Therefore let the effect of the premises take no place in your mind, specially before this circumspect audience, to the intent that you in so doing need not to have any other declaration hereafter against the misreports of your adversaries. And for your further instruction in this behalf, I would ye should the sooner come up to London, here to prepare all things in a readiness, according to such expectation as is had in you.

There is much sound sense here for preachers of all generations, especially when taking a series; but what would Latimer have thought of the modern limit of twenty minutes or so? There must have been a good deal of quiet conversation between him and the Archbishop before the first sermon was preached; and it is a thousand pities that we have no account of what he said and its reception by the King, but Sir Wm. Kingston wrote to Lord Lisle [34] on 24th February:

On Ash Wednesday Mr Latimer preached before the King, and is to do so every Wednesday in Lent. For the first part he has well begun and is very well liked.

The opening months of 1534 were fraught with immense consequences for the future, displayed in the Parliamentary

[34] *State Papers, L. & P.*, VII.228.

activity by which the King's supremacy would come to be fully acknowledged, though not all its results.

For all men deeply loyal to the Papacy it was a time of 'the prevailing of the gates of hell'. As one looks back there is something ironical in the almost exact synchronization of the sittings of Henry's Parliaments in London and those of the Pope's Consistory in Rome. Henry the Eighth's determination was now matched by Clement the Seventh's. The Tudor would not bow to the Italian's will, and Clement, irretrievably involved with Katharine of Aragon's nephew, the Emperor, was unable now even to suggest a retrogression to biblical patriarchal practices by which Henry might legally possess two wives at one and the same time. This had seriously been considered as a possible solution; but now Anne Boleyn was crowned and her child was heiress-apparent.

In January 1534 the Reformation Parliament assembled to begin that notable series of acts, all aimed at Rome, which would ensure the firmest possible grasp by the King of England upon the affairs of what was increasingly to become his Church. *The Submission of the Clergy and Restraint of Appeals* put into legal form what had been accepted by Convocation under compulsion two years before. It effectually blocked the way of appeals to Rome, making the Archbishop's courts final. This was followed by the *Annates Act*, abolishing the payment to the Pope of a Bishop's first year's stipend, and providing for the recognition of consecration without Papal consent. The entire paraphernalia of bulls and palls was swept away. Cranmer had safely received his pall: there was no need of any more. Now English Archbishops and Bishops would be elected by priors and convents, if their cathedrals were monastic, or by deans and chapters, if secular: but in any case it would be the King's nominee who would be appointed.

The English Bishops were very much the King's men, as they had been, with few exceptions, ever since the Conquest, and not the Pope's. In any tug of war between their two professed loyalties, the royal rather than the Papal was likely to win. This legislation appeared to offer financial relief—annates and first-fruits had never been popular here. In 1535 they would not be so happy when Henry not only re-imposed these exactions for his own benefit, but for his greater profit had the valuation brought up to date (the Pope's was 250 years old), and made

D*

the lesser clergy as well as the greater pay annates and first-fruits.

Swift upon the heels of these two acts came a third, forbidding the payment of Peter's Pence. The realm was to be entirely self-sufficient, and all licences or dispensations would be granted by the Archbishop of Canterbury. Visitation of monasteries normally exempt from episcopal supervision might be achieved in future by royal commissioners. This provision was menacing with possibilities for the lives of thousands who simply could not visualize the landscape of England without the abbeys as a sign of lordship, and a form of piety fast becoming obsolete in this brave new world.

An inevitable consequence of this temper and legislation was the action against foreign absentee Bishops. Latimer's own diocesan, Campeggio, was one of them. He never saw the glory of Salisbury, though he had been a visitor to these shores. Next year he would be succeeded by Latimer's friend and co-re-former, Shaxton, and he himself would succeed the deprived Ghinucci at Worcester.

Before all this spate of legislation had rushed past, Latimer had the fulfilment of his wish to preach regularly before the King. Ash Wednesday fell that year on 18th February, and so his sermons were delivered while Parliament was busy with the anti-Papal acts just noticed. More lay behind Cranmer's acquiescence to Latimer's desire to gain Henry's ear than the hope of his re-investment with royal favour. Latimer could give biblical preaching which would smooth the way for later alter-ations in worship and doctrine. But we have seen the Arch-bishop's nervousness lest the preacher might forget himself, especially in the matter of dangerous asides. Latimer could rarely resist the topical allusion or nutty reminiscence; and there would be enemies in plenty waiting to seize upon such words. He might enjoy Cranmer's confidence and come to Cromwell's favour, but it was the King who counted, and the King had men close about him still who longed for the downfall of these preaching upstarts.

Easter Day came on 5th April, and his duties were done. By this time Sir Thomas More was in danger, and there is a glimpse of Latimer as he saw him at Lambeth. More,[35] on Monday, 13th April, had gone there heavy with the sense of his fate, to

[35] R. W. Chambers's *Thomas More*, p. 302; and More's *English Works*, p. 1429.

appear before the Commissioners. He had professed readiness to subscribe to the Act of Succession but not to the oath in its set form, and the fact that so many of his former colleagues in the Lords and Commons accepted it could not dissuade him from his convictions. While his refusal was being debated, he was told to go down into the garden.

And thereupon I tarried in the old burned chamber that looketh into the garden, and would not go down because of the heat. In that time saw I Master Doctor Latimer come into the garden, and there walked he with divers other doctors and chaplains of my Lord of Canterbury. And very merry I saw him, for he laughed, and took one or twain about the neck so handsomely, that if they had been women, I would have weaned he had been waxen wanton. After that came Master Doctor Wilson forth from the Lords and was with two gentlemen brought by me, and gentlemanly sent straight unto the Tower.

Wilson was More's friend and, as a member of the minority in Convocation, had asserted the Pope's power to grant dispensations for the marriage of a deceased brother's wife, but in spite of More's exhortations he would not stand resolute. More's sense of humour and situation never deserted him: he smiled wryly upon the changed behaviour of the clergy. How much importance should be attached to his comment on Latimer's high spirits? It was just twelve months since the Bristol troubles, and Wilson apparently was only exchanging one jail for another. They were days of extravagance in gesture as in speech and clothes, and if there was elation on the part of Cranmer's friends, it may be recalled that the tide had been swinging the other way only a short time previously. It was in the days of More's Chancellorship that Bilney was burned and Latimer himself had been on trial for heresy. All the anti-Papal acts of this crucial year in English history commanded Latimer's full assent. He was intimate in the counsels of the Archbishop and Cromwell. There had been some preaching in Easter Week regarding the King's marriage which alarmed Cranmer because of its seditious nature, and he immediately held consultations with the Bishops of London, Lincoln, and Winchester. To diminish any stirrings of discontent, either domestic or on behalf of the Pope, preaching was suppressed.[36] All who were licensed to preach must obtain authority afresh before they

[36] Cranmer's *Remains*, p. 283.

mounted their pulpits. In June a detailed order was made concerning 'preaching, and bidding of the beads in all sermons to be made within this realm'.[37]

Latimer went back to his parish in the summer and had evidently been pressing upon Cranmer the claims of preachers, for he was appointed as the Archbishop's deputy [38] to grant licences which, in effect, could enable him to help forward the current policy. With people in high authority claiming his forceful speech and ready sympathy, his time as a parish priest was not likely to be long continued. We have already seen that he was absent for several months in the first half of 1534. He appears to have been chiefly at West Kington employed in his cure and as an active agent for Cranmer during the next twelve months. His absentee diocesan, Campeggio of Salisbury, and Ghinucci of Worcester having been deprived, who would be their successors? He must have appeared as a hot favourite for one of those Sees, and Chapuys, the Imperial Ambassador, hinted as much to Charles the Fifth in January, 1535.[39]

There is no trace of selfish ambition in Latimer, certainly no searching for wealth and power, but whatever he could do he would to advance reform of religion, especially for full facilities for reading and exposition of an English Bible. If Cranmer was very Erastian at this stage, Latimer would be his willing henchman. Yet there was a strange rumour abroad by 20th February that he had, in preaching before the King, 'turned over the leaf', acknowledging the Pope's authority, which could only be reformed by a General Council, and that Our Lady and the saints should be honoured and prayed to, while pilgrimages were very acceptable.[40] The rumour had reached Calais by 27th February and Lord Lisle had heard it; he wrote to Cromwell to ask if it was true. If not, he would punish the reporter.[41] In May Nicholas Shaxton was Bishop of Salisbury and so became Latimer's diocesan for a few months. Latimer is named in July as 'the King's Chaplain', as one of a commission including Cranmer, Cromwell, Barnes, and Hilsey, appointed to examine the suspect clerk, Thomas Patmer (Patmore).[42]

Latimer was a keen supporter of Cromwell's (and the King's) policy in the high summer of this year, 1535, which saw the two

[37] Cranmer's *Remains*, App. p. 460. [38] ibid., p. 296.
[39] *State Papers, L. & P.*, VIII.48. [40] ibid., p. 253.
[41] ibid. [42] ibid., p. 1063.

noblest and most consistent resisters of Henry's claims, Bishop John Fisher of Rochester and Sir Thomas More, brought to the block on Tower Hill.

Latimer knew a good deal of the real opinions of people in the country, and pressed upon Cromwell the necessity for registering the oaths and names of all landowners and gentry swearing to the succession, so that there might be no doubt as to who were thoroughly loyal.[43] He was in London and had been seeing Cromwell. Part of his business there had to do with his impending advancement. On 12th August the Royal Assent was given to his election as Bishop of Worcester, and so the news came to the clergy and people of Bristol that the preacher who had been such a lively figure of interest and trouble in their midst would now be their diocesan.

[43] *Remains*, p. 367.

CHAPTER SIX

Bishop of Worcester

T HE diocese to which Latimer was appointed was not one of the most important. It would not compare with Durham or Winchester for state and prestige, and it did not carry the same strategic responsibilities either nationally or ecclesiastically. The last three bishops had all been Italians, and the chair of the see had come to be regarded as in the Pope's bestowal. But until Bristol was separated to become the head of a new diocese in a few years' time, that city was easily the most important centre of population. The first years of the sixteenth century saw Bristol go ahead by leaps and bounds as trade along the eastern Atlantic coasts, and then across that ocean, developed. The slave trade and the tobacco trade would come presently; but the stir of merchant adventure was already felt there before the old southern and eastern centres of dealing with the Continent were awake to the fact that Columbus and Cabot between them had altered the destinies of the rising generation.

In the summer of 1535 the most notable event affecting the future of the diocese was the beginning of that visitation of monasteries, under Cromwell's direction, which would be a swift prelude to their end. A month before Latimer's election, the notorious Doctors Layton and Leigh started their peregrination—Layton in Gloucestershire and Leigh at Worcester. Leigh had with him the notary John Ap Rice. If the diocese was not remarkable for centres of civic life and trade, apart from Bristol, it had not a few monasteries of very great age and importance, among which Tewkesbury, Evesham, Gloucester, Malvern, and Winchcombe were conspicuous; and the cathedral at Worcester had been a monastic establishment since the tenth century when Bishop Oswald caused the absorption of the secular canons into the monastery of St Mary's.[1]

Latimer was therefore coming as chief pastor of a very large tract of country where there would be the two most strongly-contrasted factions in the coming clash between the old ways of medieval catholicism and those of the new reformers. If

---

[1] Stenton, *Anglo-Saxon England*, p. 147.

Lutheranism was not strong in its most obviously direct and Continental form, biblical religion had many adherents, sprung from the old Lollards whose successors throve around the head of the Bristol Channel. We have seen something of the clash in the events at Bristol in which Latimer figured; and it was only natural that the abbots and monks of long-established monasteries should cleave to the old order. As yet, to the boatmen on the Severn or the monks looking down to the Plain of Evesham from the Malvern Hills, nothing seemed changed. This was the time when, in spite of Henry's drastic religious initiation following Wolsey's downfall, it still seemed impossible that an order which had endured for so many centuries could fall because of the voice of a German monk or the passionate ambition of a Tudor King. Froude's famous summary remains true and apt: 'As yet there were uneasy workings below the surface; but the crust was unbroken and the nation remained outwardly unchanged as it had been for centuries.' [2]

The passing of the monasteries would mark, for most people, the decisive breaking of that crust. All this happened during the few years of Latimer's occupation of his diocese. When he came to his cathedral, monastic rule held there as it had for more than five hundred years in England. When he vacated his see, all that had ended, not to be renewed, except in a few places for a few feverish months in Mary's reign, until our own time, in a very different setting, and in an insignificant proportion to the general life of Church and people.

Latimer would have been untrue to his own nature if he had accepted consecration to this highest pastoral office only as giving him personal advancement and a substantial income. The rental was £975 a year [3] (which would be worth considerably more than £10,000 now), with a London residence, several manors, and Hartlebury Castle as his Worcestershire palace. His nature, like his convictions, would be in the strongest possible contrast to that of the efficient and conservative Gardiner. Latimer was not truly at home in King's councils, though he was quite prepared to play his part on any stage to which he was called. But he entered upon his work with every intention of a literal fulfilment of his vows—to be a father in God to the folk of his unwieldy diocese. Unwieldy it

[2] Froude, *History of England*, 'Henry VIII', I.
[3] *Victoria County History*, *Worcester*, II.44.

certainly was, like so many of the medieval dioceses. He would presently appoint a suffragan for Bristol; and after he had vacated the see most of the new Gloucester diocese and the populous part of the new bishopric of Bristol would be carved out of the territory of which he was from 1535 to 1539 supreme spiritual lord.

The method of his election closely followed the medieval pattern, stripped of any dependence upon Papal approval and enhancing the final authority of the King. The name of the Bishop-elect was sent down for the Chapter's approval before his consecration. Until the King had been officially informed by the Archbishop that the new Bishop had been consecrated, and had issued a deed of appointment, all the temporalities of the see remained in the royal custody—a useful means of help to finance, as Henry's daughter, Elizabeth, would also discover. Though, to be fair to them, this was not a Tudor device, for it had often been used by medieval kings.

The King assented to Latimer's election on 12th August and to a modern reader it seems a curious coincidence that six days later he should have given a bond to Anne Boleyn for £200.[4] This looks like first-fruits with a difference, but we have no clue to the inner significance of this transaction.

There were irritating delays before Latimer could enter fully into his position. His name had been duly sent down for the approval of the Prior and Chapter at Worcester, and he was installed as Bishop on 20th August. 'Two royal assents and *significavits* for the Bishops of Worcester and Salisbury' were forwarded by John Gostwyk, an ecclesiastical commissioner, to Cromwell on 22nd August [5] and seven days later Gostwyk had evidently been embarrassed by Latimer's inquiries:

This Sunday August 29th the late [lately?] elected bps. of Worcester and Rochester sent for me to the Blackfriars and showed me that you had written me a letter, expressing your wish that I should compound with them for their first-fruits. No such letter has come. They beg for the same arrangement as that made with Shaxton [Salisbury]. Otherwise they cannot find sufficient sureties. They have asked for their royal assents and *significavits* without which they cannot be consecrated.[6]

On 2nd September poor Gostwyk still does not know Cromwell's pleasure concerning the documents and describes Hilsey

[4] *State Papers, L. & P.*, XI.117.   [5] ibid., IX.151.   [6] ibid., IX.203.

and Latimer as 'hot suitors'.[7] (Hilsey was the prior of the
Dominicans at Bristol who had swung over to Latimer's side in
the disputes there and was now to succeed Fisher at Rochester.)
Two days afterwards Latimer wrote direct to Cromwell:

We have been here now all this fortnight in vain, obtaining as yet
neither confirmation, nor yet of temporalities restitution. For lack
of the royal assent with your signification, my lord of Canterbury
cannot proceed.[8]

On that same day, the 4th, Latimer was with Polsted, another
ecclesiastical commissioner, trying to arrange for a composition
for first-fruits, but was still without sureties, and hoped his own
bond would be deemed sufficient. He intended to speak to the
King about it.[9] But on the 11th September they were still
unsettled, both for Rochester and Worcester.

We have taken order with the bishop-elect of Worcester that he
shall pay £900 for his first-fruits, and more if the Commissioners
certify it of greater value; and he has promised to sign new obligations after his consecration.[10]

Towards the end of September the King called the Bishops
to Winchester, and on the 29th Cromwell directed that Latimer
should receive half the year's rent of the whole bishopric, the
other half going to the Crown.

Hilsey of Rochester and Fox of Hereford were both consecrated on the same day at Winchester, 26th September 1535,
and Demaus is surely right in his surmise that Latimer was
consecrated with them.[11] Cranmer's Register is silent, but
Fox's and Hilsey's consecrations are recorded in their separate
diocesan records and the temporalities of the three new Bishops
were all settled on the same date, 4th October.[12]

The King had summoned the Bishops to meet him because he
was anxious to ensure that they should preach up the royal
supremacy in their dioceses and explain to their people the
reason why the Pope was now excluded from all jurisdiction in
his realms.[13]

This was work very much to Latimer's liking, and just the
kind of programme he would want for his first winter's work as

[7] ibid., 252.
[8] *Remains*, p. 369.
[9] *State Papers, L. & P.*, IX.273.
[10] ibid., 342.
[11] Demaus, *Latimer*, p. 198.
[12] Rymer, *Foedera*, XIV.553.
[13] Strype, *Cranmer*, I.63.

a diocesan. He seems to have been pushing Cranmer for directives, for the Archbishop remarked to Cromwell:

The bishop of Worcester lately wrote unto me in your name that I looked upon the King's business through my fingers, doing nothing in that matter wherefore we were sent for unto Winchester.[14]

At the beginning of October Latimer had a touch of ague which prevented him from seeing Cromwell regarding 'the draft you wot of' (the substance of what was to be preached regarding the King's Supremacy), and he wants it all the more urgently because the Abbot of Westminster desires him to preach at the Abbey. On the 26th October he is still in London, behind with his business because of preparing for his journey homewards. The London house of the Bishops of Worcester was Stroud Place, destroyed to make way for the Protector Somerset's palace in 1549. He asks Cromwell whether he has the old seal of his see, for which he is quite prepared to pay according to its weight.[15]

Fully equipped with all necessary authority, Latimer turned to his pastoral work at the beginning of November 1535.

Latimer's chief house was Hartlebury Castle, and he could not have been very conversant with the affairs of his cathedral before the threat of dissolution loomed over its convent. The Prior at Worcester since 1518 had been William More, and the life of the monastery had been long disturbed by personal feuds, and the greed or ambition of some of its chief members. More was typical of many monks who had used their profession as a means of helping relatives, as well as affording opportunity for personal enjoyment. He seems to have been fond of display; he had a pretty taste in copes, carpets, and wines. There is evidence of debt which caused the arrest of the Prior during Convocation[16] in London, and there were members of the brotherhood who did their utmost to force him out. Lady Margery Sandys—a member of the well-known family long established in the west—had befriended the Prior by writing to Cromwell about him.[17] Leigh and Ap Rice had here precisely the kind of conditions they wanted. Their visit to Worcester in

---

[14] Cranmer's *Letters*, CLX.314.
[15] *Remains*, Letters XIII and XIV, pp. 370–1.
[16] Baskerville, *English Monks and the Suppression of the Monasteries*, p. 42; *State Papers, L. & P.*, IX. 653.
[17] *State Papers, L. & P.*, IX.656.

October 1535 gave opportunities to the various parties to reveal their jealousies.[18] If a prior could spend the equivalent of more than £2000 on a new mitre, as More had done, reckoning his bill in modern values, Cromwell could suggest a better use for the money.

More was wise in this world's ways, and made a bargain that if he went out he should be given a well-furnished room in the monastery, with necessary fuel, be excused a debt of £100 and have his house at Crowle put into good repair. No doubt he judged that what complaints against him from his brethren might not do, Dr Leigh's comperts would achieve. Yet on 8th January 1536 Latimer was writing to Cromwell about him in some concern because 'the King's grace, moved with pity, and having also divers other considerations stirring to the same is inclined to restore the Prior of Worcester to his room and office again'. Latimer has been asked for his opinion. He does not seem to have any intimate personal knowledge of his Prior, but he is very anxious not to have him close at hand, and makes the plea that he is in 'extreme age'. Is it likely that he will succeed in his post now 'which thing (perchance) he was never able to discharge in midst of his youth'? Latimer had in fact named two other men to the King;[19] and on 13th March 1536 Henry Holbeach was elected as the new Prior. Latimer's judgement as to More's decrepitude was faulty; for he was still living in 1558, and was buried at Crowle some time afterwards, having lived more than eighty-six years.

The Act for the Dissolution of the Smaller Monasteries was passed in February 1536, but few people could seriously have thought that larger establishments would be allowed to remain untouched. Latimer had so far never expressed opposition to the religious as such, though his marked sympathies were with the more open virtues possible in parish work. But the cloister was closely associated in too many instances with the abuse of pilgrimages, and he would presently show himself quite ready to seize any opportunities for exploding any hoaxes that had been practised upon the credulous. The monastery, however purely it might have once fulfilled its proper function, was now the stronghold of those views and practices which were to evoke

[18] Vide Baskerville, op. cit., pp. 134–6; and *Journal of Prior More* (Worcs. Historical Society), I.167.
[19] *Remains*, Letter XV.

his growing protest. His sense of fair play would be aroused on behalf of individuals, but the policy of the King and Cromwell would have his full support, as it had Cranmer's, though he could speak out even to Henry's face if he thought that Church property was being wrongfully used. A reminiscence came tellingly into his first sermon preached before Edward the Sixth:

Horses for a king be good and necessary, if they be well used; but horses are not to be preferred above poor men. I was once offended with the king's horses, and therefore took occasion to speak in the presence of the king's majesty that dead is, when abbeys stood. Abbeys were ordained for the comfort of the poor: wherefore I said, it was not decent that the king's horses should be kept in them, as many were at that time; the living of poor men thereby minished and taken away. But afterwards a certain nobleman said to me, What hast thou to do with the king's horses? I answered and said, I spake my conscience, as God's word directed me. [20]

The reference was to the suggested use of Jervaulx, the Cistercian abbey in Yorkshire whose abbot identified himself fatally with the Northern Rebellion. It was suppressed by attainder, and Sir Arthur Darcy afterwards reported to Cromwell, that for Henry's 'sstoodes of mares',

I think thatt at Gervayes and in the grangyes incident, with the hellp off ther gret commones, the kynges hyenes by good overseers scholld have ther the most best pasture that scholld be in Yngland. [21]

Another memory of the times of suppression came into the second sermon before Edward the Sixth.

I would not that ye should do with the chantry priests as ye did with the abbots, when abbeys were put down. For when their enormities were first read in the parliament-house, they were so great and abominable, that there was nothing but 'down with them'. But within a while after, the same abbots were made bishops, as there be some of them yet alive, to save and redeem their pensions. [22]

Latimer, as a Bishop and spiritual lord, was now necessarily involved in the affairs of Parliament. His activities, however, were not so much concerned with initiating legislation as with

[20] Latimer's *Sermons*, p. 93.
[21] Thomas Wright's *Letters relating to the Suppression of the Monasteries*, Camden Society, Vol. XXVI (1843), p. 158. (Vide *Sermons*, p. 93 n.)
[22] *Sermons*, p. 123.

implementing it. Historians as opposed in view as Froude and James Gairdner agree that he was touched with the superiority which often comes upon men who have suddenly found themselves in power where formerly they were in prison. He followed Cranmer and Cromwell, and Shaxton of Salisbury was often his associate. He had not been in the saddle long enough to know how best to use his authority, and no doubt his enthusiasm often betrayed him into speech which was more exaggerated than the occasion offered. Thomas Dorset,[23] the curate of St Margaret's, Lothbury, writing to the Mayor of Plymouth on 13th March 1536, gives a picture of Latimer at Lambeth with Shaxton and Cranmer, examining a heretical visionary named Crewkhorne who had claimed to see Our Lady and been instructed by her to preach that she should be honoured as she had formerly been, especially at Ipswich and Willesdon. Dorset had gone to Lambeth in the same wherry as Dr Crewkhorne. He had also heard Latimer preach:

On Sunday last, the Bishop of Worcester preached at Paul's Cross, and he said that bishops, abbots, priors, parsons, canons, resident priests, and all, were strong thieves; yea, dukes, lords, and all. The king, quoth he, made a marvellous good act of parliament, that certain men should sow every of them two acres of hemp; but it were all too little, even if so much more, to hang the thieves that be in England. Bishops, abbots, with such others, should not have so many servants, nor so many dishes, but to go to their first foundation; and keep hospitality to feed the needy people—not jolly fellows, with golden chains and velvet gowns; ne let these not once come into houses of religion for repast. Let them call knave bishop, knave abbot, knave prior, yet feed none of them all, nor their horses, nor their dogs. Also, to eat flesh and white meat in Lent, so it be done without hurting weak consciences, and without sedition; and likewise on Fridays and all days.

All his days Latimer was true to his concern for the common people, and especially the poor; no one ever charged him with personal luxury or indifference to the claims of Christ's flock. Still, it smacks of being 'unco' guid' to denounce one's peers before the crowd. In fairness to Latimer, it can be said that he would not fail to speak as definitely, if more politely, when face to face with them.

On 14th April 1536 the Parliament that had passed such acts

[23] *State Papers, L. & P.*, X.462.

as beggared the imagination of representatives of the old order
was finally dissolved. It had lasted from 3rd November 1529.

In the following month Queen Anne was beheaded (19th
May) and the King was swift in marrying her successor, Jane
Seymour, on the 30th. A new Parliament was called for
8th June, and on the next day Latimer obeyed Cranmer's order
and preached two Latin sermons to Convocation.

His plea to his fathers and brethren was for fidelity in their
calling, and he surveyed what seemed to him the chief present
deficiencies in the pastoral office. He brought forward his
favourite matters for denunciation—especially the payment of
money for release of souls from purgatory, and the decking of
images in gold or jewels. Too many teachers had been 'adulter-
ating the word of God, or else mingling it (as taverners do,
which brew and utter the evil and good both in one pot)'.

Latimer was never completely at ease on such official occasions, preaching, as he had to do, in Latin to the clerisy, but the
homely similes would come out! Phrases which would later be
wrought frequently into the texture of his best English preaching
occur:

They thus preached to the people, that dead images (which at the
first, as I think, were set up, only to represent things absent) not
only ought to be covered with gold, but also ought of all faithful
and christian people, (yea, in this scarceness and penury of all
things,) to be clad with silk garments, and those also laden with
precious gems and jewels; and that beside all this, they are to be
lighted with wax candles, both within the church and without the
church, yea, and at noon days; as who should say, here no cost can
be too great; whereas in the mean time we see Christ's faithful and
lively images, bought with no less price than with his most precious
blood, (alas, alas!) to be an hungred, a-thirst, a-cold, and to lie in
darkness, wrapped in all wretchedness, yea, to lie there till death
take away their miseries.[24]

The emphasis lies, as it increasingly would do, on the need
for preaching. In an imaginative exhortation of His stewards
by God, Latimer's own points are put: the simple and direct
proclamation of God's Word and access to it.

You preach very seldom; and when ye do preach, do nothing but
cumber them that preach truly, as much as lieth in you: that it were
much better such were not to preach at all, than so perniciously to

[24] *Sermons*, p. 36.

preach. . . . To be short, I would that christian people should hear my doctrine, and at their convenient leisure read it also, as many as would: your care is not that all men may hear it, but all your care is, that no lay man do read it: surely, being afraid lest they by the reading should understand it, and understanding, learn to rebuke our slothfulness.

The discourse was in two parts, and in the afternoon Latimer dealt more fully with the need for reform of religious practice that derived, he contended, from the medieval Popes' contrivances to acquire money because of the worldliness that had infected the Church. Again he spoke of 'our old ancient purgatory pick-purse' and superstitious devices, 'a Franciscan's cowl put upon a dead man's back' by which the wicked noble or knight hoped to gain heaven. The dilatoriness and the corruption of Church courts, the drunkenness and gluttony that sprang from too many holidays, images and relics ('sometime we chance to visit pigs' bones instead of saints' relicks') and pilgrimages all came under his lash.

Last of all, how think you of matrimony? Is all well here? What of baptism? Shall we evermore in ministering of it speak Latin, and not in English rather, that the people may know what is said and done?

The Bishops and abbots were no less accustomed to hear the catalogue of abuses than the Popes had been. In 1512 Dean Colet had been just as outspoken when preaching to Convocation though emphasizing different points that showed the need for reform. He, too, had spoken of the pride of life, the lust of the flesh, the covetousness and the worldly occupation which absorbed the attention of the great Church dignitaries; and he had not contented himself with expounding the evils without going on to suggest remedies. But Warham as Archbishop in 1512 was one thing, Cranmer, with Cromwell as the King's Vicar-General in a Church where Henry the Eighth definitely exercised his Headship, was another. The older and conservative Bishops were galled by the preaching of such a new member of their Bench as Latimer. But there was the solid fact that the smaller houses of religion had been dissolved; and what might be waiting round the corner?

It was at this Convocation they saw Cromwell's proctor, Petre, claiming the right of the chief seat, and on the next day

(17th July) Cromwell himself presiding over them as the King's representative. This would not alarm the Bishop of Worcester. On the whole he must have been well pleased with the prospects made possible by the passing of the Ten Articles in Convocation followed by the King's Injunctions, and already Coverdale's translation of the Scriptures had been licensed in this same year.

Each of these items calls for some notice.

The *Ten Articles*,[25] divided into two sections, five touching matters of belief and five on ceremonies, could not have gone far enough to satisfy Latimer or his friends; but they went farther than men like Gardiner of Winchester wished. The three Sacraments of Baptism, Penance, and the Altar all conformed to the orthodox pattern of the time. It is plainly stated 'that they that are once baptized must not be baptized again. That the opinions of Anabaptists and Pelagians are to be held for detestable heresies.' There is an emphasis, not marked but definite, on the spiritual sincerity of the recipient of a Sacrament—as concerning penitence, that contrition 'consists of faith, trust and confidence in the mercies and goodness of God; whereby the penitent must conceive certain hope and repute himself justified, not for any merit or work done by him, but by the only merits of the blood of Jesus Christ. That this faith is begotten and confirmed by the application of Christ's words and promises.' Men are not by any means to despise auricular confession, and the voice of the absolving priest is as the voice of God. There is no deviation from the received catholic doctrine concerning the change that comes in the elements of the Sacrament of the Altar—

That under the form and figure of bread and wine is verily and substantially contained that very same body and blood, which was born of the Virgin Mary, and suffered upon the cross. And that the selfsame body and blood of Christ is distributed unto, and received by, all the communicants.

Justification as it is defined would scarcely satisfy a true disciple of Luther, though the English Protestants could take some hope from the admission,

That neither our contrition and faith, nor any work proceeding thence, can merit or deserve the said justification. That the mercy

[25] Strype, *Cranmer*, I.85–90.

and grace of the Father, promised freely for Christ's sake, and the merit of his blood and passion, be the only sufficient and worthy causes thereof.

In the matter of ceremonies—and it was on the abuse of ceremonies more than on points of belief that Latimer had until now been concentrating—nothing was abandoned of contemporary custom, but in every instance a reform of its implications was attempted. Images are to remain, but the clergy are to ensure that the people are so taught the true purposes of images that there shall be no danger of idolatry. Similarly, saints 'are to be honoured, but not with that confidence and honour that is due only unto God', and sins can be remitted and grace received only from God by Christ's mediation. But 'it is very laudable to pray to saints in heaven to be intercessors, and to pray for us unto God'. Long-established rites, like candles on Candlemas-day, ashes on Ash-Wednesday, palms on Palm-Sunday, and so forth are not to be condemned or discontinued: in themselves, however, 'none of these ceremonies have power to remit sin'. Christians should continue to pray for souls in purgatory—but all the abuses, stemming back to the pretended power of the Bishop of Rome by which monetary payment had come often to be regarded as a guarantee of the departed soul's immediate release, must be abolished.

Strype's pious comment on these 'Articles devised by the King's Highness to stable Christian quietness, &c' could be ante-dated by a hundred and fifty years to express the mixed feelings of Latimer and his group.[26]

We find indeed many popish errors here mixed with evangelical truths; which must either be attributed to the defectiveness of our prelate's knowledge as yet in true religion, or being the principles and opinions of the king, or both. Let not any be offended herewith, but let him rather take notice, what a great deal of gospel doctrine here came to light; and not only so, but was owned and propounded by authority to be believed and practised.

Convocation had passed the Ten Articles, however much or little its members were free to express their own minds truly in them. The first Injunctions [27] of Henry the Eighth were published in the same summer, and it has been said of them 'This

[26] ibid., p. 90.
[27] Vide Gee and Hardy, *Documents Illustrative of English Church History* (Macmillan), p. 270.

was the first act of pure supremacy done by the king, for in all
that had gone before he had acted with the concurrence of
Convocation.'[28] Their purpose is quite clear, and direction is
given to all practising the cure of souls. In the very forefront is
the necessity that all the anti-Papal laws are to be faithfully
obeyed 'for the abolishing and extirpation of the Bishop of
Rome's pretensed and usurped power and jurisdiction within
this realm and for the establishment and confirmation of the
king's authority and jurisdiction within the same, as of the
supreme head of the Church of England'. The Ten Articles are
to be expounded to the people in sermons and addresses, the
abrogation of superfluous holydays should prove a benefit to the
commonwealth (a point Latimer had pleaded in Convocation).
People will be serving God better by sticking to their work in
field and parish than by gadding about on pilgrimages, and
the money they might have bestowed upon images and relics
could be better given to the poor and needy. The clergy are to
teach, and cause parents and masters to teach, the *Pater Noster*,
the Articles of the faith and the Ten Commandments 'in their
mother tongue'.

So much for the teaching of the people. Latimer had been
pleading zealously for these points in his preaching for the past
three years. As to the behaviour of the clergy, the Injunctions
not only bade them improve their conduct, but claimed, particularly from non-residents, portions of their income which
could be devoted to the poor, and to the provisions of exhi-
bitions for scholars at Oxford, Cambridge, or some grammar
school. This also was a cause dear to Latimer's heart, and often
to be proclaimed as a primary Christian duty, not only for the
clergy who could afford it, but for laymen as well. There
should also be available in every church a Bible, in Latin and
English, to be placed in the choir before the feast of St Peter
ad Vincula, 1537 [29] (August).

The appearance of Coverdale's Bible,[30] sent out with an
English printer's frontispiece (Nicholson of Southwark) early in
1536 and the 'Address to the Reader', links up with those pub-

[28] *Wriothesley's Chronicle*, p. 55.
[29] This last-named injunction has been disputed, and suspected as an inter-
polation, but Gairdner acknowledges its genuineness, in common with Protestant
historians (e.g. Foxe, Strype, Lindsay). See Injunctions as printed in Strype's
Cranmer, I.119; Lindsay, *History of the Reformation*, II.339; Gairdner, *History of the
English Church in the Sixteenth Century*, p. 178.
[30] Cranmer's *Letters*, 344.

lished *Articles* and *Injunctions*. Whatever the faults of Coverdale as a translator (and he was not in the same street as Tyndale for scholarship in the original tongues), he had a good flowing English style, and there was no doubt of his loyalty to the King. He cribbed from Tyndale, but kept off Tyndale's dangerous ground, and he has left his lasting mark on English life and devotion in his version of the Psalms which, revised for the 1539 Bible, passed into the Prayer Book.

Thus in the summer of 1536 the Bishop of Worcester could see some solid gains. Much he had contended for was in process of appearing—a reform of present customs which lent themselves to superstition, a more spiritual presentation of religion, and an English Bible. He could go about his diocese with good hope for the future.

A letter which belongs to this period shows something of his pastoral vigilance, and refers to a sermon preached by one Coots, most probably a monk of the abbey, at Hailes. Cromwell had sent for him, and now Latimer is forwarding what can only be the bare bones of a sermon which had aroused suspicion. Latimer—an extempore preacher himself—knows well enough that this cannot be the whole matter that was delivered to the congregation . . . 'not as he spake it, (if he spake it as his hearers reported,) but rather as he had modified and tempered it, since he perceived that he should be examined of it. And yet, peradventure, you will not judge it everywhere very well powdered.' [31]

Coots was evidently a disciple of Sir Thomas More, whose writings against Tyndale and others were anathema to Latimer and his friends. 'He [Coots] appeareth to stick stiffly to unwritten verities' and would put Church traditions on a level with Biblical truth. Latimer would like to be rid of him:

He is wilfully witted, Dunsly learned, Moorly affected, bold not a little, zealous more than enough; if you could monish him, charm him, and so reform him &c. Or else I pray you, inhibit him my diocese; you may send another and appoint him his stipend; which God grant you do.

But there was restlessness in his diocese, and Thomas Bell, Sheriff of Gloucester, did not hesitate to write to the Bishop of London, protesting against Latimer's appointment of preachers,

[31] *Remains*, p. 374.

especially James Ashe, parson of Staunton, Beret, and Garard, his Chaplain. Beret had proclaimed in Gloucester that, 'If the Purgatory priests do pray with their tongues till they be worn to the stumps their prayers shall not help souls departed.' [32]

In the autumn of 1536 rebellion broke out in the northern counties in protest against Henry's dissolution of the monasteries. Tax-gatherers, claiming a Parliamentary subsidy, had followed swiftly on the heels of the departing monks and, first in Lincolnshire in September, and in the next month in Yorkshire, the rebels raised their standard. They demanded the restoration of the monasteries, and Latimer was named by them in their plea for the removal of Cranmer and Cromwell. Robert Aske's followers in this *Pilgrimage of Grace* were stout in their affirmation of loyalty to Henry, though they went so far as to express preference for Papal rather than royal supremacy. The abbots of Whalley, Sawley, Jervaulx, and Barlings, together with the former Abbot of Fountains, paid the extreme penalty, with a number of noblemen and gentry. But the immediate consequence was a threat to the larger monasteries. What could be more plain than that the greater houses must be a menace if the smaller houses could be such seedplots of rebellion?

Quite apart from the difference between South and North in other respects, it is certain that the monasteries mattered much more in Yorkshire than they did in the Thames Valley. Population was much thinner, and the life of the countryside centred round the large Cistercian houses. But the heads of the big establishments had seen the red light, and between 1536 and 1539 their abbots and priors came in increasing numbers to surrender before the inevitable compulsion was used.

Latimer was at Hartlebury in the middle of October, but he came hurrying to London at Cromwell's call [33] because of the troubles, and he preached at Paul's Cross against the rebellion on Sunday, 5th November, taking as his theme the Epistle for the day, the 21st Sunday after Trinity, 'Put on all the armour of God' &c. (Ephesians 6^{10} sqq.).

The sermon [34] was chiefly directed to his present hearers in their daily loyalties and temptations. Even in the printed record one catches the touch of the preacher that arrests the wandering attention with allusions to weapons and armour,

[32] *State Papers, L. & P.*, X.1099.   [33] *Remains*, p. 375.   [34] *Sermons*, p. 25.

things of as much interest to Tudor men and youths as petrol engines are to us. To modern listeners some of the allegorical allusions would seem highly amusing. The devil 'is a crafty warrior, and also of great power in this world; he hath great ordnance and artillery'. He proceeds, 'Yea, what great pieces hath he had of bishops of Rome, which have destroyed whole cities and countries, and have slain and burnt many! What great guns were those'! He proceeds to identify the members of religious orders with the dark powers:

Ye must live rightly in God's law, following his commandments and doctrine, clothed righteously in his armour, and not in any feigned armour, as in a friar's coat or cowl. For the assaults of the devil be crafty: to make us put our trust in such armour, he will feign himself to fly; but then we be most in jeopardy: for he can give us an after-clap when we least ween.

The men in the North Country have thus been deceived: they think they wear God's armour because 'they arm them with the sign of the cross and go clean contrary to Him that bear the cross and suffered those wounds . . . they rise with the church, and fight against the church, which is the congregation of faithful men'. His definition of the Church as 'the congregation of faithful men' shows his Protestant belief.

Evidently Latimer had not seen Cromwell during this visit to London. He alludes to being 'occupied at Paul's Cross upon Sunday next after your departure from London', and is pleased with the thanks expressed to him by the lords who were present to hear his plea for unity, preached in accordance with Cromwell's instructions. Latimer is writing to Cromwell requesting that two benefices in his diocese, held by an Italian, Silvester Dario, recently sequestered, may be bestowed upon Dr Thomas Baggard, his Chancellor, and Dr Rodolph Bradford, his Chaplain. His feelings about holding benefices in plurality did not yet extend to his immediate officers, though it could at least be maintained that the Englishmen were in the diocese, whereas Dario was overseas. He had spoken to the King about the matter, and 'The king's grace said no more to me but, "Give 'em, give 'em." You know my chancellor's scrupulosity; and I myself, though I am not altogether so scrupulous, yet I would it were done inculpably and duly.' [35] The scrupulosity only extended to the legal sanctions before entering into possession.

[35] Letter, *Remains*, p. 375.

Latimer was anxious to make a thorough visitation of his diocese, but duties in London held him from it for several months.

Although rebellion had only been open in the North disaffected persons had been letting their tongues wag, and Bristol figures in the news once more. There was renewed hubbub, preaching and counter-preaching about the old ways and the new. The Report of a Royal Commission [36] which was held there on 7th May 1537, shows the two ancient orders of friars had been at loggerheads during Lent. The Prior of the Dominicans, William Oliver, was his Bishop's man, proclaiming justification by faith, and that the garb of friars and monks was of no avail: he had a cartload ready for burning. He was loyal to the King and detested the Northern Rebellion. The Warden of the Grey Friars was of the old ways and preached the opposite. In Christ Church, Bristol, the parson, John Kene, omitted the prayer for the King and called the Bishop of Worcester 'a false harlot in his preaching since Christmas'. Others, it was deposed, thought their Bishop a heretic, and the Rev. John Rawlins hoped he might bring a faggot to burn him. They rejoiced over the Northern Rebellion. There were 'dyverse other persons hath been in pryson for their sedycious and slanderous words hadde of the bishop of Worcester'.

Severe treatment was meted out to the rebels. Latimer, as a member of the Lords as well as being a faithful servant of the King and Cromwell, was involved to the extent of being sent, in June, to plead with some of the leaders who were in the Tower. He referred to it once when preaching before Edward the Sixth. [37]

I was travailed in the Tower myself, (with the king's commandment and the council), and there was Sir Robert Constable, the lord Hussey, the lord Darcy: and the lord Darcy was telling me of the faithful service that he had done the king's majesty that dead is. 'And I had seen my sovereign lord in the field', said he, 'and I had seen his grace come against us, I would have lighted from my horse, and taken my sword by the point, and yielded it into his grace's hands.' 'Marry', quoth I, 'but in the mean season ye played not the part of a faithful subject, in holding with the people in a commotion and a disturbance.'

But the work which chiefly occupied Latimer and all the other

---

[36] *State Papers, L. & P.,* XII(1).508, 1147.   [37] *Sermons,* p. 163.

Bishops in the first half of 1537 was the publication known as *The Bishops' Book*. A council of Bishops and Divines was ordered by the King to review the Articles published in the previous year and 'devise a wholesome and plain exposition upon those subjects, and to set forth a truth of religion purged of errors and heresies'.[38] They were at work from February to the end of July. The incidence of plague hurried their lordships to a conclusion, and Cranmer was anxious to disperse the members of the commission into safer climes. He asked for Cromwell's help in gaining the King's permission,

that we may have his grace's license to depart for this time, until his grace's pleasure be further known; for they die almost everywhere in London, Westminster, and in Lambeth they die at my gate, even at the next house to me.[39]

They had already subscribed to their declarations on the *Pater Noster*, *Ave Maria*, Creed, and Ten Commandments, and there only remained some notes on the Creed. Fox, the Bishop of Hereford, was the chief agent of his brethren in clarifying their findings and conveying them to Cromwell.

Latimer adds to the gruesome details of the menacing plague. Writing to Cromwell on 21st July,[40] he remarks,

Sir, we be here not without all peril: for beside that two hath died of my keeper's folks, out of my gatehouse, three be yet there with raw sores; and even now master Nevell cometh and telleth me that my under cook is fallen sick, and like to be of the plague. *Sed duodecim sunt horæ diei, et termini vitæ sunt ab eo constituti, qui non potest falli; neque verius est tamen, quod nascimur, quam quod sumus morituri.*

This letter shows Latimer's uneasiness. The Bishops, like too many modern committees, had spent time and effort which showed, indeed, their ability to find phrases which could be passed *nem con.*, but the interpretation of the words would be very different if spoken by Gardiner of Winchester from that understood by Cranmer, Shaxton, or Latimer.

As for myself, I can nothing else but pray God that when it is done it be well and sufficiently done, so that we shall not need to have any more such doings. For verily, for my part, I had lever be poor parson of poor Kinton again, than to continue thus bishop of Worcester; not for anything that I have had to do therein, or can do, but yet

[38] Strype, *Cranmer*, Chap. XIII, p. 106. [39] ibid., p. 107.
[40] *Remains*, p. 380.

forsooth it is a troublous thing to agree upon a doctrine in things of
such controversy, with judgments of such diversity, every man (I
trust) meaning well, and yet not all meaning one way. But I doubt
not but now in the end we shall agree both one with another, and
all with the truth, though some will then marvel. And yet, if there
be anything uncertain or unpure, I have good hope that the king's
highness will *expurgare quicquid est veteris fermenti*; at leastway give it
some note, that it may appear he perceiveth it, though he do tolerate
it for a time, so giving place for a season to the frailty and gross
capacity of his subjects.

Evidently booksellers and printers were anxious to get Cromwell's ear and were soliciting the Bishops' interest. Latimer's
relations with Cromwell would mark him out as a most influential friend at court. This letter to Cromwell was carried by
the hand of Thomas Gybson, the printer of a Concordance to
the English New Testament, 1534,

that he may by your favour have the printing of our book. He is an
honest, poor man, and will set it forth in a good letter, and sell it
good cheap: whereas others do sell too dear, which doth let many
to buy.

The King was not ready to allow his name to be attached to
a book of such mixed content as the Bishops had produced. He
read it and annotated it, but when at length it appeared
(printed by Berthelet, the King's Printer) some months later,
its title was, *The Godly and Pious Institution of a Christian Man.*
Its Preface was signed by the commissioners, not by the King.
Two years later, very much altered, it appeared as authoritatively royal, 'A necessary Doctrine and Erudition of any
Christian Man', and became known as *The King's Book.* By
that time the King was prepared to state his position a good
deal more definitely, as Latimer would find to his cost.

A short written debate [41] between Latimer and the King
regarding purgatory most probably belongs to this period. It
obviously falls between the dissolution of the smaller monasteries and the surrender of the larger. Earlier writers (Demaus,
for instance) saw in Latimer's quotations from the Scriptures
and the Fathers adequate evidence for his contention that there
is only the possibility of going direct to hell or heaven; but the
modern reader will probably find less satisfaction in them. To
believe his doctrine is one thing—to applaud his proof-texts and

[41] *Remains*, p. 245.

exegesis another; and it is quite evident from the remarks annotated in Henry's own hand that the King was intent on saying 'No!' as pungently as possible to everything that the reformer would adduce. Henry never wavered in his belief in an intermediate after-state, and his will made provision for prayers for him hereafter.

Latimer sums up his belief thus:[42]

As touching purgatory, I might, by way of disputation, reason this against it: God is more inclined to mercy than to justice. He executeth justice upon those that be damned, mercy upon those that be saved. But they that be damned, as soon as the soul is separate from the body, goeth straight to hell. Ergo, if God be more inclined to mercy, them that be saved, as soon as the soul is out of the body, goeth by and bye to heaven. Of these there is no purgatory.

The King retorts:

This is a false argument, and also a wrong example. For God is as merciful and indifferent in this world to him that may be damned as to him that may be saved; yet the obtsinacy of the man lets not: whereby one may perceive that his justice and mercy dependeth on the will of the creature, and as you, in a text before, allege the merits of the person.

As in almost all his writings and arguments, Latimer relates his belief to some contemporary policy or event.

The founding of monasteries argued purgatory to be; so the putting of them down argueth it not to be. What uncharitableness and cruelness seemeth it to be to destroy monasteries, if purgatory be! Now it seemeth not convenient the Act of Parliament [i.e. of February 1536] to preach one thing, and the pulpit clean contrary.

Latimer came away from London and the plague in late July or early August 1537 to spend the next three months in the pleasing countryside of his diocese. He was now able to turn to the real work of a Father in God to the people of Worcestershire and Warwickshire. His injunctions to the parish clergy keep close to what one would expect of a friend of Cranmer. They [43] reveal the emphasis he put upon the need for acquaintance with the Bible, especially the English [44] Bible, and the

---

[42] ibid., p. 249. [43] ibid., pp. 240–244.
[44] Cranmer was pressing Cromwell to obtain a licence for Matthew's Bible which pleased him so much.

need for preaching to the people. He would purify religion from many of the prevalent customs and superstitions. The parish clergy are to beware of allowing 'religious persons, friar or other, to have any services in your churches'. Preaching is to have the pre-eminence and not to be set aside for the sake of any other observances—he mentions processions as an instance of the more undesirable kind of service. An interesting point is his care that communicants should know at least a little intelligently of what belongs to worship. 'Do not admit any young man or woman to receive the sacrament of the altar, until that he or she openly in the church, after mass or evensong, upon the holiday, do recite in English the Pater.' He was asking for a higher standard from the ploughman and the dairy girl than he would be likely to find among some of his clergy. The clergy were to study at least one chapter of the Bible every day in Latin and English, comparing the two, and going straight forward from the beginning of a book to its end. They must also have a copy of *The Institution of a Christian Man*. They are to keep watch 'lest long bead-telling let [hinder] fruitful preaching of God's word'.

It was his concern for an enlightened laity as well as clergy that prompted Latimer to issue the following simple verses for use in the parishes.[45]

In giving Holy Water

> Remember, your promise in Baptism,
> Christ, his mercy and blood-shedding,
> By whose most holy sprinkling
> Of all your sins you have free pardoning.

What to say in giving Holy Bread

> Of Christ's body this is a token,
> Which on the cross for our sins was broken.
> Wherefore of your sins you must be forsakers,
> If of Christ's death ye will be partakers.

Except that there is less pastoral responsibility laid upon the monks of St Mary's than upon the parish clergy, their injunctions are very similar. The obligation to read or hear the Bible read in English is definite, and no professed religious persons

[45] *Remains*, p. 294.

should discourage the laity from reading good books, either in Latin or English.

Such were the measures by which he would himself judge, and expect his brethren to be judged. That a very different kind of Bishop had come among them, as compared with the stewards of absentee Italians, would declare itself very plainly, and the next couple of years would see many changes—especially because of the surrender of the larger abbeys which would occur increasingly.

There was such an abbey at Pershore, where he was on 6th October. He would probably meet Abbot Stonywell, typical of the religious who combined the advantages of the cloister and worldly advancement at one and the same time. The Abbot and his fourteen colleagues would presently surrender their old Benedictine abbey and accept good pensions or employment in the diocese.[46]

His disappointment [47] with the eastern part of his diocese is expressed in the letter he wrote to Cromwell from Warwick on 14th October. He is troubled about Stratford-on-Avon. Anthony Barker, warden of the collegiate church there, is not resident. Barker has succeeded Dr John Bell (who would himself succeed Latimer as Bishop of Worcester) and there is a pension of £22 per annum payable to him. He wants Cromwell to put pressure upon Barker 'to keep house in it, preach at it and about it, to the reformation of that blind end of my diocese. For else what are we the better for either his great literature or good conversation, if my diocese shall not taste and have experience thereof?' But Barker was a pluralist as well as an absentee.

The visit of a diocesan was something more than a test of the clergy's fidelity. Latimer was quick to observe the condition of houses, the leanings of the gentry—anything that affected the commonweal; and if we are to judge only by the few letters which we can read now, he must have been a very useful source of information to the Lord Privy Seal in the King's interest.

Five days later he is back home at Hartlebury, penning an effusive letter of congratulation to Cromwell, reporting the joy of the neighbourhood because of the birth of a prince. The future Edward the Sixth was born on 12th October. The event had evoked as much rejoicing, he says, as the birth of John the

[46] Vide Baskerville, op. cit., pp. 80–1, 186–7.
[47] cf. Description in Sermon VI before Edward VI.

Baptist. Then Latimer lets himself go and shows with complete sincerity sentiments which it is difficult for men of the middle years of the twentieth century to read without some disdain. Yet there is no doubt of his real conviction:[48]

God give us all grace to yield due thanks to our Lord God, God of England! for verily he hath shewed himself God of England, or rather an English God, if we consider and ponder well all his proceedings with us from time to time. He hath overcome all our illness with his exceeding goodness; so that we are now more than compelled to serve him, seek his glory, promote his word, if the devil of all devils be not in us. We have now the stop of vain trusts, and the stay of vain expectations: let us all pray for his preservation; and I for my part will wish that his grace always have, and even now from the beginning, governors, instructors and officers of right judgements. . . . And thus the God of England be ever with you in all your proceedings!

Erastianism run riot? Blind following of a selfish monarch? It is also the sign of profound thankfulness on the part of a sturdy Englishman that here, at last is a living guarantee that, should Henry die, a male heir may succeed him. The existence of only the two half-sisters, Mary and Elizabeth, must previously have caused many a debate where men talked of the future with apprehension.

Queen Jane only lived for twelve days after the birth of her child. Henry had real affection for her and she was given burial at Windsor with great pomp. On 8th November Latimer was in London to preach a funeral sermon but was ill, and in the house of Master Statham in Milk Street, whose wife was a good friend and nurse to him. He wrote to Cromwell that he hoped to be well enough for the sermon in honour of Queen Jane.[49]

I would have waited upon your lordship myself, as my duty had been; but surely, sir, I do what I can to enable myself to stand in the pulpit upon Tuesday. I am in a faint weariness all over my body, but chiefly in the small of my back: but I have a good nurse, Mistress Statham, which seeing what case I was in, hath fetched me home to her own house, and doth pymper [pamper] me up with all diligence: for I fear a consumption.

A tribute to Latimer's worth as a preacher of biblical religion is shown in the will of Humphrey Monmouth, the London draper who had been Tyndale's patron. The will is dated

[48] *Remains*, p. 385.   [49] ibid., p. 386.

16th November 1537 and names Latimer, with Crome, Barnes, and Taylor (the rector of St Peter's, Cornhill) to be preachers of thirty sermons in All Hallows, Barking instead of the customary thirty Masses for the repose of his soul. For this service he left £20.[50]

Latimer was at Hartlebury for Christmas. Correspondence with Cromwell shows his readiness to help forward his friends' causes by introducing them to the Lord Privy Seal. The bearer of one letter is Master Acton, of Sutton Park, Tenbury, Worcestershire, who had married the niece of Humphrey Monmouth. Latimer recommends [51] that Acton should have Anthony Throgmorton's property at Wynche, unless Throgmorton should prove to be a true subject of the King. Latimer's doubt proved to be correct. Throgmorton double-crossed Cromwell by pretending to spy on his master, Cardinal Pole, in the King's interest, but acted in the reverse direction.

Barnes was Latimer's guest at Hartlebury. He is mentioned in a letter dated Christmas Day. It was a far cry from the Cambridge days when he had given Latimer permission to preach in his pulpit, which was then free from the supervision of the University and episcopal authorities. Now Latimer was a Bishop and often frustrated because he found his own authority stopped short at some monastery doors.[52]

Mr doctor Barnes hath preached here with me at Hartlebury, and at my request at Worcester,[53] and also at Evesham. Surely he is alone in handling a piece of scripture, and setting forth of Christ he hath no fellow. I would wish that the king's grace might once hear him: but I pray you let him tell you how two monks hath preached alate in Evesham: I wist you will hearken to them and look upon them; for though they be exempt from me, yet they be not exempt from your lordship. I pray God amend them, or else I fear they be exempt from the flock of Christ, very true monks; that is to say, pseudo-prophets and false christian men, perverters of scripture; sly, wily, *disobedientiaries* to all good orders; ever starting up, as they dare, to do hurt.

Latimer is keyed up to take advantage of every piece of information that will help forward the purifying of religion. The very next day finds his pen busy once more, recommending to Cromwell,

an honest poor gentleman, whose chance hath been to travel much

---

[50] Strype, *Ecclesiastical Memorials*, I.II.   [51] *Remains*, p. 387.   [52] ibid., p. 389.
[53] Wrongly printed as 'Winchester' in *Remains*.

in Wales, and in the borders of the same, as in the diocese of
Llandaff and otherwhere; and by the reason of the same hath perceived something seeming to him not well.[54]

It is not surprising that Latimer was not popular with some of
his brother Bishops, if he was willing to be the influential informer that he appears to have been.

Soon after Christmas Drs Leigh and Layton set out once more
on their travels, intent to procure evidence which would guarantee the closing of the remaining larger monasteries. Latimer
would not be unsympathetic to their project.

[54] *Remains*, p. 389.

CHAPTER SEVEN

The Campaign Against Superstition

IT had been suggested that the larger monasteries would be purer than the smaller, and therefore could absorb their personnel and continue the functions of religion. But they were all liquidated by the spring of 1540. About two hundred had remained after the first suppression, but it did not need the inquisition of Messrs Leigh and Layton in 1538 to convince the vast majority of abbots and priors that they had better surrender on favourable terms before compulsion came. Leigh began his investigations in the Midlands and worked northwards. Among the houses thus 'voluntarily' surrendered were the notable foundations of Evesham, Malvern, Pershore, Tewkesbury, and Gloucester, besides the cathedral convent at Worcester.

The most casual tourist of today cannot fail to be impressed by the grandeur of the considerable remains of monastic building in the Severn Valley. The tower at Evesham, priory churches at Malvern and Pershore, and the noble abbey church at Tewkesbury, together with the cathedral at Gloucester and its associated buildings, all give us some conception of their domination of the countryside as the Bishop of Worcester saw them in the last days of their decaying state.

Historians of our century have given ample demonstration that, however dismayed the inmates of the great monasteries were at the prospect of enforced release from their vows and habits, they lost comparatively little so far as wellbeing was concerned. Their pensions were adequate, even generous, and they were honoured. The heads of houses were certainly not in need of pity. The priors of the cathedral monasteries became the deans of the new secular chapters (except at Canterbury, where Cranmer's wishes ran counter to the prior's). The shaven monk became the not-so-shaven priest. Newly appointed prebendaries and canons in cathedral precincts wore the familiar faces of former monks.

At Worcester, the new prebendaries did not even have to shift from their old houses, for the officers of obedientiaries of a large monastery like this had long ago provided themselves with separate houses.[1]

Latimer does not appear to have been hitherto a marked opponent of the religious as such. Some of his best friends were from their ranks. His personal convictions would change and harden in the years to come; but there can be no doubt regarding his consistent enmity towards superstition, and the customs he detested had long been associated with some famous monasteries. Pilgrimages were ostensibly an aid to pure devotion. He had long been an exposer of their dangers, and if relics, housed in monasteries, were a lure away from simple, biblical religion, he would be only too happy to investigate supposed miracles or to destroy 'graven images'.

A strong campaign against superstition was set afoot in 1538, the chief targets being well-known shrines and wonder-working relics or roods.

As early as 29th January, Cromwell's agents received the surrender of Boxley Abbey,[2] two miles out from Maidstone, where was the famous Rood of Grace. Geoffrey Chamber was the official appointed for the defacement of this popular crucifix. The Abbot and the oldest monks, on examination, said they knew nothing of the Rood. It must be assumed they referred to the history of this ingenious crucifix. They could scarcely deny that the abbey had greatly profited by it, and been famous for generations as a place of pilgrimage on account of it. But they were well pensioned, John Dobbes, the Abbot, receiving £50 p.a.[3]

Chamber's report said that it had,

certain engines and old wire, with old rotten sticks in the back of the same, that did cause the eyes to move and stir in the head thereof, like unto a lively thing, and also the nether lip likewise to move as though it should speak.[4]

It was taken first to Maidstone, and thence to London, where it was set up at Paul's Cross, and on Sunday, 24th February, Hilsey, the Bishop of Rochester, preached while its eyes and lips were moved. As John Husee, servant to Lord Lisle, Captain of Calais, had prophesied, 'there shall the abusion be divulged'.[5]

[1] Baskerville, *English Monks*, p. 254.　　[2] *State Papers, L. & P.*, XIII.1.173.
[3] *Augm. Book* 232, II.5; *State Papers, L. & P.*, XIII.1.583.
[4] *State Papers, L. & P.*, XIII.1.231.　　[5] ibid., 339.

Latimer was present. After the sermon the image was toppled over for the crowd to wreak its vengeance or ridicule, and it was very soon smashed to bits before being burned. Then—according to a report contained in a letter of John Finch [6]—

Bishop Latimer, in the western part [in Occidentali parte] carried a small image in his hand, which he threw out of the church, though the inhabitants of the country whence it came constantly affirmed that eight oxen would be unable to remove it from its place.

Gairdner suggests [7] that the words 'in Occidentali parte' refer, not to the west part of the church but to the part of the country where Latimer's diocese lay and that the incident does not refer to the same day and occasion. But the rest of Finch's letter seems to belong to that Sunday.

In the same sermon Hilsey alluded to the Blood of Hailes as a relic to which attention might well be given. As a former Prior of the Dominicans at Bristol, he knew the lure this relic had possessed in the West Country, just as Latimer had observed while rector of West Kington. They also were probably aware that the Abbot of Hailes, Stephen Sagar (or Segar), was already (February 1538) [8] in touch with Cromwell regarding it.

The destruction of the Boxley Rood was only the beginning. The King's intention was to permit the despoiling of shrines for the benefit of the royal purse, though the motive was well disguised. Letters passed to and fro among reformers at home and abroad, jubilant over the news.[9] John Hoker of Maidstone wrote to Bullinger at Zurich:

Dagon is everywhere falling. Bel of Babylon has been lately broken to pieces, a wooden god of the Kentish men, a Christ hanging who might have vied with Proteus, for he nodded his head, winked his eyes, turned his beard, bent his body to receive the prayers of worshippers. . . . The thing was worked by wires through little pipes. For ages they have deluded the people of Kent and of all England with much gain.

The tricks of ingenious and mechanically-minded monks of a former age were thus exposed to public ridicule. John Hoker's words reflect the exultation of what must have been, in 1538, only a small minority of Englishmen.

It seems to surprise some writers that Protestant reformers

---

[6] *Original Letters*, p. 607.   [7] *Lollardy and the English Reformation*, I.129 n.
[8] *State Papers, L. & P.*, XIII.1.347.   [9] ibid., 348.

should have become so indignant or happy when the Rood of
Boxley and its like were smashed to atoms by the crowd. But it
is idle to pretend that the devotions offered at Boxley, as at
Hailes or Walsingham, were anything other than sincere, or
that the monks did not profit eagerly by them. Journeys were
made by simple folk, often with ailing bodies, and at great
expense, for the precise purpose of obtaining physical and
spiritual benefit. Boxley had been a famous place of pilgrimage
—and Warham did not have his tongue in his cheek when he
had once described it to Wolsey as 'so holy a place where so
many miracles are showed'.[10]   Perhaps for the past few years
the Cistercians at Boxley had not taken conspicuous advantage
of folk who came there. But people had come there, with
however much less reason than they might have gone to
Canterbury where 'the blissful holy martyr' had certainly been
murdered, buried, and venerated. At Boxley they had not been
discouraged.

Latimer and his friends were on the side of the people, and
sought to give them religion free from any taint of superstition
or monetary traffic in holy things. To that extent they were
one with Luther. These images were not quaint toys to them;
they were masquerading as agents of health and salvation from
God to man, and they were shown now to be nothing of the
sort. One wonders how Gairdner could ever have missed that
point, as he surely did when he wrote:

What ideas the ignorant vulgar may have entertained about it
may, perhaps, be a question: but the veriest numskull could hardly
have taken a puppet for anything but a puppet, or supposed that its
motions were controlled by anything but mechanism. Those, however, who hated monasticism, or loved to expose ecclesiastical
abuses, were delighted at seeing the work done for them by authority
of the King himself.[11]

The grasping policy of Henry in these years did provide
English reformers with an opportunity to speak and act as never
before, but very soon—the gold and jewels of the shrines having
been seized—the reaction of the royal conscience would be
expressed in the Act of Six Articles, and Latimer would be
silenced for the rest of the reign. When there was no more
treasure to be had, the King would react to the orthodox belief

[10] Vide Baskerville, op. cit., p. 22.   [11] Gairdner, *Lollardy*, II.24.

of his earlier years which, in his heart, he had never really disbelieved.

Meanwhile the opportunity was here, and it was used. John Husee wrote on 21st March from London [12] to his master. The letter ranged in interest from an emerald ring to four barrels of herrings, but also included news that 'Pilgrimage saints goeth down apace'.

The famous statue, the Virgin of Walsingham, was among the first to fall. Soon after his accession, Henry had once walked two miles barefooted from Barham to pay his homage to it, when there was as yet no shadow upon either his orthodoxy or his matrimonial status.

It would have been strange if Latimer's policy and reputation escaped bitter criticism, and the little evidence we possess is a very small fraction of opinion that must have been the subject of gossip on many an alehouse bench as well as in the great houses. In March 1538, evil speaking was sufficiently noteworthy to call for inquiry, and William Lucy,[13] King's Commissioner in the diocese, got busy with his colleagues.[14] They fastened on Richd. Cornewell, a country priest, who was reported by witnesses as having said in the churchyard of Hyll, Worcestershire, that Latimer had cursed him; but he had 'no more authority to curse me than I have to curse him, for if he were a rightful bishop I would regard his curse, but the rightful bishop is in Rome'. Cornewell also flaunted his relations with his 'housekeeper'. 'Let me see who dare meddle with her.' He sneered at his Bishop's former trials—'There ought no man to sit in judgment after he is once suspected in heresy till such time they have made their purgation.'

Henry Horton was another whose tongue brought him before the authorities. Bishop Roland Lee of Coventry and Lichfield, President of the Council in the Marches of Wales, reported to Cranmer and the Bishops of Worcester and Rochester the slanders that he had spoken against them.[15]

The bishop of Canterbury was a knave bishop, an heretic and a lowler [lollard] and so were the bishops of Worcester and Rochester.

---

[12] *State Papers, L. & P.*, XIII.1.564.

[13] Lucy also asked Latimer to use his influence with Cromwell to recover 'a small house of the Trinity (Thelesford) near him', of which he was founder! If Lucy were allowed to negotiate with the head of the house for both house and land, he would continue payment of yearly tenths to the King.

[14] *State Papers, L. & P.*, XIII.1.543, 545.   [15] ibid., 715.

He hoped to see them burned and would carry a faggot 16 miles to help.

Latimer had imprisoned Horton for five weeks prior to this, and then released him. Roland Lee, however, wanted to know their lordships' pleasure, and meanwhile held him in jail.

Latimer was employed in April and May with the trial of Dr John Forest, an observant friar of that convent at Greenwich which had resisted the King. He had been accused of using the confessional to belittle the King's Supremacy. Cranmer wrote to Cromwell on 6th April that 'concerning Friar Forest, the Bishop of Wurceister and I will be tomorrow with your lordship' to draw up articles against him.[16]

Forest had previously been Queen Katherine's confessor, and her sturdy advocate in the discussions on the divorce. There can be no doubt of his deep conviction regarding the Pope's spiritual authority and the King's lack of it.[17] But he had vacillated after strict imprisonment in the London house of the rival branch of the Franciscans, the Conventuals. At length his conscience and true loyalty to the old religion brought him to martyrdom. He had been permitted to act as confessor, and appears to have admitted to his penitents his own uneasiness concerning his purchase of comparative freedom and life itself at such a heavy price as the denial of what he really believed. Brought before the Court, he acknowledged that concerning his previous acceptance of the King's Supremacy—

he took his oath with his outward man, but his inward man never consented thereunto: then being further accused of divers heretical opinions, he submitted himself to the punishment of the Church.[18]

He abjured on the 8th May, and Latimer was to preach on the next Sunday, the 12th, when he came to Paul's Cross for open penance. Forest's changes of mind can well be understood. So much that had been firm rock in his youth had proved to be shifting sand, and the day would come when the Archbishop before whom he now abjured, would himself deny his deep conviction and then return to it. The ordeal of Peter in the hall of judgement was known to men on both sides. But Latimer's sermon had to be of a different sort. Almost immediately after abjuring, Forest refused to do the prescribed pen-

---

[16] Cranmer, *Remains*, CCXXI.365.   [17] *State Papers, L. & P.*, XIII.i.1043.
[18] Stow's *Chronicle*, p. 574; Cranmer's *Remains*, p. 366 n.

ance, and stood fast by his original beliefs. There could be only one result. It jars when one reads Latimer's letter to Cromwell dated 18th May—

And, sir, if it be your pleasure, as it is, that I shall play the fool after my customary manner when Forest shall suffer, I would wish that my stage stood near unto Forest: for I would endeavour myself so to content the people that therewith I might also convert Forest, God so helping, or rather altogether working: wherefore I would that he should hear what I shall say.[19]

It seems incredible that any preacher could write so lightly of so awful an occasion, but there is no department of life in which we are more different from our Tudor forebears than in this of our attitude to suffering entailed by punishment. The reforming group was at present enjoying marked success. Whether Forest was a good man or an indifferent is, to our way of thinking, beside the point. But Latimer was perturbed by the news that he was not lodged with sufficient strictness in Newgate, for his companions—dissident White Friars from Doncaster and ten Carthusians—might confirm him in his stand. 'Some think he is rather comforted in his way than discouraged; some think he is allowed both to hear mass and also to receive the sacrament; which, if it be so, it is enough to confirm him in his obstinacy, as though he were to suffer in a just cause.'

Perhaps, if Forest were assured that recanting from heresy would not leave him still to face a charge of treason, he might submit. 'If he would yet . . . return to his abjuration, I would wish his pardon; such is my foolishness.'

Forest came to his terrible fate at Smithfield on 22nd May, and Latimer preached as arranged. Cromwell himself, the Lord Mayor and the City Fathers were all present. Latimer's eloquence was in vain: Forest told him that he could not have dared to preach thus seven years before.[20] And so the fire was lighted; but instead of binding him to the stake and heaping the fire around him, which could often be a quick death, the unfortunate friar was suspended with chains by the arms and middle over the flames. Part of the fuel was a famous image that had been brought from North Wales—Darvell Gadarn. It was said that there had been a Welsh prophecy that one day

---

[19] *Remains*, p. 391.   [20] *State Papers, L. & P.*, XIII.xvii, xviii.687, 877.

this image would set a forest on fire. Whether this were so or not, to use an image to burn a friar would appeal to some men's sense of humour as a fitting end for both.

The destruction of images, shrines, and relics continued. Latimer returned to his diocese and its business. His correspondence with Cromwell shows his interest in various suits for lands and privileges, for 'many men doth think that my poor remembrance with a word or two unto your lordship should further their causes with you'. To gain Latimer's ear appeared to some of these West Midland aspirants after more lands the shortest way to success. His heart could not have been in this part of his work. He would, no doubt, not be sorry to be rid of all the administrative troubles that attended him, though if he was busy directly in the cause of reformed religion, he would be the last to complain.

After recommending Master Evans's suit for the demesne of Bordesley—which Latimer himself was tempted to ask for, since he was short of ready money—and Master Nevill's who had 'got the widow' but was in quest of land (which he failed to get), he reminds Cromwell that he hopes his nurse will not be disappointed. He also pleads that Cromwell will permit the destruction of the famous local image, 'Our Lady of Worcester'.

I trust your lordship will bestow our great Sibyll to some good purpose, *ut pereat memoria cum sonitu*. She hath been the devil's instrument to bring many (I fear) to eternal fire: now she herself with her old sister of Walsingham, her young sister of Ipswich, with their other two sisters of Doncaster and Penrice,[21] would make a jolly muster in Smithfield; they would not be all day in burning.[22]

He was writing on 13th June 1538, and the next few weeks saw all his wishes fulfilled regarding the images. Our Lady of Walsingham—second only in fame to the shrine of Becket as a place of pilgrimage—was taken by Cromwell's agents on 14th July [23] and reached London on the 18th, the priory surrendering on 4th August.[24] The statue from Ipswich arrived in London at the end of the month, and Thomas Thacker reported to Cromwell, 'There is nothing about her but two half shoes of silver and four stones of crystal set in silver.' [25]

The Worcester virgin was nothing like so well known as 'her

[21] Near Swansea.
[23] *State Papers, L. & P.*, XIII.i.1376, 1407.
[25] ibid., XIII.i.1501.

[22] *Remains*, p. 395.
[24] ibid., XIII.ii.31.

sisters', but the image had long been venerated in the West Midlands. Latimer had shown his practical interest in the matter twelve months before by stripping the statue of its clothes and jewels. It was reported by Herbert in his *Henry VIII* that the image proved to be only the effigy of some deceased Bishop of Worcester. Little credence can be given to such a belief. A travesty of that sort would very certainly have been seized by Latimer for public exposure and pulpit reminiscence. Moreover, the Bishop had immediate evidence that there was at least one faithful soldier of the old religion at the heart of his diocese. On 14th August in the previous year, the Eve of the Assumption of the Virgin, Thomas Emans went to the chapel at the cathedral monastery, and in the presence of his neighbours, said:

Lady, art thou stripped now? I have seen the day that as clean men hath been stripped at a pair of gallows as were they that stripped thee.

He showed his devotion, kissing the image, and telling the people, 'Ye that be disposed to offer, the figure is no worse than it was before and the lucre and profit of this town is decayed through this.' The keeper of the chapel heard him add the dark words that he hoped to see the day when her despoilers would be as stripped themselves. Dangerous words! He had to make his confession on 19th August and Latimer, the Bishop, and Holbeach, the Prior, were among the witnesses to it.[26]

Approximately twelve months after that little defence, Latimer had his wish: the Worcester image was destroyed in London with those of Walsingham and Ipswich. It was a general holocaust, and it is not surprising that Nicolas Partridge wrote to Bullinger in tremendous excitement:

Religion is making favourable progress among us. By order of the king, persons are sent to preach the truth in all parts of England. You have, I suppose, heard long since respecting the lady of Walsingham and the breaking in pieces of the other idols. The boiling flames of purgatory are now extinguished among us.[27]

The destruction of images on such a scale, and the cessation of pilgrimages, inevitably brought loss of livelihood to more than the monks who were most nearly affected as the guardians

[26] ibid., XII.II.587.   [27] *Original Letters*, p. 612.

of the shrines. Apart from the lay servants of the monasteries, shops and inns were affected by loss of trade, and Thomas Emans at Worcester was probably voicing the opinion of many citizens when he foresaw this. The Bishop took another view of the matter, and could write to Cromwell on 6th October

by reason of their lady they have been given to much idleness; but now that she is gone, they be turned to laboriousness, and so from ladyness to godliness. [28]

Worcester is responsible for three costly matters—the school, the bridge over the Severn (of obvious importance for communication with the lands to the West, including Hereford and the Marches of Wales), and the city wall. The school is impoverished. The religious reforms have caused the cessation of its chief income from a guild 'not without some guile, popishly pardoning, and therefore now worthily decayed'. [29]

Latimer speaks warmly in praise of the schoolmaster and keeps him with livery and food during holidays, with part of his living as well. The schoolmaster brings up the Worcester boys in the best way. The bridge and wall are essential to the nation, and Latimer is as anxious as a modern corporation trying to get its bills for repairs footed by Whitehall. He suggests a way. Let the possessions of the Black and Grey Friars be used for the maintenance of these three essential priorities for Worcester's and the nation's benefit. Latimer thus backs up a similar appeal which was written on the previous day from the Bailiffs, Aldermen, and Common Council of Worcester, pressing their claim to the friars' houses. 'The store of the said houses is very meet for the purpose.' They had been suppressed in August by Richd. Ingworth, Bishop of Dover, Cromwell's special visitor of Friars' Houses, and he had given Latimer a certificate to this effect. Latimer was evidently (23rd August) in London when Ingworth wrote to him of his visitation of friars' properties in the Midlands, where he left only Black Friars, Shrewsbury, standing. He had been a Prior of the Black Friars himself.

Far and away the most detailed account of Latimer's investigation of a famous relic concerns the Blood of Hailes. He had long ago protested against the superstitious pilgrimages to it. Now he was not the 'poor parson of Kington' but the Lord

[28] *Remains*, p. 403.
[29] Wrongly printed as 'decried' in *Remains*. Vide *State Papers, L. & P.*, XIII.II. 543.

Bishop of the diocese in which Hailes Abbey stood; he was a close friend of Cromwell, and the Abbot—Sagar—was uneasy, ready to promote any investigation, and had written early in 1538 to Cromwell. This letter speaks for itself. The modern reader is more likely to observe the Abbot's anxiety to be in Cromwell's good books than to be assured of his purity of motive.

Hilsey, Bishop of Rochester, on the famous occasion at St Paul's (24th February 1538) when the Rood of Grace was destroyed, had said in his sermon [30] that, twenty years before, a woman from Hailes (the miller's wife) had confessed to him at Oxford that she had close friendship with the then Abbot. He had given her jewels offered to the relic, and would have given her one, in particular, that 'handed about the Holy Blood', but although she had evidently not been as good as she might have been, this kind of gift scared her. The Abbot retorted, 'Tush, thou art a fool, it is but a duck's blood.'

When Hilsey broadcast this information, he was divulging something originally said in confession. The Abbot most intimately concerned was dead—possibly the woman was also. But here, in February 1538, is Abbot Sagar, writing to Cromwell and making a similar allusion. First, he wanted to thank Cromwell for his great goodness to him (possibly in the matter of recommending him for a royal chaplaincy),[31] next most piously thanking God that he now lives in an enlightened time in which he has 'liberty to read the Scripture in English', and he is most anxious to help in the putting away of superstition. Then he comes to his point, that there is in his monastery a

blood which has been reputed a miracle for a great season. I am perplexed, not wishing to put it away of my own authority, but fearing, as it has been shown there to such as seek for it, lest I should condemn myself to be guilty in misusing of it, as changing and renewing it with drake's blood.

It was never so renewed with his knowledge, and an old monk who had kept it for wellnigh forty years would say the same. The Abbot suggests that a commission should be sent to examine the matter.[32] Then he kept in touch with Cromwell during the summer, and took every possible step to be in his good books.

[30] *Wriothesley's Chronicle*, I.75, 76. Quoted by Gairdner, *Lollardy*, II.142.
[31] *State Papers, L. & P.*, XII.1.1323.   [32] ibid., XIII.1.347, 1203.

On 25th August Latimer wrote [33] to Cromwell on a number
of matters, and referred to 'the bloody abbot' as having said to
his brethren that the Bishop's making him go to London had
cost him £140 over and above his travelling expenses, so that
he had raised money on the security of the best mitre and cross,
as well as other things belonging to the abbey. It is generally
assumed that the impolite adjective must apply to Sagar. If
Sagar was hoping to trick Cromwell, and not have the abbey's
jewels fully valued, he was a fool as well as a knave. But on
23rd September he was again writing, [34] thanking Cromwell for
his 'inestimable goodness' and stating that the feigned relic is
still housed in a shrine. He implores that it may be completely
dismantled so that no trace of the forgery may remain 'so long
as it pleases the King that this poor house may stand. The silver
and gold in it is not worth £40, scarce £30.'

Sagar's real hope was to keep his house in being, and there
are notes in Cromwell's papers [35] of 'Two bills of the abbot of
Hallys, one to make a college of the monastery, the other touching the blode.' The idea was to save the monastery for educational purposes at the price of surrendering the relic, but
evidently Cromwell was taking no chances. Before Stephen
Sagar was allowed to leave London he was bound for £500 from
the time of his going home to prevent him from alienating any
moveables or making grants under the seal of the convent 'from
the day of his privy surrender'. So Cromwell's servant, Richard
Layton, reported to his master.

The commission was appointed on 4th October and was at
the monastery on 28th October to make full inquiry into the
composition of the relic. Latimer [36] reported that he had been
'boulting and sifting the blood of Hayles all this forenoon'. The
apparent blood 'was enclosed within a round berall garnished
and bound on every side with silver'. The case was opened in
the presence of many people. The commissioners agreed that
the contents were gum-like, sticky and amber-coloured when
out of the glass, though appearing red like blood when seen
through it. They enclosed the fake in red wax, sealed it and left
it in the keeping of the Abbot; but the key was kept by Richard
Tracy until the King's pleasure should be known. The commissioners were Latimer, Henry Holbeach (Prior of Worcester

[33] *Remains*, p. 400.   [34] *State Papers, L. & P.*, XIII.II.409.
[35] ibid., 488.   [36] *Remains*, p. 407; and *State Papers, L. & P.*, XIII.II.707–10.

and Suffragan Bishop of Bristol since 2nd March 1538), Stephen Sagar, the Abbot, and Richard Tracy.[37]

In April of the next year Tracy is still keeping a watchful eye on Abbot Sagar. Although he is sworn as Chaplain to the King he most falsely deceives him. None the less [38] the Abbot went back to his native Yorkshire after the surrender and fared well for the remainder of his days on a good pension, a house in the country, and a prebend of York Minster.

Sagar was not the only abbot in Latimer's diocese who sought to keep his establishment in being by having it diverted to educational purposes. The Benedictine monastery at Evesham was a large establishment. Latimer regarded its Abbot, Philip Hawford, as a very civil and honest man and requested Cromwell to consider him favourably [39] (28th October). During the next month the Abbot and his monks petitioned Cromwell, as Sagar had done, that theirs should be one of the colleges the King was about to create from surrendered monasteries. The petition reads like a modern prospectus for a select hotel. Evesham Abbey is the best house in the whole country for such a purpose, situated in wholesome air and on a great road to Wales.[40] The buildings are in good condition, suitable to receive the King and his court or the Council of the Marches, and it is close to Warwickshire which now has no monastery left. Apart from a debt of £800 to the King for firstfruits, it is solvent; there is no other monastery within twelve miles, and it is famous for its hospitality. The monastery supports the town of Evesham which is well inhabited and repaired at their cost. Apart from the monastery, the inns would be insufficient to lodge noblemen who might come there: besides, there are the poor and sick folk of the countryside who every day receive charity.[41]

But Evesham was swept away. Letters survive which range from requests for the purchase of its stone to the plea of a student, Thos. Coventree,[42] to Cromwell to continue the exhibition he has hitherto received from the abbey ('now as I hear to be dissolved') so that he may continue his learning Hebrew, Greek, and Latin ('I studied these tongues to refute papistical sophistry').

[37] Richard Tracy, *State Papers, L. & P.*, XIII.i.545, had reported on the priest Richd. Cornewell who had seriously disparaged Latimer (supra VII, p. 137).
[38] *State Papers, L. & P.*, XIV.i.388.   [39] ibid., XIII.ii.709.
[40] ibid., XIII.ii.866, and XIV.i.1191.   [41] ibid., XIV.ii.418.
[42] ibid., 437, Thos. Coventree to Cromwell.

The Second Royal Injunctions of Henry the Eighth, drawn up by Cromwell and communicated to Cranmer at the end of September, went out to the diocesan officials on 11th October. They were precisely in harmony with the Archbishop's aims, and legislated for almost everything that his friend Latimer had preached about. The chief emphasis of the Injunctions falls upon the imperative necessity that the English Bible shall be open and available for all parishioners. The study of the Bible is to be encouraged. No let or hindrance is to be permitted, and parish priests are to take steps forthwith for the instruction of their people in the Scriptures, and also in the learning of the Our Father, the Creed, and the Ten Commandments in English. As a corollary, instructions are given for the discouragement of superstition, especially such as has been fostered by 'wandering to pilgrimages, offering of money, candles, or tapers to images or relics, or kissing or licking the same, saying over a number of beads, not understood or minded on, or in such-like, superstition'.

The positive contribution to religion given by Bible-reading and biblical preaching and catechizing was Latimer's ideal, and the sweeping away of almost all the familiar shrines, candles, and offerings would be, in his judgement, the removal of the Pope's closest possible hold upon the homes of England.

It is not surprising that families were divided by loyalty to the old or the new, or that priests were by no means of one mind regarding the steps initiated by Cromwell. Wolsey had indulged in pluralities and turned his divine office into a worldly career; but Cromwell also took every opportunity of trying to serve God and Mammon. He invested money in the production of Bibles which would be sold by compulsion to the churches of the realm and bring a handsome return for his spiritual diligence.

The story of such family divisions and the passionate loyalties aroused is well illustrated by Strype's account of Foxe's search for details:

One William Maldon, happening in the company of John Foxe, in the beginning of the reign of Queen Elizabeth, and Foxe being very inquisitive after those that suffered for religion in the former reigns, asked him if he knew any that were persecuted for the gospel of Jesus Christ, that he might add it to this book of martyrs; he told him that he knew one was whipped by his own father in King

Henry's reign for it. And when Foxe was very inquisitive who he was, and what was his name, he confessed it was himself; and upon his desire he wrote out all the circumstances. Namely, that when the king had allowed the Bible to be set forth to be read in all churches, immediately several poor men in the town of Chelmsford in Essex, where his father lived, and he was born, bought the New Testament, and on Sundays sat reading of it in the lower end of the church. Many would flock about them to hear their reading; and he among the rest, being then but fifteen years old, came every Sunday to hear the glad and sweet tidings of the gospel. But his father observing it, once angrily fetched him away, and would have him to say the Latin matins with him, which grieved him much. And as he returned at other times to hear the Scripture read, his father still would fetch him away. This put him upon the thoughts of learning to read English, so that he might read the New Testament himself: which when he had by diligence effected, he and his father's apprentice bought the New Testament, joining their stocks together; and, to conceal it, laid it under the bed-straw, and read it at convenient times. One night, his father being asleep, he and his mother chanced to discourse concerning the crucifix and kneeling down to it, and knocking on the breast then used, and holding up the hands to it, when it came by on procession: this he told his mother was plain idolatry and against the commandment of God, where he saith, 'Thou shalt not make any graven image, nor bow down to it, nor worship it'. His mother enraged at him for this said, 'Wilt thou not worship the cross, which was about thee when thou wert christened, and must be laid on thee when thou are dead?' In this heat the mother and son departed and went to their beds. The sum of this evening's conference she presently repeats to her husband; which he impatient to hear, and boiling in fury against his son, for denying worship to be due to the cross, arose up forthwith, and goes into his son's chamber, and, like a mad zealot, taking him by the hair of his head, with both his hands pulled him out of the bed, and whipped him unmercifully. And when the young man bore this beating, as he related, with a kind of joy, considering it was for Christ's sake, and shed not a tear; his father, seeing that, was more enraged, and ran down and fetched an halter, and put it about his neck, saying he would hang him. At length, with much entreaty of the mother and brother, he left him almost dead. I extract this out of the original relation of the person himself, wrote at Newington, near London, where he afterwards dwelt. Which relation he gave to John Foxe.[43]

In the middle of November 1538 Latimer was in London.

[43] Strype, *Memorials of Cranmer*, I.142–3.

It is difficult enough for the modern reader to follow the trend of the King's varying purposes. How much harder it was for the men for whom correct interpretation, and obedience, were literally matters of life and death! In September there had been injunctions for the setting up of an English Bible. In October there was a royal commission to investigate the dangers of Anabaptism, thanks to something more than a broad hint from Protestant rulers in Germany that undesirable characters were wanting to come to England. Henry the Eighth was always quick to take that sort of hint; but he was really more anxious to become safe from the attentions of the Emperor and the King of France than to be in close league with Lutheran princes, and the forecast for diplomatic weather was not favourable. Of one thing, however, we can be sure. Whatever willingness the King had shown in listening to pleadings for the English Bible and a religion purified from superstition, he was never truly weaned from the customs of devotion which had been his from the cradle. He was always anxious to establish his orthodoxy, saving the undesirable presence of the Pope.

Under the terms of Humphrey Monmouth's will, Latimer was due to preach on 17th November at All Hallows, Barking. The day before, he wrote to Cromwell sending details of certain relics which accompanied the Blood of Hailes and explaining that he would have called on the Lord Privy Seal himself, had he not been engaged for this sermon.

By a queer coincidence, that very day saw the proclamation of an order prohibiting the import, sale, or publishing of English books unless they were licensed by the Council. Moreover, dispute concerning the Sacrament was not to be tolerated unless by learned clerics. Customs, long-established but now opposed by the Protestant preachers in practice, if not openly in their pulpits, were to be kept up, unless and until the King should change them. These customs included creeping to the Cross on Good Friday (one of the King's constant devotions), the use of candles at Candlemass, and the continuance of holy bread and water. Any priests who were married were to be deprived, and any marrying in the future would be imprisoned.

This was the turning of the tide. Did Latimer see it? Apparently not, or if he did, he was now bent on as faithful an adherence to his course of conduct as he could accomplish. At all events, there is no comment from him.

That same day also saw the King sitting as the Supreme Head of the Church at the trial of John Nicholson (or Lambert), Bilney's convert, who had been in trouble and prison in Warham's time, and was before Cranmer, Latimer, and Shaxton in 1536, denying the rightfulness of prayer to saints, with which his judges would presently agree. But now he was denying the corporal presence of his Saviour in the Sacrament of the altar; and for that there was only one end. Henry thoroughly enjoyed himself as a lay pope, displaying his own brand of theology for the benefit of his Bishops on the right and his nobles on the left hand. Nicholson would be one of those figures that would rise in the memory of Cranmer and Latimer, when they themselves stood before their last tribunal; but Henry, to whom he had appealed, wished 'to make an open signification that though he had cast off the papal supremacy, yet he intended not to be a favourer of heresy so-called'.[44] Within a week Nicholson came to the flames at Smithfield, in lurid evidence that the King would tolerate no Sacramentaries or Anabaptists.

There is no reason to believe that either Cranmer or Latimer at this time had begun to waver in their belief concerning transubstantiation. Latimer had written to Morice when at West Kington:[45]

And if it were that they that did violently and injuriously pluck it out of his body, when they scourged him and nailed him to the cross, did see it [his blood] with their bodily eye, yet they were not in clean life. And we see the selfsame blood in form of wine, when we have consecrated, and may both see it, feel it, and receive it to our damnation, as touching bodily receiving.

It was to Cranmer's writing that Latimer at last attributed his complete conversion to the position which he held when he died.[46]

Latimer came home to Hartlebury before the middle of December to busy himself with diocesan matters and to square his accounts before spending what was to be his last Christmas as Bishop of Worcester. On the 13th he wrote a long letter [47] to Cromwell stressing the claim of the Prior of Great Malvern for special consideration. He can himself vouch for the honesty of the Prior, and so can Sir William Kingston, the Constable of the Tower. 'The man is old, a good housekeeper, feedeth many,

---

[44] Strype, *Memorials of Cranmer*, p. 145.   [45] *Remains*, p. 364.
[46] ibid., p. 265.   [47] ibid., p. 410.

and that daily; for the country is poor, and full of penury.'
Latimer does not forget to mention that 500 marks could be
found for the King and another 200 for Cromwell if this house
could be left 'to many good purposes: not in monkery, he mean-
eth not so; God forbid! but in any other ways as should be
thought and seem good to the king's majesty: as to maintain
teaching, preaching, study, with praying'. This priory was
not subject to the Bishop's jurisdiction but to the Abbey of
Westminster.

There is an interesting end-of-the-year statement of his financial position.[48] In all the charges and counter-charges made
against the prominent churchmen of the time regarding their
ambitions and pride of place, no word is ever spoken in suspicion of Latimer's way of life. In an age when the tiniest
request was conventionally accompanied by a gift, he would
not omit the supplicant's readiness to fall in with custom; but
he himself asked for nothing, expected nothing, and lived
simply.

Since becoming Bishop he had received over £4000 (an
average of more than £1000 a year), of which £1700 had gone
in first-fruits, reparations, and outstanding debts. At this audit
(Christmas Eve, 1538) he has £180 in ready money, but he
owes £105 for his tenths in 1538 and £20 must go in his New
Year gift. For keeping Christmas and then going up to London
there remains £60.

All the rest is spent: if well, that is my duty; if otherwise, that is my
folly. As any man can complain, I must make answer; else, God
knoweth all. It is spent, I say, saving that I have provision for
household, in wheat, malt, beeves, and muttons, as much as would
sustain my house this half year and more, if I should not go forth of
my diocese: and in this standeth much the stay of my house; for I am
more inclined to feed many grossly and necessarily, than a few
deliciously and voluptuously. As for plate and hangings, hath not
cost me twenty shillings. In plate, my new year's gifts doth my need
with glass and byrral; and I delight more to feed hungry bellies than
to clothe dead walls. Thus it is, my lord, therefore you may me
credit; and as you have been always my good lord, so I desire you
to continue, and to take this rude signification of my condition for a
new year's gift, and a poor token of my good will toward you, for
this time. Another year, and I live, it shall be better; for, I thank
my Lord God, I am within forty pounds out of debt, which doth

[48] *Remains*, p. 412.

lighten my heart not a little. And shortly cometh on my half-year's rent; and then I shall be afloat again, and come clean out of debt. Latimer ends this letter with the request that if 'my brother suffragan, the prior of Worcester' (Henry Holbeach, Bishop of Bristol) is to preach before the King during the coming Lent, he would be glad to know the date—an understandable need for any preacher, but especially if he were engaged to preach before Henry the Eighth at this juncture.

There is quite often a tone of cordiality in Latimer's letters to Cromwell, but whether it implies real liking for him or is only a reflection of naturally robust spirits it is difficult to determine. Cromwell's policy coincided with many of Latimer's cherished desires; but it would be strange if so warmhearted a man could have evoked real friendship from a man so chill, aloof, and generally detested as Cromwell was fast becoming. The Lord Privy Seal had gathered immense power into his own hands, but he lacked both aristocratic background and high ecclesiastical orders, and his isolation would reveal itself more and more. But he was the King's vicegerent in matters spiritual, as well as the first great lay bureaucrat in English history—forerunner of a whole race of underlings; and Latimer supplied him with every kind of information that might be useful, and in turn asked boons and effected introductions to him.

If Cromwell had lived in our time, one can well suppose that his connexions with religion would have been of the slightest. But he lived when all men were religious, and the affairs of daily life were bound up with churchmanship. His position was of such paramount influence that his correspondence grew to an enormous extent, and this was especially so when abbeys were falling and their lands became available to noblemen at a fairly easy price, or when benefices were vacant and candidates for them were not slow in coming forward. We catch many glimpses of this traffic in lands and livings in the letters of the Bishop of Worcester to the Lord Privy Seal. To be in Latimer's favour might bring real advantage to families building up their fortunes in these brave new days—like the Lucy family of Charlcote, Warwickshire. Lucy was [49] King's Commissioner in the diocese: what would Latimer have thought of Shakespeare's skit on the owner of Charlcote as Justice Shallow with his 'dozen white luces'? There was an abundance of material

[49] ibid., p. 413; *State Papers, L. & P.*, XIV.i.79.

for Shallows in the Cotswold country that he came to know so
well. Or there is Henry Tracy of Todington, Glos:

your lordship doth know what manner of man he is; I would wish
there were many of that sort. He had a lease of the demesnes of
Winchcombe, as other more had. The others have theirs renewed
without a condition; if you would of your goodness write to the
Abbot and Convent, that he might have his renewed again, without
a condition, your lordship should do an act not unworthy yourself.
He is given to good hospitality, and hath need of such things for the
maintenance of the same; and he is always ready to serve the king
in commissions and other ways, with most hearty fashion, according
to his duty, letting for no costs nor charge at any time.[50]

Amid all this petitioning and counter-petitioning, with its
scurry of riders and servants bearing letters or to plead in their
own persons, Latimer always has his eye on the needs of the
people at large. That is one of his reasons for favouring men,
religious or lay, who are given to hospitality. And he is confident in his approach to Cromwell on such matters.

I doubt not, but the king's highness, of his gracious and accustomable
goodness, will remember his poor subjects now in Lent as touching
white meat, of the which I now motion your lordship, to the intent
it may come betime among them; for heretofore it hath been
Midlent as ever it hath come to the borders of the realm.

But he does not sound too pleased with the Warden of Strat-
ford, Anthony Barker, Cromwell's nominee. 'I like not these
honey-mouthed men, when I see no acts nor deeds according
to their words.' As for his own motives,

I never presented any matter unto you, of any malice or ill will to
any person, but only of good zeal to the truth and discharging of my
duty. And as for the Arches, [The Court of Arches] I could have had
fewer matters there with more money in my purse, by not a little, if
I would have followed the old trade in selling of sin and not doing
of my duty.[51]

There would not be many more weeks in which Latimer
would be approached by men wanting him to win the Lord
Privy Seal's ear on their behalf.
In February the Act was passed by which the greater monasteries were to be dissolved, though as we have seen, there had

been a steady stream of surrenders, and the Act was only needed to push the most stubborn abbots to the point of decision.

A couple of letters written to Cromwell in April show Latimer moving through his diocese—at Sutton Acton's place in Tenbury on 2nd April and Stroudend, Painswick, on the 16th. He has received a letter from his chaplain, William Benett,[52] assuring him that Wattwood, the President of Warwick College, is a changed man. In the previous June the Bishop was not a little troubled about Wattwood [53] and the collegiate church of St Mary at Warwick. He had told Master Wattwood to get back from London and its pleasures to his proper work, but he seemed to prefer being in London, especially as it was at the college's expense. He had told Wattwood to refer the whole matter of the welfare of the college to the Lord Privy Seal. It was desperately poor, and it would greatly help if 'his highness should do graciously to remember them with some piece of some broken abbey'. On the spiritual side, Latimer had ensured that there should be a course of lectures on the Scriptures, though he must find the reader's payment himself. Further inquiries about Wattwood's [54] character left Latimer in the autumn still uneasy, though he did not seem to be quite so black as rumour had said—'so that he be reformed and I discharged, I care not how little I have to do with him; saving only I pray for him that God would made him a good man'.

Now, in April 1539, Wattwood has begun to yield to this intensive pastoral care. William Benett says that he shows more gentleness day by day than all the rest, and he sets forth the King's and Latimer's injunctions. Wattwood now approves of Benett's lecturing, but he is not having the same success with 'the other two canons, but only grudging at it but plainly denying it'.

The insight we are given in his letters into the continual duties of a conscientious Bishop should dispel any lingering illusion that, because means of communication were slow and uncertain, life was less busy in Latimer's day than in ours. Facilities were certainly very limited, and through much of the year, when he was in his diocese, riding would be all too often a struggle against foul ways and weather.

We are so easily led to think of his ministry in terms of the later triumphant preaching, that it is necessary to remember he

[52] ibid., 638.   [53] *Remains*, p. 396.   [54] ibid., p. 402.

did not always command the crowd. The people of the countryside were not so eager to gather for their Bishop's preaching as
the merchants and people of London. A reminiscence of this
sort occurs in the sixth sermon preached before Edward the
Sixth:[55]

I came once myself to a place, riding on a journey homeward from
London, and I sent word over night into the town that I would
preach there in the morning, because it was holiday; and methought
it was an holiday's work. The church stood in my way, and I took
my horse and company, and went thither. I thought I should have
found a great company in the church, and when I came there, the
church door was fast locked. I tarried there half an hour and more:
at last, the key was found and one of the parish comes to me and
says, 'Sir, this is a busy day with us, we cannot hear you; it is Robin
Hood's day. The parish are gone abroad to gather for Robin Hood:
I pray you, let them not.' I was fain there to give place to Robin
Hood: I thought my rochet should have been regarded, though I
were not; but it would not serve, it was fain to give place to Robin
Hood's men. It is no laughing matter, my friends, it is a weeping
matter, a heavy matter; a heavy matter, under the pretence of
gathering for Robin Hood, a traitor and a thief to put out a preacher,
to have his office less esteemed; to prefer Robin Hood before the
ministration of God's word: and all this hath come of unpreaching
prelates. This realm hath been ill provided for, that it hath had
such corrupt judgments in it, to prefer Robin Hood to God's word.

The opportunity to preach was what he coveted, and what his
authority, if not his reputation, should have guaranteed to him;
but we have none of the sermons which he delivered to the folk
of his diocese. He knew their needs, he knew their interests in
life, and how to speak of them; but they did not possess steno-
graphers in the villages of the West Midlands as in London, and
so they are lost to us for ever.

His correspondence was necessarily taken up with administrative matters, and these must have claimed far more hours
than a preacher would gladly accord to them. We have seen,
among these reports of affairs, how anxious some abbots and
priors were to procure the continuance of their houses by having
them made into colleges. Neither Evesham nor Hailes survived
in that way. But Latimer was never lacking in support of efforts
to give country boys their chance. We have noticed his interest

[55] *Sermons*, p. 208.

in the school at Worcester which was, in fact, established more securely by Henry the Eighth in 1542, in the time of Latimer's successor, for forty poor scholars. At Gloucester, too, there was a scheme which Cromwell appears to have favoured [56] for the provision of a school. This is the well-known Crypt School. What is possibly the last letter to Cromwell of those surviving from Latimer's official correspondence deals with this matter:

And now, sir, your good lordship hath begun right graciously with the school of Gloucester: if of your goodness you would now make an end, your perseverance cannot be unrewarded. If the king's highness doth use to sell of such lands as hath been belonging to monasteries, lady Cooke, foundress of the school, would give after twenty years' purchase for a parcel which lieth near unto the town, and was belonging to Llanthony. This bill inclosed doth specify the value, and I did send this bearer, Mr Garrett, my chaplain, to speak with lady Cooke, and to know further of the same. . . . But I refer all to your known both wisdom and goodness; and upon your pleasure known herein lady Cooke shall make ready thereunto.[57]

The lady referred to was the widow of John Cooke, an alderman of Gloucester, and she did endow the school, in fulfilment of her husband's will. Lands formerly belonging to Gloucester and Llanthony Abbeys contributed to the endowment. This last letter to the Lord Privy Seal probably belongs to the spring of 1539 immediately before the meeting of Convocation. There was greater need than Latimer could have realized for the prayer ending it—'Thus God preserve you in long life to the finishing of many things well begun, and to the performance of many things yet unperfect!' Within a few weeks the reaction which had been presaged since the previous autumn would show Henry's unwillingness to proceed with worship or belief that would depart openly from the Catholic pattern.

Convocation assembled on 2nd May at St Paul's, and on the 5th a committee of nine met to frame a religious statement. The Lord Privy Seal, Cranmer, Latimer, and Goodrich of Ely represented the reforming interest, the other five members being Lee, Archbishop of York, Tunstal (Durham), Aldrich (Carlisle), Clark (Bath), and Salcot (Bangor). It is not surprising that settled agreement was not possible among them, but six points were remitted to the Lords. Thus the matter of the Six Articles was brewing, and one lay member of the House of Peers left his

[56] *Remains*, pp. 393, 409, 417.   [57] ibid., p. 417.

impressions in a letter written on the eve of the passing of the
Act. It puts beyond dispute the King's personal interest and part
in the discussion, however much he may have been 'hereunto
stirred by the crafty insinuations of the bishop of Winchester
[Stephen Gardiner] and other old dissembling papists'.[58]

I assure you never prince shewed himself so wise a man, so well
learned, and so catholic, as the king hath done in this parliament.
With my pen I cannot express his marvellous goodness which is
come to such effect, that we shall have an act of parliament so
spiritual, that I think none shall dare say, in the blessed sacrament
of the altar doth remain either bread or wine after the consecration:
nor that a priest may have a wife: nor that it is necessary to receive
our Maker 'sub utraque specie', nor that private masses should not
be used as they have been: nor that it is not necessary to have
auricular confession. And notwithstanding my lord of Canterbury,
my lord of Ely, my lord of Salisbury, my lords of Worcester,
Rochester and St. David's, defended the contrary long time; yet
finally his highness confounded them all with God's learning. York,
Durham, Winchester, London, Chichester, Norwich and Carlisle,
have showed themselves honest and well learned men. We of the
temporalty have been all of one opinion: and my lord chancellor,
and my lord privy seal, as good as we can devise. My lord of
Canterbury and all these bishops have given their opinion and come
in to us, save Salisbury, who yet continueth a lewd fool. Finally, all
in England have cause to thank God, and most heartily to rejoice
of the king's most godly proceedings.[59]

The reforming Bishops had as yet no open supporters among
the nobility, and this unknown lord's verdict probably reflects
the tenor of much conversation in and about the court. Cromwell was, when all is said and done, a creature of the King; he
had been very powerful, and able to supply lands at fairly cheap
rates so long as abbeys were falling. He was likely to fall himself if he made one slip. The Englishman is by nature conservative, and Gardiner approximated more closely to a noble
lord's conception of a Bishop than Cranmer or Latimer. Both
Cromwell and the Lord Chancellor (Sir Thomas Audley) had
taken a safe place among the majority. Who were they, laymen
and servants of Henry, to dispute with him in matters theological? He was the Supreme Head of the Church; and what he
wished men to believe, they should believe, leaving scruples to
Bible lovers and preachers whose convictions might get the

[58] Strype, *Cranmer*, I.160.   [59] *State Papers, L. & P.*, XIV.i.1040.

better of their common sense. If the King were not quite so infallible as the Pope in matters of doctrine, at least he was able to show that it was not far from Convocation in St Paul's to Tower Hill, and the headsman was also his paid servant.

We can peep a little behind the scenes. During those days before the Act obtained its final shape, the Bishops were debating six questions on transubstantiation, priests' marriage, vows of chastity, and whether they were binding or not, the necessity of auricular confession according to God's law, whether private Masses 'stand with the Word of God or no', and whether it was 'necessary by the word of God that the sacrament of the altar should be ministered under both kinds or not?' [60]

Latimer, like Cranmer, said priests may marry; but Cranmer took no chances, and sent off his wife to Germany. The two friends both agreed that confession was not expressly enjoined in God's word, but they held its use was 'very requisite and expedient'. It is interesting to see that Latimer, and all the others, agreed that private Masses might stand. There was, as yet, among the English Reformers, nothing like the antipathy to the private Mass which was conspicuous on the Continent.

Thus in this not so merry month of June the Act was passed which was anathematized by Protestants more than anything else done by 'Junker Harry', as Luther would dare to call him. 'The Whip with the Six Strings', 'the terrible bloody act of the Six Articles' (Strype) was not, in fact, carried out to the last syllable or there would have been a holocaust. Doctrinally, what it affirmed would stand for the rest of Henry the Eighth's reign. What had been put forward as questions for discussion were now affirmed as doctrines and necessities. Whether the terrible punishments outlined in the act for denial of transubstantiation or the marriage of priests would be actually inflicted, who could tell? Probably not the King himself; but he was aware of the disturbed state of mind in which his Archbishop was, and sent counsellors, including the Dukes of Norfolk and Suffolk,[61] to visit and comfort him, lest he should think that his resistance had brought him under royal displeasure.

Latimer and Shaxton were in different case and resigned on 1st July. Shaxton would relent and recant later on, but Latimer would be out of public life for the rest of the reign, and in prison for some of it. Precisely how much of the time was spent in prison no one is ever likely to know. Foxe is certainly wrong in saying that he was 'cast into the Tower, where he continually remained prisoner till the time that the blessed King Edward entered his crown'.[62] He is possibly giving a true picture of what happened,

> At what time he first put off his rochet in his chamber among his friends, suddenly he gave a skip on the floor for joy, feeling his shoulder so light, and being discharged (as he said) of such a heavy burden.

It is precisely the kind of thing a man with Latimer's temperament would do, though he was no buffoon; and he never agreed to wear the rochet again, but he did say before the Privy Council in May 1546 that Cromwell had deceived him in persuading him that the King wanted his resignation.[63]

The penalty for denying the first article (on transubstantiation) once was death by burning, and two denials of any of the others would bring the reward of a felon's death. Latimer was wise to take the hint of current events, for on 6th July a letter went to Lord Lisle [64] describing a priest carrying his faggot at Paul's Cross for saying, 'Christ nor any creature had any merit by his Passion'. The writer, Thos. Warley, reports that the late Bishop of Worcester, now Latimer, had gone to Gravesend but was brought back, and on the next day Husee gives the same news. 'What his intent was God knows.' [65] It does not require much imagination to hazard Latimer's destination. At the same time Francis Hall wrote to Lady Lisle of Latimer's and Shaxton's resignations, 'They be not of the wisest sort methinks, for few nowadays will leave and give over such promotions for keeping of opinion.' [66] Yet a fourth letter [67] went to the Lisles from Leonard Holland on 7th July, written from Dover. He is on his way to London and will verify the facts:

> The bysshop of Worssyther whas syne [seen] with the bysshop of Canturbury in a prest gowne, and a sarsynyd typyd [sarsenet tippet] a bowthe hys necke, and never a man affter hym, and as the sayinge ys that the bysshop Lattomer fledde and ys taken at Rochester and browthe tyll the Tower.

[62] Foxe, *Acts and Monuments*, VII.463.   [63] *State Papers, L. & P.*, XXI.i.823.
[64] ibid., XIV. i. 1219.   [65] ibid., 1227.
[66] ibid., 1220.   [67] ibid., 1228.

Latimer was certainly in the news.

Official action had already been taken regarding his bishopric, for on 7th July the *congé d'élire* [68] had gone to the Prior and convent of Worcester Cathedral regarding the resignation of Hugh Latimer, clerk. On 11th August the appointment of his successor [69]—Dr John Bell, Archdeacon of Gloucester and a King's Chaplain—was confirmed at Lambeth.

These matters did not escape comment in the London pulpits, for preachers have always been liable to indulge in slightly dangerous remarks on current events when congregations nod; and it was high summer, the dog days. Dr Crome (most vacillating of reformers, but keeping his skin whole to the end) had preached in July on Relic Sunday, which, according to the Use of Sarum, was on the first Sunday following 7th July, the Feast of the Translation of St Thomas of Canterbury. In a deposition made on 13th August Thomas Herd, [70] priest of the church, admitted he had given little ear to the preacher until he began to speak about Latimer and Shaxton:

Friends, would to God that ye would leave your slanderous tongues. Ye say that these bishops be false knaves and whoresons.

But they were as good in their living as anybody, and if their honesty only consisted in their promotions, it was like saying that the Lord Mayor and the Sheriffs ceased to be honest when they went out of office.

Continental sympathizers watched what was happening with grave concern. Bucer lamented the reaction in a letter to Philip, the Landgrave of Hesse: [71]

Two of the most pious bishops have been taken. In Nov. there is to be a new synod [Parliament] at London, in which they will proceed to extremities with these persons who are at present only prisoners and many others: for there are many in England who know Christ truly and cannot keep silence. The King has therefore ordered strict watch to be kept at the ports that very few may escape. The crafty bp. of Winchester bears rule, who has warned the King that if he proceed with the Reformation, it will lead to commotion and the principal lords of England will be against him.

Bucer, like Foxe, and others, attributed more interest in the Reformation to the King than we would assign today.

[68] ibid., 1354 (30).
[69] Strype, *Cranmer*, I.169.
[70] *State Papers, L. & P.*, XIV.II.41(2).
[71] ibid., 186.

Latimer did not know—no one could know—what his future might be, whether death, strict imprisonment, or nominal restriction. A reminiscence of these times from a sermon [72] preached before Edward the Sixth shows that he was not able to obtain his 'Pentecostal'—the annual composition paid by households in a diocese to the cathedral for general absolution, given at Pentecost. He expected £55. 'I set my commissary to gather it, but he could not be suffered, for it was said a sedition should rise upon it.' But he was not cut off quite without a penny, for in the Augmentation Accounts, among payments of pensions made to heads of former religious houses, appears, 'Hugh Latymer, clerk, *quondam* bishop of Worcester, for the last half of his year ending Michaelmas, £33 6s. 8d.[73] His friend, Nicholas Shaxton, was similarly treated.

He was placed in the care of Sampson, the Bishop of Chichester, and remained mostly in London with sufficient liberty for his friends to visit him, though he might not go out.[74] They could bring him news of impending executions, and he was apprehensive of his own fate. 'I was desirous, I say, to hear of execution, because I looked that my part should have been therein. I looked every day to be called to it myself.' But there is a petition to the King belonging to the autumn of 1539 [75] which mentions him as being actually at Chichester in August.

A Staffordshire man, Thomas Pylson of Abbots Bromley, sought royal letters for his restoration to a fellowship at King's Hall, Cambridge. In the previous Lent one of Latimer's servants, John Tyndall, had recommended a barber and surgeon to cure a trouble Pylson had contracted in a brothel in Southwark. The barber had, however, ill treated him with starvation and physic, finally turning him out of doors unhealed in April, and in such a state that for three days he lay out in the weather, for no one would dare to take him in, he was in such a sorry plight. Then Tyndall and another of the Bishop of Worcester's servants, William Farley, a lawyer, pressed Pylson to resign his fellowship in favour of one of Latimer's chaplains, Hugh Rawlyns. He refused, and returned to Staffordshire, and thence to Cambridge. But that was not the end of it. Tyndall sent Rawlyns to Cambridge with a letter which compelled him, while sick, to ride from Cambridge to London on 1st August.

[72] *Sermons*, p. 135.
[74] *Sermons*, I.136.
[73] *State Papers*, L. & P., XIV.II.236, p. 73.
[75] *State Papers*, L. & P., XIV.II.255.

The next day they persuaded him to make a formal resignation before a notary of Paternoster Row, and then afterwards to ride to Chichester to see Mr Hugh Latimer, sometime his master. On the way to Chichester, at Midhurst on Monday, 4th August, he revoked his resignation. All to no avail, for Rawlyns had the greater influence with Dr Skyp the almoner, got a bill on 7th September, secured the fellowship and went to Cambridge.

That typically Tudor story of vice, graft, and self-seeking does no harm to Latimer's reputation; but it shows three of his former staff in an unpleasant light, and it also seems to prove that, at least in August 1539, he was not merely in the Bishop of Chichester's keeping, but in Sussex, and not in London.

Latimer was almost certainly in London for most of the time until the spring of 1540 when his warden fell under the royal displeasure and was committed to the Tower in May for leanings towards Rome. Sir Richard Sadler was commanded to write to Cromwell,[76] 'Touching Latimer, his Majesty would have him yet to remain in the Bishop's house till he may speak with you, and devise what is best to do with him.'

The new glory of being Earl of Essex which had just been given to Cromwell was no guarantee of his continuance in power. His policy of seeking union with German Protestant princes had small chance of success if Anne of Cleves was to be a main inducement for Henry's support. It would be easier for Cromwell to lose his head than the King his heart. When his mind was made up, Henry swooped like a hawk; and only a few weeks passed between Cromwell's arrest on 10th June and his execution—botched by the headsman—on 28th July, Convocation having obligingly decided that the marriage with Anne was null and void. Anne, with a pension of some £4000 a year and two houses in the country, was able to indulge her passion for new dresses, and live in considerably greater safety than if the marriage had been consummated. She remained here until the year of Elizabeth's accession and was buried in Westminster Abbey.

In the meantime the petite and fascinating Katherine Howard had appeared on the scene. Londoners then, as now, were not blind to the private delights of the great, and they 'saw the King very frequently in the daytime, and sometimes at midnight, pass over to her on the river Thames in a little boat.

[76] ibid., XV.719.

The bishop of Winchester also very often provided feastings and entertainments for them in his palace.' So Richard Hilles wrote to Henry Bullinger in Switzerland in a long letter surveying the events of 1539–40 [77] and bemoaning the sins which must have contributed to the downfall of Cromwell and the return to influence of Stephen Gardiner with his conservative catholicism and aristocratic friendships, particularly with the Howard family. Reaction was setting in, literally with a vengeance. Three ardent reformers were burned at Smithfield in the persons of the unfortunate Dr Robert Barnes, Thomas Garrard (or Garrett), and William Jerome. They had all been associated with Protestant activities, and Barnes most conspicuously in the move towards Lutheran alliances. These three men were all condemned without trial by Act of Attainder and brought to the stake on 30th July, two days after Cromwell's execution. Wolsey had long ago warned Barnes that persistence in pulpit sallies could bring him to burning; but he never learned the lesson and had been tilting a little too joyously against Gardiner. Henry demonstrated his proper independence as Supreme Head, and matched the burning of the three preachers on the same day by executing for treason, with all the customary horrible procedure, three friars who were loyal to the Pope.

Barnes, Garrard, and Jerome, with Cromwell himself, had been explicitly excluded from a general amnesty which Henry had found it necessary to declare a little more than a year after the passing of the Six Articles Act, that 'no further persecution should take place for religion, and that those in prison should be set at liberty on finding security for their appearance when called for'.[78]

This amnesty left Latimer without the fear of paying the extreme penalty for what his friends called his 'singularity' [79] in not retaining his bishopric at the price of agreement with the Act. But it speaks much for Latimer's faithfulness to friends that he did not hesitate to show what he thought. On 21st May Barnes had written to Aepinus, 'A fierce controversy is going on between the Bishop of London [Bonner], Gardiner and myself, respecting justification by faith and purgatory.' [80] In point of fact, Barnes had already been forced to recant because of his 'errors' when he had very pointedly objected to Gardiner's

[77] *Original Letters*, p. 202.
[79] *Sermons*, p. 136.
[78] *State Papers, L. & P.*, XVI.271.
[80] *Original Letters*, p. 616.

preaching, who had preceded him as one of the Lenten preachers at Paul's Cross. Barnes never possessed the happy knack of
being able to say the daring thing about or to authority as
Latimer repeatedly did. On paper, their words might not seem
very different, but the one only irritated where the other often
commanded respect, if not liking. Gardiner had been taking
what was the traditional view of works, purgatory, and Masses
and Barnes regarded himself as the champion of Lutheran
doctrine

But I, on the other hand, in opposition to all these things, vindicate
the efficacy of the blood of Jesus Christ my Lord; but hitherto I
stand alone in doing it. For although many persons approve my
statements, yet no-one stands forward except Latimer. You shall
hear the result of this controversy.[81]

It was a different result in July from the one poor Barnes
expected in May.

Latimer and Shaxton were not free to do whatever they liked.
The King specifically forbade them to come within half a dozen
miles of their former dioceses, Oxford, Cambridge, and London:
and they were prohibited from preaching.[82] During the next
six and a half years, therefore, Latimer was kept from his chosen
and favourite work.

He was by no means without friends, but no one has left any
considerable detail as to where and how he spent his time. Foxe
probably obtained his information about Latimer's accident,
when he was badly hurt by a falling tree, from Augustine
Bernher, his faithful servant. Certainly, when he emerged into
full public life again on Edward the Sixth's accession, he was 'a
sore bruised man'.

Thomas Becon mentions [83] that when he was in trouble
in Henry's reign (*circa* 1545) he saw Latimer in Warwickshire, and was greatly cheered by his conversation. Foxe says
that Latimer, after being hurt by the tree, came up to London
for treatment. 'He was molested and troubled by the bishop,
whereby he was again in no little danger; and at length was
cast into the Tower, where he continually remained prisoner,
till the time that blessed King Edward entered his crown.'
Latimer was certainly not in the Tower for most of the years
from July 1539, when he resigned his bishopric. If he sustained

[81] ibid., p. 617.   [82] ibid., p. 215.   [83] Becon's *Works*, II.426.

damage from the tree in 1545 or thereabouts, instead of 'a little
after he had renounced his bishopric', it would be more true to
the happenings. For we do know that he was summoned before
the Council on 13th May 1546,[84] at Greenwich. Dr Crome had
once more got himself into trouble by preaching fearlessly
against purgatory during Lent, and once more he recanted. But
Latimer and others were involved in the purge which the
authorities had instituted. The report of the Council reads:

We had yesterday Latimer before us and after a declaration made
unto him that he was accused for one that had devised and
counselled with Crome—he made answer that he had indeed been
sundry times in his company since he was at the house of me the
Lord Chancellor and that he had said somewhat touching his
recanting or not recanting, couching his words so as he neither confessed the matter, nor yet uttered his mind so cleanly but somewhat
stak and appeared by the way. Whereupon we ministered an oath
unto him, and delivered him certain interrogatories to answer,
appointing him a place for the quiet doing of the same; where, when
he had answered to two or three of them, he sent unto us, desiring
that he might eftsoons speak unto us, without the which, he could
proceed no further in his answer. Upon which request, being much
busied with the examinations of Huick, Lascelles, the Vicar of
St Bride's and the Scottish friar, it was ordered that I, the Bishop
of Durham [Tunstal] and I, the controller [Sir John Gage] should
go to him to know what he would with us: to whom making general
answer that he could not proceed with his conscience till he might
again speak with us, we left all the rest and sent for him. At his
coming he told us he was light to swear to answer the interrogatories
before he had considered them, and that charity would that some
man should have put him in remembrance of this. He told us it was
dangerous to answer such interrogatories, for that he might by that
means be brought into danger; noting the proceedings therein to be
more extreme than should be ministered unto him if he lived under
the Turk as he liveth under the King's majesty, for that he said it
was sore to answer for another man's fact; and besides, he said, he
doubted whether it were his Highness' pleasure that he should be
thus called and examined; desiring therefore to speak with His
Majesty himself before he made further answer. For he was once,
he said, deceived that way when he left his bishopric; being borne in
hand by the Lord Cromwell, that it was His Majesty's pleasure he
should resign it, which his majesty after denied and pitied his
condition.

Latimer accused Gardiner [85] of malice against him, which he denied, though he admitted he had no love for his doctrine. The end of the matter was that the Council was little the wiser concerning Latimer's real views. He showed himself to be shrewd, unhurried, and self-possessed, and he did not hesitate to appeal to the King. Cranmer was still Archbishop, and that could count for much in Latimer's favour, but he had shown sufficient sympathy with the offenders to justify the authorities in restraining his liberty. He was not bereft of means, for his pension still came to him.[86] He was kept in the Tower for the remaining twelve months of Henry's reign, and the Privy Council footed a bill for £10 for Thomas Gifford who was appointed to search his possessions in the country for any incriminating evidence.[87]

That last summer of Henry the Eighth's reign saw the martyrdom of Anne Askew, the gentlewoman who denied the accepted doctrine of the Sacrament with a patience and bravery which put many men to shame. She was brought before the Council at Greenwich at the beginning of June and endured several days of continuous cross-questioning. 'Then on the Sunday I was sore sick, thinking no less than to die: therefore I desired to speak with Master Latimer [88] (who was in the Tower) but it would not be.' She was transferred to Newgate. Brought before her judges once more at the Guildhall on 18th June, Shaxton was her companion in distress; but he yielded, and so avoided the stake. Anne—whatever some historians may say of the pertness of women heretics in bandying words of Scripture with their clerical betters—had something of Blandina's spirit. Did Shaxton, who had forfeited his see with Latimer over the Six Articles, really become persuaded concerning transubstantiation? Anne Askew had no doubt of her own convictions. She endured racking in which the Lord Chancellor, Wriothesley, literally lent a hand, to the chagrin of the Lieutenant of the Tower, who chased off by boat to Henry to acquit himself of compliance without specific orders from the King. Wriothesley was after other prey. Anne Askew said:

Then they did put me on the rack because I confessed no ladies or gentlewomen to be of my opinion, and thereon they kept me a long

[85] ibid., 823.
[86] ibid., 643, f. 54. Pension: Hugh Latimer, £66 13s. 4d., 30 March, 8 October.
[87] *State Papers, L. & P.*, XXI, Pt. I, 1086, 18 June.
[88] ibid., 1181, Foxe, op. cit., V.544 ff.

time; and because I lay still and did not cry, my lord chancellor and Master Rich took pains to rack me with their own hands, till I was nigh dead. Then the lieutenant caused me to be loosed from the rack. Incontinently I swooned, and then they recovered me again. After that I sat two long hours reasoning with my lord chancellor upon the bare floor; where he, with many flattering words, persuaded me to leave my opinion.[89]

This lady was for burning if Wriothesley and Gardiner had their way. She was carried to Smithfield in a chair, helpless from her torture, and died there on 16th July, in the presence of the Lord Mayor, the Lord Chancellor, and a noble assembly. It was characteristic of the King that he should appoint as the preacher to the condemned woman and her three male companions (Nicholas Belenian, a Shropshire priest, John Adams, a tailor, and John Lacels of the King's Household) no less a person than Shaxton, who had so narrowly himself missed being at the stake instead of in the pulpit.

At the end of the following January the King died, and with the general amnesty, on Edward the Sixth's accession, Latimer was freed from the Tower.

[89] Foxe, op. cit., p. 547.

CHAPTER EIGHT

The Full Tide of Reform

L ATIMER'S fame is most secure as a preacher. It was in that way he best served in the days of Henry the Eighth: it was almost the only way in which he served during the short reign of his son. The six years of Edward the Sixth's reign gave him fullness of opportunity to follow his natural bent, and what he conceived to be his chief vocation. The considerable remains of his sermons, largely garnered and published by his very faithful Swiss servant, Augustine Bernher, belong almost entirely to these years.

Although the advantage seemed to lie during Henry's last years with the conservatives, the sting had been drawn from the anti-Protestant legislation. The Bishop of Winchester remained as the chief menace to the reformers, but Cranmer had survived all the troubles of the reign, and now would have opportunities beyond his farthest reach hitherto. Though Gardiner would show, in Mary's reign, his readiness to accept Papal authority, there were not many enthusiasts for absolutism in that direction. But it must also be acknowledged that there were not many people who were eager for sweeping reforms in doctrine or worship. Religion, at least as much as politics, can be altered by minorities who are possessed of zeal and conviction.

Religiously, the main influence in policy and action would be Cranmer, politically two very different men—Hertford, the King's uncle, almost at once to become Duke of Somerset, the Protector, and, after October 1549, Dudley, the Earl of Warwick. This crafty, unscrupulous and ambitious man would end his days as a traitor, execrated by his fellow-countrymen for his selfish use of Lady Jane Grey as his tool. It could have happened that, after Dudley's coming to power, there would have been reaction from the religious policy of Protector Somerset's régime; but in fact, it was not so. The tide of reform flowed faster and fuller towards the closing years of the reign.

Latimer, and men of similar fortune, were released at the opening of the reign under a general pardon [1] and he came at

---

[1] *State Papers*, Ed. VI, II.34.

once into close association with his old friend, the Archbishop. Lambeth was his home whenever he chose to avail himself of it. Pollard has deftly summarized the character of the Protector, who was King in all but name:

He was born before his time, a seer of visions and a dreamer of dreams. . . . He believed that the strength of a King lay not in the severity of his laws or the rigour of his penalties, but in the affections of his people; and not one instance of death or torture for religion stains the brief and troubled annals of his rule.[2]

In religious matters Cranmer was able to pursue a policy which would give effect to convictions which had become increasingly dear to him during the last years of Henry's reign. Some of his friends—especially those who had been abroad—found him slower to move forward than they wished; but his influence was everywhere, in the placing of men in key positions in the Church and, supremely, in the ordering of its worship. He prevailed without being too forceful, and in the preaching of Latimer we find complete agreement with what the Archbishop intended. Of course, it was an Erastian conception of Church government. The Church, after the defeat of the Papal policy, was deprived of anything like equal bargaining power with the State. A king's religion should be the norm of faith for all men in his borders. The Church in England was rapidly becoming the Church of England, dependent on Crown and Council and Parliament. But there was now a chance of liberty of opinion in greater degree than it had been known before. It would sometimes degenerate into licence. The apprentices might indulge in some too boisterous 'ragging' of priests, and the incumbent of St Martin's in Ironmongers' Lane would be swift to anticipate eighteenth-century squarsons by setting up the Royal Arms and texts in English, having removed images and the crucifix.

By September 1547 both Gardiner and Bonner were in prison—not surprisingly; and in November the first Parliament of the reign, called by Somerset, repealed all the laws against heresy. It was almost a complete amnesty, for all the laws against expounding or reading the Scriptures in English were swept away, with the *Act of Six Articles*. The clergy could marry unashamedly; and so it is not to be marvelled at that, in

[2] *Cambridge Modern History*, II.476.

London, where the 'known men' had hidden and expounded English Scripture before Luther had written his theses, there now came immigration from the Continent of zealous men interested in the Reformation. Among them were exiles returning home. They had been under Lutheran, Zwinglian, or Genevan influence, and no doubt their hopes were high; but neither they nor the foreign divines who followed later had any marked effect upon the trend of events. They would show their disappointment at the mildness of Cranmer's tone in the First Prayer Book in 1549, and although there would be definite traces of a Zwinglian kind at the heart of the Communion Service in the Second Book of 1552, the tenor of the way was that which Cranmer would have followed in the last six or seven years of the old King's reign, had he been permitted. The Archbishop affirmed that it was the intention of the King to turn from the Mass towards a Communion Service; and certainly this was the direction he himself desired.

The increased liberty given to preachers did not reduce confusion. Foreign influences as well as native would all find their opportunity in the pulpit unless there were to be imposed a strict censorship which would consort ill with the prominence the reforming party gave to the preaching of God's Word. It had, however, long been Cranmer's intention to stabilize doctrine, and to proclaim sound ways of behaviour by means of a Book of Homilies. In Henry the Eighth's time he had not been successful in obtaining permission for their publication, but the chance soon came in the boy King's reign. A visitor from a Catholic country about the time of Henry's death would have found little in an English parish church to differentiate the service from that to which he was accustomed; but within six months the great liturgical changes began which would show the insularity of the English Reformation and its unique beauties in vernacular worship. The first sign of alteration was shown in the Royal Chapel. Compline was said in English on Easter Monday, 1547. Had it been an English Mass on Easter Sunday, that would have been an innovation daring indeed, and might have provoked widespread protest; but once the start had been made English came quickly into its own as the language of devotion as well as exhortation. The 'First Book of Homilies' appeared in July and these sermons were 'to be declared and read by all parsons, vicars or curates every

Sunday in their churches where they have cure'. The author-
ship of all the homilies cannot be definitely assigned, though it
seems reasonable to believe that Cranmer was responsible for
the first four. The book opened with 'A Fruitful Exhortation
to the Reading of Holy Scripture'. It is possible that Latimer
was responsible for No. 12 'Against Strife and Contention'—a
subject on which he could speak with the note of experience.

Ridley and Becon were others who helped in this work, and
therefore the Book gives some clue to the minds of men in the
front rank of English reformers.

Sir Edwyn Hoskyns, who did so much to emphasize the
importance of 'The Word of God' for Cambridge men in the
1920's and '30's, assessed their aim thus:

The authors of the Homilies did not, however, for one moment
suppose that to have translated and published the English Bible was
in itself sufficient. The themes of the Bible required to be known and
apprehended, and it was still necessary to make their relevance to
English life plain and unmistakable. It was for this reason that the
Homilies were ordered to be read in the churches, for this reason also
that the titles were so carefully chosen, in order that the relevance of
the Bible to the ordinary, straightforward and fundamental things
of all human life should be at once recognisable. The visible world,
men, marriage, babies and the manner in which they come into the
world, war, famine, prosperity, success, bread, death, the relation
of a man to his neighbour, these are the themes of the Homilies, just
as they are the themes of the Bible: and after all these are not
irrelevant things; they cannot be dismissed as uncomfortable relics
of antiquity.[3]

This was to be the intended diet of instruction for the
parishioners in the towns and villages, a standard to which an
illiterate clergy could scarcely reach and a safe one for times
when open preaching would be denied because unrest and
plotting were feared. No one as yet could foresee the necessity
or the success of that Middle Way which would be the triumph
of Anne Boleyn's daughter.

Latimer was included among those who were officially recognized as having licence to preach under the ecclesiastical seal
since July 1547. The list includes that fiery particle, John Knox,
and two future Archbishops of Canterbury, Matthew Parker
and Edmund Grindal. He habitually spoke on matters which

[3] *Cambridge Sermons* (S.P.C.K.), p. 163.

were treated in the Book of Homilies—but with a difference.
He became a champion, not only of the spoken word, but of
the word preached directly to the present congregation. His
preaching all through the days of Edward the Sixth was consistently relevant to the condition of the nation as he saw it,
and with special reference to the men and women immediately
before him. Two years after the Homilies were published and
had been taken into the dioceses by the King's Visitors together
with the Injunctions for the abolition of any lingering loyalty to
the Pope, Latimer referred to them as he preached before the
King:

But how shall he read this book? [The Bible.] As the Homilies are
read. Some call them homelies, and indeed so they may be well
called, for they are homely handled. For though the priest read
them never so well, yet if the parish like them not, there is such
talking and babbling in the church that nothing can be heard; and
if the parish be good and the priest naught, he will so hack it and
chop it, that it were as good for them to be without it, for any word
that shall be understood.[4]

Latimer had been in full sympathy with the publication of
the Homilies and the Injunctions. What he had contended
for was now plainly set forth as the law of the land, Parliament
ratifying what the Council designed. The abuse caused by
images would cease by their destruction—the Gospel and the
Epistle would be read in English, the English Litany would
now be said kneeling and not, as formerly, in procession.
Where there could not be sound preaching because of lack of
education on the part of the local clergy, there could be the
guarantee of the weekly homily, though he was well enough
aware of the soporific effect of the read sermon—especially
when it had been written by someone else.

But why, in these first changeful months of the new King's
reign, was not Latimer in his old place as Bishop? The question
can be answered as definitely as Latimer met the request. He
would not again wear the rochet. Moreover, Heath had succeeded him at Worcester. He was old—but not so old as to be
incapable. He was never again to be physically robust; but his
preaching was robust, and it was for the work of preaching the
gospel of practical Christianity in a day of new opportunity

[4] 2nd Sermon before Edward VI, *Sermons*, p. 121.

that he would live and spend his remaining years. He would have grudged the time a diocesan must give to Convocation, Councils, and administration. If he were not involved in affairs so intimately as when he was Bishop of Worcester, his view could gain in objectivity and his counsel might be even more effective.

Latimer had always been a popular preacher. His forthright manner of speech and strength of personality had been a guarantee of awakening and sustaining interest. This had been so in his Cambridge days as well as in the time spent at his cure in Kington and his bishopric. But he had never before felt completely free to express his own convictions without some embarrassing qualification. The Protector Somerset was not of Henry the Eighth's mind in religion, and although he had always enjoyed Cranmer's friendship Latimer had never previously been sure that the policy of the Crown and the Church would be unobstructive. If he made enemies (and he did) it would be on personal grounds and not through conflict with official policy.

By the end of the year 1547 Parliament had ratified all the wishes expressed in the Council. The Act of Six Articles had not only been abolished, but Communion in both kinds had been instituted. Here was change indeed at the central point of Christian worship as it had been known in England continuously for almost a thousand years. Foxe takes special pleasure in recording this enactment [5]—

his majesty, with the lords spiritual and temporal, and the commons in the same parliament assembled, thoroughly understanding by the judgment of the best learned, that it was more agreeable unto the first institution of the sacrament of the most precious body and blood of our Saviour Christ, and also more conformable to the common use and practice both of the apostles, and of the primitive church, by the space of five hundred years and more after Christ's ascension, that the said holy sacrament should be ministered unto all christian people under both the kinds of bread and wine, than under the form of bread only; and also that it was more agreeable unto the said first institution of Christ, and the usage of the apostles and primitive church, that the people, being present, should receive the same with the priest, than that the priest should receive it alone.

It seems incredible that Latimer should have remained silent

[5] Foxe, *Acts and Monuments*, V.715.

for almost a year, but the first allusion to his return to public preaching is that made by Stow: [6]

On January 1st Doctor Latimer preached at Paul's Cross, which was the first sermon by him preached in almost eight years before; for at the making of the Six Articles, he, being Bishop of Worcester, would not consent unto them, and therefore was commanded to silence, and gave up his bishopric. He also preached at Paul's Cross on January 8 where he affirmed that whatsoever the clergy commanded ought to be obeyed but he also declared that the clergy are such as sit in Moses' chair and break not their Master's commandment, adding nothing thereto nor taking anything therefrom; and such a clergy must be obeyed of all men, both high and low. He also preached at Paul's on the fifteenth and on the twentyninth of January.

This series was the famous sequence 'On The Plough', of which the last has come down to us in such full detail that we can gauge its passionate sincerity as well as savour its terse colloquialism. This fourth sermon was preached in *The Shrouds*, the covered place at the side of the cathedral to which preacher and congregation resorted in inclement weather.

In the first three sermons the preacher had sought to show 'what seed should be sown in God's field, in God's ploughland' —the doctrine that should be taught. Now he approached the matter of defining 'what men should be the teachers and preachers of it'.

Sermons are not usually capable of retaining their life for succeeding generations. Preaching is the mediation of God's truth by a personality convinced first of all in itself of the importance of the message. It is conveyed directly by a man speaking to men; and very rarely indeed does it happen that the words spoken in the pulpit can come home with the same compulsion to the reader as to the hearer. They suffer a seachange, like those specimens of seaweeds gathered by Victorian damsels and doomed to lose their colour in glass cases. Latimer carefully prepared his sermons—but what we have seems to be a verbatim report rather than a preacher's manuscript. The Sermon on the Plough [7] shows us Latimer at his work, speaking in his own person, with reminiscence and topical allusion, but also with invective and passionate warning. If he sought to stir the clergy to their duty, he also was not blind to the get-

[6] Stow, *Chronicles.*   [7] *Sermons*, p. 59 ff.

rich-quick mood of the London citizen and the new nobility. Thus he speaks to the preacher's duty:

Ye may not, then, I say, be offended with my similitude, for because I liken preaching to a ploughman's labour, and a prelate to a ploughman. But now you will ask me, whom I call a prelate? A prelate is that man whatsoever he be, that hath a flock to be taught of him; whosoever hath any spiritual charge in the faithful congregation, and whatsoever he be that hath cure of souls. And well may the preacher and the ploughman be likened together: first, for their labour of all seasons of the year; for there is no time of the year in which the ploughman hath not some special work to do: as in my country in Leicestershire the ploughman hath a time to set forth, and assay his plough, and other times for other necessary works to be done.

He then indulges in comparisons that come close indeed to the soil, but would be understood by all Londoners in a day when no citizen was far from the furrows.

His plea was of the necessity for constant, regular preaching:

For the preaching of the word of God unto the people is called meat: scripture calleth it meat; not strawberries, that come but once a year, and tarry not long [a dig at non-resident and non-preaching bishops and curates] but are soon gone: but it is meat, it is no dainties. The people must have meat that must be familiar and continual, and daily given unto them to feed upon. Many make a strawberry of it, ministering it but once a year; but such do not the office of good prelates.

The theme of the duty of a good prelate would be one to which Latimer would return often. He had spoken of it, greatly daring, in his first sermon before Convocation when he was himself a new Bishop. Now he was intent on making plain to the people—lords or citizens as well as clergy—what was rightly to be expected of the ministers of Christ's Church. Latimer would not score high marks in a modern school of homiletics either for firmness of structure in his sermons or for consistency of treatment. He would wander away from a point and come back to it—which has always been a fault of extemporary preachers, except that some forget their way back to their original argument.

But the citizens of London did not escape his admonition and pleading. Many of them were newly rich—for the days were full of opportunity for men skilled in trade; but it had never been in Latimer's mind that release from the old compulsory duties of unreformed religion should free a man from the better dictates of conscience and compassion. He had been sadly disillusioned, and would never cease to proclaim it, by the selfishness now shown so brazenly.

But London was never so ill as it is now. In times past men were full of pity and compassion, but now there is no pity; for in London their brother shall die in the streets for cold, he shall lie sick at the door between stock and stock, I cannot tell what to call it, and perish there for hunger: was there ever more unmercifulness in Nebo? I think not. In times past, when the rich man died in London, they were wont to help the poor scholars of the Universities with exhibition. When any man died, they would bequeath great sums of money toward the relief of the poor. When I was a scholar at Cambridge myself, I heard very good report of London, and knew many that had relief of the rich men of London: but now I can hear no such good report, and yet I inquire of it, and hearken for it; but now charity is waxen cold, none helpeth the scholar nor yet the poor. And in those days what did they when they helped the scholars? Marry, they maintained and gave them livings that were very papists, and professed the pope's doctrine: and now that the knowledge of God's word is brought to light, and many earnestly study and labour to set it forth, now almost no man helpeth to maintain them.

He is particularly severe on Bishops who are more eager to remember their status as great men in the world than as ministers of the Word.

But this much I dare say, that since lording and loitering hath come up, preaching hath come down, contrary to the apostles' times: for they preached and lorded not, and now they lord and preach not. For they that be lords will ill go to plough: it is no meet office for them; it is not seeming for their estate. . . . For ever since the prelates were made lords and nobles, the plough standeth; there is no work done, the people starve. They hawk, they hunt, they card, they dice; they pastime in their prelacies with gallant gentlemen, with their dancing minions and with their fresh companions, so that ploughing is set aside: and by their lording and loitering, preaching and ploughing is clean gone.

These paragraphs show the words tumbling out, with not a little alliteration that reminds one of the older sort of English poetry which died with *Piers Plowman* and *Gawain and the Green*

Knight. It is the speech of the people being forged as a weapon. Much of it can be read with far greater interest by a man of the twentieth century than the sermons of admittedly greater learning and theological wisdom composed by preachers of later centuries. Sometimes—at least to the modern ear—he overdoes it, though he may well have been arresting a wandering attention or evoking new interest in his audience by such sentences as—

They are so troubled with lordly living, they be so placed in palaces, couched in courts, ruffling in their rents, dancing in their dominions, burdened with ambassages, [was this a dig at Gardiner?], pampering of their paunches, like a monk that maketh his jubilee; munching in their mangers, and moiling in their gay manors and mansions, and so troubled with loitering in their lordships that they cannot attend it.

We look at this kind of preaching from the farther side of the gulf that divides us from his generation, and it is easy to forget how small were the numbers of men in the country as a whole who would be sympathetic with the changes that had so recently been given official sanction, but were by no means as yet accepted in the life of the churches. No doubt the years of silence that had been imposed upon Latimer since his retirement from the See of Worcester had made him more than ever sure of the inherent wrongness of doctrines and practices which he had once accepted. Cranmer had in him the sturdiest of henchmen, who could 'put it over' most effectively to the laity —for it was by the laity that the future would be made or marred, and William Cecil was only one, though destined to be the greatest, among those who might be influenced by such preaching. Latimer aimed at producing character—character which would be effective in the shaping of a new England, and though he might not use the phrase 'the priesthood of all believers', it was such an office of Christian living that he proclaimed. He had no doubt at all that, whatever idleness might be seen in the prelates, the Devil would not be lazy. He went so far as to say, paradoxically, that the devil was 'the most diligent preacher of all other; he is never out of his diocess'.

Where the devil is resident, and hath his plough going, there away with books, and up with candles; away with bibles, and up with beads; away with the light of the gospel, and up with the light of candles, yea, at noon-days.

Latimer ended his last sermon on the Plough with a straight-forward plea for a simple trust in the Death of Christ as the all-atoning Sacrifice.

Then let us trust upon his only death, and look for none other sacrifice propitiatory, than the same bloody sacrifice, the lively sacrifice; and not the dry sacrifice, but a bloody sacrifice. For Christ himself said, *consummatum est*: 'It is perfectly finished: I have taken at my Father's hand the dispensation of redeeming mankind, I have wrought man's redemption, and have despatched the matter.' [8]

Latimer's servant said that his master usually preached twice a Sunday; but there is no detailed register of his sermons to give us the clue as to his itinerary in and about London or the provinces. He was in London for the winter and spring of 1548, and especially was Court Preacher during Lent, as he was in the two succeeding years.

These sermons were not delivered in the Chapel Royal but in the inner private garden [9] where a pulpit was set up and the boy King could hear at an open window. The courtiers stood to listen longer than a modern crowd does at a football match, and no doubt some of them would have been very pleased if they could have hauled the preacher down; for it was his habit to do a good deal more than tackle general abuses. He could indicate people by pointed allusion and sometimes by openly naming them. His fearlessness is something to be marvelled at, for he knew well enough that the King's health was precarious, and the succession would come to Mary, consistently staunch in her devotion not to the religion her father professed at his death but to the complete acknowledgement of the Pope's authority. He would face the enmity of Bonner and Gardiner, but apart from the Catholic hierarchy, there would be the embittered and hardened men of fortune who were unscrupulously taking advantage of the King's minority. Graft was spreading like measles.

Prescience of his fate would not, however, deflect Latimer from his duty for one moment. Foxe [10] rightly comments that 'as touching himself, he ever affirmed that the preaching of the gospel would cost him his life'. It is difficult for us, in a time when news and opinion can be broadcast by wireless and press, to realize the importance of the pulpit in Tudor England.

[8] *Sermons*, p. 74.   [9] Foxe, op. cit., VII.463.   [10] ibid., p. 464.

Opinion can still be moulded regarding ethical questions, but the most popular preacher does not enjoy personal contact with so great a proportion of 'all sorts and conditions of men' as formerly. It is especially true that the preacher would not today have the chance of speaking authoritatively face to face with men influential in affairs at the highest level.

The directness of speech shown in his preaching at Paul's must have been continued during Lent at the court. With the exception of one allusion of his own we have no account of his subjects. They would be addressed chiefly to a lay audience. But there was a very definite result to his plea for restitution, a theme to which he would return again and again during these years. Three years later, on 10th March 1550, he preached his last sermon before Edward the Sixth [11] and took as his text, 'Take heed and beware of covetousness' (Luke 12[15]). His own words describe what happened as the result of his earlier preaching in 1548:

I have now preached three Lents. The first time I preached restitution. 'Restitution,' quoth some, 'What should he preach of restitution? Let him preach of contrition,' quoth they, 'and let restitution alone; we can never make restitution.' Then, say I, if thou wilt not make restitution, thou shalt go to the devil for it. Now choose thee either restitution, or else endless damnation. But now there be two manner of restitutions; secret restitution, and open restitution: whether of both it be, so that restitution be made, it is all good enough. At my first preaching of restitution, one good man took remorse of conscience and acknowledged himself to me, that he had deceived the king; and willing he was to make restitution: and so the first Lent came to my hands twenty pounds to be restored to the king's use. I was promised twenty pound more the same Lent, but it could not be made, so that it came not. Well, the next Lent came three hundred and twenty pounds more. I received it myself, and paid it to the king's council. So I was asked, what he was that made this restitution? But should I have named him? Nay, they should as soon have this wesant [windpipe] of mine. Well, now this Lent came one hundred and fourscore pounds ten shillings, which I have paid and delivered this present day to the king's council: and so this man hath made a godly restitution. 'And so', quoth I to a certain nobleman that is one of the king's council, 'if every man that hath beguiled the king should make restitution after this sort, it would cough the king twenty thousand pounds, I think',

[11] *Sermons*, pp. 239 ff.

quoth I. 'Yea, that it would', quoth the other, 'a whole hundred thousand pounds.' Alack, alack; make restitution; for God's sake, make restitution: ye will cough in hell else, that all the devils there will laugh at your coughing. There is no remedy, but restitution open or secret; or else hell.

The man who was stricken with remorse and came to Latimer for advice was none other than John Bradford, one of the best known of the second generation of English reformers and himself to become one of the Marian martyrs. He was not yet in train for the ministry but had been employed by Sir John Harrington of Exton, Rutland. Harrington was treasurer in the King's camps and buildings at Boulogne in 1544, and Bradford had been deputy paymaster under him at the siege of Montreuil. Later (8th April 1547) [12] he entered the Inner Temple as a student of the common law, and there became friendly with Thos. Sampson who was instrumental in effecting his conversion. Then came Bradford's hearing of Latimer's first sermon at court and its plea for restitution. The grief and difficulty in which Bradford found himself are plainly shown in letters [13] from or to his friend Traves (or Travers) a fellow-Lancastrian. Bradford while on service in France was involved in a fraud for which his master, Harrington, was responsible. He sought out Latimer who gave him sound advice, and at length Bradford's pressure on his master resulted in his agreeing to restore the King's money he had wrongfully acquired (but not before Bradford had told him that, in the last resort, he would lay the whole matter before the Council). By 12th May 1548 it was settled:

Concerning the great matter you know of, it hath pleased God to bring it to this end, that I have a bill of my master's hand, wherein he is bound to pay the sum afore Candlemas next coming. This thinks Master Latimer to be sufficient.

(Letter to Traves.) [14]

It is not surprising that Bradford, on seeing some criminals, should have been the speaker of the phrase, 'But for the grace of God there goes John Bradford'.

The sums mentioned by Latimer are confirmed by entries in the Council Book for 1549 and 1550.

[12] *Dictionary of National Biography.*
[13] *Writings of John Bradford* (Parker Soc.), Letters, I, II, IV, VI.
[14] ibid., Letters, p. 17.

March 28th, 1549. This day Sir Mychall Stanhopp, knight, by commandment and order of the Lord Protector's Grace and Counsaill received of Mr Latymer of suche the King's money as came of concelement and now delivvered by the exhortacion of the said Mr Latymer £373.[15]

Of this they gave £50 to Latimer as the King's reward 'in respect of his attendaunce at Courte this Lent' and the rest was to be used for payments in his charge.

10th March [Monday] 1550. Mr Doctor Latymer brought in £104.[16]

This sum was used as the King's reward to two Germans who had come over from the Duke of Brunswick, a useful windfall.

It is abundantly clear that Latimer's chief interest now was in practical religion, and his thought and studies were directed towards this end. His preaching was for the sake of righteousness, and his studies for the sake of his preaching. He would entirely approve of something said in the preface to the sermons preached before the King and published in his lifetime, 'God's word must not be talked of only, for that is not enough, it must be expressed. Then must we as well live the word as talk the word.' [17] Augustine Bernher, in his preface to the 'Sermons on the Lord's Prayer' (which Foxe followed closely) remarks that 'every morning ordinarily, winter and summer, about two of the clock in the morning, he was at his book most diligently'.[18] But Latimer was not one of the formative theologians of the time. His veneration of the Bible was noticeable in his Cambridge preaching, and especially his detestation of any practices which exploited people's credulity. He knew what other men were reading and talking: he was a reader himself, though little exists to show that he read much of the writings of the Continental reformers. But he could not fail to be Cranmer's friend, especially in the reign of Edward the Sixth and as his guest at Lambeth, without entering into conversation and discussion, concerning the central point of doctrine— what was the interpretation of Christ's words, 'This is my Body'? Cranmer could not put his liturgical projects into effect without consideration of this, though in fact his prayer-books were never completely satisfactory to his Continental friends.

[15] *Acts of the Privy Council*, II.266.
[17] *Sermons*, p. 106.
[16] ibid., pp. 409–10.
[18] ibid., p. 320.

These foreign visitors—among whom John a Lasco, Bernardine Ochino, Peter Martyr and Martin Bucer would be conspicuous —began to arrive in this country in the winter of 1547 and the spring of 1548 and to be provided with incomes and opportunities for teaching.[19] Thus both Ochino and Peter Martyr were given royal pensions in May, and both had spent several weeks at Lambeth. It would be the following spring (1549) before Peter Martyr openly lectured upon the Eucharist at Oxford (where he was Regius Professor of Divinity) [20] and raised a mighty stir in that still Catholic university.

Inevitably Cranmer, and Latimer with him, must make up their minds. Hitherto they had kept to the old formularies, though they had been advocates of communion in both kinds. They had never been, and they never were, fully Lutheran in their views, and it is as difficult to label their ultimate positions definitely as to catalogue other features of the English Reformation. They were, however, now being influenced by the men from Switzerland and their English followers.

Traheron, an English layman sympathetic to the Swiss Reform and now a member of Parliament, wrote on their change of view to Bullinger on 1st August: [21]

As to our own affairs, and the extent to which we have made progress in matters of religion, I do not think you can be ignorant. You must know that all our countrymen, who are sincerely favourable to the restoration of truth, entertain in all respects like opinions with you; and not only such as are placed at the summit of honour, but those who are ranked in the number of men of learning. I except the archbishop of Canterbury and Latimer, and a very few learned men besides; for from among the nobility I know not one whose opinions are otherwise than what they ought to be. As to Canterbury, he conducts himself in such a way, I know not how, as that the people do not think much of him, and the nobility regard him as lukewarm. In other respects he is a kind and good-natured man. As to Latimer, though he does not clearly understand the true doctrine of the eucharist, he is nevertheless more favourable than either Luther or even Bucer. I am quite sure that he will never be a hinderance to this cause. For, being a man of admirable talent, he sees more clearly into the subject than the others, and is desirous to come into our sentiments, but is slow to decide, and cannot without much

[19] Strype, *Cranmer*, II.142 ff.
[20] C. H. Smyth, *Cranmer and the Reformation*, p. 118.
[21] *Original Letters*, I.320.

difficulty and even timidity renounce an opinion which he has once imbibed. But there is good hope that he will some time or other come over to our side altogether. For he is far from avoiding any of our friends, that he rather seeks their company, and most anxiously listens to them while discoursing upon this subject, as one who is beyond measure desirous that the whole truth may be laid open to him, and even that he may be thoroughly convinced. But more upon this subject when I have more time.

Eight weeks later Traheron was writing again to Bullinger [22]—

But that you may add yet more to the praises of God, you must know that Latimer has come over to our opinion respecting the true doctrine of the eucharist, together with the Archbishop of Canterbury and the other bishops, who heretofore seemed to be Lutherans. Let us implore God with our united prayers, to complete a work so favourably begun; and may he long preserve you and yours! . . . Farewell. London, Sept. 28.

Bullinger may have remembered a letter he had received from Nicholas Partridge a little more than ten years before (dated, Frankfort, 17th September 1538) saying that whereas Cranmer had only civilly accepted the present of his book on the Holy Scriptures Latimer had been enthusiastic about it. [23]

In April 1554 Latimer told Weston, in the Disputation at Oxford [24]

I have long sought for the truth in this matter of the sacrament, and have not been of this mind past seven years: and my lord of Canterbury's book hath especially confirmed my judgment herein. [25]

The view that Latimer came to hold was, then, that expressed by the Archbishop. However much that may have seemed to be Zwinglian—and Traheron was quick to think it was—the final position was not purely Zwinglian. The first three years of Edward the Sixth's reign were those in which Cranmer (and therefore Latimer) were listening to the arguments of a Lasco, Peter Martyr, Bucer, and other visitors who were part of the Archbishop's familia so often at Lambeth. But there is no reason to doubt Latimer's word that what he believed in 1554 he first began to believe in 1547. Tresham,

[22] *Original Letters*, p. 322.
[24] *Remains*, p. 265.
[23] ibid., p. 612.
[25] 'Answer to . . . Gardiner.'

one of the disputants at Oxford, reminded him of his earlier acceptance of the catholic dogma: [26]

To be short, I myself have heard you preaching at Greenwich before King Henry the Eighth, where you did openly affirm, that no Christian man ought to doubt of the true and real presence of Christ's body in the sacrament, forasmuch as he had the word of scripture on his side; *videlicet, Hoc est corpus meum,* 'This is my body:' whereby he might be confirmed.

Latimer's assertion was that, 'He gave not his body to be received with the mouth, but he gave the sacrament of his body to be received with the mouth: he gave the sacrament to the mouth, his body to the mind.' [27] Over and over again the emphasis of Latimer falls on the word 'spiritually' in his final attempts to define what he believed of the reception of the Sacrament. And this accords exactly with the analysis of Cranmer's position which has been put most cogently by Canon C. H. Smyth as follows: [28]

Cranmer himself always claimed to have been consistent. At his Examination before Brokes [September 1555] it was to the *Defence* that he appealed for his vindication: 'My book was made seven years ago, and no man hath brought any authors against it. I believe, that whoso eateth and drinketh that sacrament, Christ is within them, whole Christ, his nativity, passion, resurrection and ascension, but not corporally that sitteth in heaven.' 'I taught but two contrary doctrines', he declared on the same occasion: the first was of course, transubstantiation: the second, this . . . doctrine of the spiritual eating, learned from Ratramnus through Ridley's agency, modified by a Lasco, fortified by Bucer. Nor was this claim to consistency unjustified. Except for that brief period of doubt and confusion in the winter of 1548–49, Cranmer's doctrine was always clear: and it was not Zwinglianism.

For some years Cranmer had been busy with projects that would alter the services of the Church and enlarge their scope by the use of English. How far he had actually got in the framing of those orders which have been most familiar to his countrymen for upwards of four hundred years, no one can gauge precisely. But if uniformity was to be attained, acceptable liturgies would be necessary; and inevitably this would mean consultation regarding the doctrine of the Sacrament.

We have noticed something of the prevailing excitement in

[26] *Remains*, p. 268.   [27] ibid., p. 267.   [28] Smyth, op. cit., p. 71.

Traheron's letters to Bullinger. He wrote again at the end of the year reporting that Parliament had been busily engaged concerning the new forms of worship, and particularly that there had been a disputation 'concerning the eucharist in the presence of almost all the nobility of England'. He is referring to the fact that the Bill which embodied the new Book of Common Prayer was introduced to the Lords on 14th December, and thereafter followed debate before it was read in the Commons' House on 19th December. It was now that the country could become definitely aware that their Archbishop no longer believed in transubstantiation. Traheron is a little too optimistic when he tells Bullinger that Cranmer 'learnedly maintained your opinion upon this subject' and that 'it is all over with Lutheranism, now that those who were considered its principal and almost only supporters, have altogether come over to our side'.[29]

Peter Martyr, writing from Oxford to Martin Bucer on 26th December,[30] contented himself with the main fact, which was so glaringly apparent to the catholics, and did not blink at the uncertainties:

And even in the supreme council of the state, in which matters relating to religion are daily brought forward, there is so much disputing of the bishops among themselves and with others, as I think was never heard before. Whence those who are in the lower house, as it is called, that is, men of inferior rank, go up every day into the higher court of parliament, not indeed for the purpose of voting, (for that they do in the lower house) but only that they may be able to hear these sharp and fervent disputations. Hitherto the popish party has been defeated, and the palm rests with our friends, but especially with the archbishop of Canterbury. whom they till now were wont to traduce as a man ignorant of theology and as being only conversant with matters of government; but now, believe me, he has shown himself so mighty a theologian against them as they would rather not have proof of, and they are compelled, against their inclination, to acknowledge his learning, and power and dexterity in debate. Transubstantiation, I think, is now exploded, and the difficulty respecting the presence is at this time the most prominent point of dispute: but the parties engage with so much vehemence and energy as to occasion very great doubt as to the result; for the victory has hitherto been fluctuating between them.

When the reformers of the left, however, read the Prayer

Book, there was not so much at the heart of the Communion Service that they could rejoice over, and quite a lot that made them shake their heads. The book did not go as far as Cranmer wished, but Cranmer himself never went as far as they wanted him to go.

Latimer, not being a Bishop, was out of the fray; but he must have watched with chagrin that Heath, the Bishop of his old see, was a champion on the reactionary side.

The Act of Uniformity of 21st January 1549, finally established the authority of the new book which was to be everywhere in use not later than the following Pentecost. The older various 'uses', of which that of Sarum was the chief, were thus intended to give way to 'a uniform quiet and godly order', which would have 'as well eye and respect to the most sincere and pure Christian religion taught by the Scripture, as to the usages in the primitive Church'.[31]

Perhaps it was because of Heath's opposition, more probably it was because of the help they thought Latimer could bring, that a petition was sent to the Protector on 8th January that he should be reinstated in his former diocese of Worcester.[32] Latimer, however, steadfastly refused to return to the wearing of the rochet he had doffed. But the next few months would provide him with opportunities of exceptional importance, especially during Lent when he preached what were, perhaps, his most important sermons before the court, and the only full sequence we possess that show his true vein in this responsible work.

The reader of these Lenten sermons should recall something of the political and personal disturbances of these weeks, which had little to do with the religious matters mentioned above.

It was in January that frauds acknowledged by Sir William Sharington, in connexion with the Mint at Bristol, revealed the unholy liaison between himself and Somerset's brother, Thomas Seymour, the Lord High Admiral. Ever since the reign began Thomas had been a thorn in his elder brother's flesh, resentful of his high place and hoping that he might—preferably by marrying the Princess Mary, or Elizabeth, perhaps even Anne of Cleves—secure for himself more power and rewards. In

[31] First Edwardine Act of Uniformity, 1549. Gee and Hardy, *Documents Illustrative of English Church History*, p. 359.
[32] *Journal of the House of Commons.*

the end he consoled himself with Catherine Parr, Henry the Eighth's widow, to whom he had been a suitor before he was warned off as from a royal preserve, to Catherine's chagrin. Catherine Parr was definitely Protestant, and far too good for Thomas Seymour. She died in the summer of 1548. A man of physical and social parts, the Admiral had been seeking to build up support for himself unscrupulously—even to the point of staying at home when he should have been commanding the fleet in connexion with the Scottish campaign of the autumn of 1547. Moreover he had been disgracefully enriching himself by easing the watchfulness against the pirates in the Channel and taking payment from them.

This kind of revelation of treachery, corruption, and selfish ambition, earned punishment which was condignly meted out when Seymour was at length attainted by Parliament, following upon examinations in which Warwick and Southampton (rivals to the Seymours in all things) were conspicuous. The Protector agreed to the execution of his brother, and this took place on 20th March. Thereby it was made easier for Warwick later on to carry out his own schemes for depriving Somerset of his power and position.

Such was the atmosphere of suspicion, intrigue, and fear (for who knew what the discoveries of plots might reveal?) in the court to which Latimer must preach every Friday in Lent.

These sermons give a most vivid and unpleasing picture of the times. If ever canonical prophets are given an occasional glimpse of their successors one can imagine Amos and Isaiah peeping in at the court of Edward the Sixth and being thoroughly pleased with the way Latimer went about his work. At four hundred years' distance one is amazed at his boldness, which could very well be, and was interpreted as brazen impertinence by some of his hearers, especially the climbing courtiers. We are fortunate in possessing the full sequence of these seven Lenten sermons, preached on every Friday, beginning on 8th March and ending on Good Friday, 19th April 1549. They reveal on every page the freedom of extemporary speech—the topical allusion, the arresting anecdote or amusing incident, and the detailed retelling of Biblical incidents. They fascinated a boy King, pleased men of probity and lashed into fury, if they did not melt into penitence, those whose corruption or ambition was plainly described.

These court sermons were published soon after their delivery. They are not a verbatim report. The editor, Thomas Some, in dedicating them to Katherine, Dowager Duchess of Suffolk, said,

And let no man be grieved though it be not so exactly done as he did speak it; for in very deed I am not able so to do, to write word for word as he did speak: that passeth my capacity, though I had twenty men's wits, and no fewer hands to write withal.[33]

Latimer's theme was that the Bible gives the pattern for all human activities, be they of king or commoner, judge or prelate; and for each sermon the general text was Romans 15[4], 'Whatsoever things are written aforetime are written for our learning; that we through patience and comfort of scripture might have hope.' But in each sermon he treated of other texts or incidents more precisely, as in the first sermon addressed to the King specifically, Deuteronomy 17[14] ff. ('When thou art come into the land which the Lord thy God giveth thee, and enjoyest it' &c), or in the third, greatly concerned with bribery and the law's delays, Luke 18 (The parable of the importunate widow and the judge). But he rides to or from his theme with a very loose rein. He obviously does not expect from his audience that knowledge of Scripture which was assumed in later generations, brought up on the Authorized Version read in church, and retells the narratives of the Bible with imaginative gusto, as when he reports the Pharisees answering the police sent to arrest Jesus and returning empty-handed, 'What, ye brain-sick fools, ye hoddy-pecks, ye doddy-pous, ye huddes, do ye believe him? Are you seduced also?'[34]

Much of what he said to the young King strikes us as being too near the bone. Could he not have said this privately rather than before the whole court? But no, he had his conception of the preacher's office, based firmly upon the prophets—'Let the preacher therefore never fear to declare the message of God unto all men. . . . If he preach before a king, let his matter be concerning the office of a king; if before a bishop, then let him treat of bishoply duties and orders. . . .'[35]

A preacher has two offices, the first is 'To teach true doctrine'. But he must also often use another 'To reprehend, to convince, to confute gainsayers, and spurners against the

[33] *Dedication Sermons*, p. 82.   [34] *Sermons*, p. 136.   [35] ibid., pp. 86–7.

truth'.[36] In these court sermons there is perhaps more of the latter than the former kind, though by doctrine Latimer would mean a sound rule of living and not merely orthodox theology. Thus he used his text from Deuteronomy to drive home warnings to the young King. He must not have too many horses (he himself had protested against Henry the Eighth's keeping 'excess of horses').[37]

Next he speaks of the King's marriage, 'Let him not prepare unto himself too many wives.' This, to the son of Henry the Eighth by his third wife, must have caused a few smiles. Has any other preacher in a royal chapel ever spoken face to face like this?

It is a very hard thing for a man to rule well one woman. Therefore, let our king, what time his grace shall be so minded to take a wife, choose him one which is of God; that is, . . . of the household of faith. Yea, let all estates be no less circumspect in choosing her, taking great deliberation, and then they shall not need divorcements, and such mischiefs, to the evil example and slander of our realm. And that she be such one as the king can find in his heart to love, and lead his life in pure and chaste espousage; and then he shall be the more prone and ready to advance God's glory, and to punish and to extirp the great lechery used in this realm.[38]

Latimer knew well that it is often a preacher's apparently casual asides and illustrations that stick in a congregation's memory. So he indulges in sarcasm about the new coinage:

We have now a pretty little shilling indeed a very pretty one: I have but one, I think, in my purse; [which he probably produced in evidence] and the last day I had put it away almost for an old groat: and so I trust some will take them,[39]

and is scathing on the way children are wed to each other while mere infants, because grasping noblemen will thus pile up riches.[40] Latimer is ahead of his time in pleading that parents should not press marriage where the parties do not love each other. The King must beware of riches and the exploitation of his people. The preacher gives some startling evidence of what is happening, and we see the rapidity of the changes that were coming in England.

[36] *Sermons*, p. 129.   [37] Supra, VI, p. 114.
[38] *Sermons*, p. 94.   [39] ibid., p. 95.
[40] ibid., pp. 95, 170; cf. Trevelyan, *English Social History*, p. 69, on infant marriage.

At merchant's hands no kind of ware can be had, except we give for it too much. You landlords, you rent-raisers, I may say you step-lords . . . you have for your possessions yearly too much . . . poor men, which live of their labour, cannot with the sweat of their face have a living, all kinds of victuals is so dear; pigs, geese capons, chickens, eggs.[41]

Arable land has been turned into pasture, 'where as have been a great many householders and inhabitants, there is now but a shepherd and his dog'. The aim seems to be 'to make the yeomanry slavery, and the clergy shavery' for whereas the clergy formerly had too much, now they have too little. He concluded his sermon to the King with the famous description of his own boyhood and home [42] and a plea for the safeguarding of such households 'for by yeomen's sons the faith of Christ is and hath been maintained chiefly'.

The next five sermons ran true to this type, but he returned again and again to a few contemporary needs. All that he said has been borne out by historians; but he was standing there in the changing scene, quick to notice what was for the whole-some growth of human life so that the Gospel might be glorified, and quick to denounce by its standards anything that was amiss. His was no cloistered spirit: he was familiar with the talk and ways of men in every direction, and he was especially approachable by the folk of the riverside, the city street, and the lonely farm; for though he spent so much time necessarily in London, he was always in touch with the country, the real England, to which he was proud to belong.

Today it is chiefly left to the press to reveal unhealthy ten-dencies. A modern Bishop addresses a letter to *The Times* from 'The Athenaeum'. Latimer spoke, often in the presence of the people who were most closely concerned with what he exposed. There was corruption in trade: fraudulent cloth-makers doped their stretched and inferior cloth with powder to give it weight.[43] There were the law's delays, so that he could not walk in the Archbishop's garden at Lambeth, studying his sermon, but people saw him through the gate and clamoured for his help to right their wrongs,[44] and judges were afraid to hear the cases of the poor against the rich.[45] Indeed, bribery was so bad that a woman of no high reputation, but with

[41] *Sermons*, p. 99.   [42] Supra, I, p. 9.   [43] *Sermons*, p. 138.
[44] ibid., pp. 127–8.   [45] ibid., pp. 145, 158.

friends, had given birth secretly to triplets, strangled and drowned them, but escaped execution, whereas a poor woman who had stolen a few rags from a hedge was condemned in the same court and hanged.[46]

Bribery existed everywhere. Murder had been committed by a rich merchant who was caught evading customs duty by one of the King's searchers. The merchant went home, sharpened his wood-knife and, returning, killed the man. A Spaniard quarrelled with an Englishman about a woman, killed his rival and escaped hanging,[47] as did the merchant.

If he did not concentrate so much upon the Bishops at court, because he had other game to shoot at, he did not forget their duties. They should keep to their proper tasks and be real fathers in God, preaching in their dioceses, not holding civil offices, like that of Lord President. They should not remain in office when in extreme age, but should provide effective preachers with part of their income.[48] 'If they be found negligent or faulty in their duties, out with them. I require it in God's behalf, make them quondams, all the pack of them.' Chantries have been put down. He does not want to see the chantry priests treated as were abbots and monks, so that their pensions might be saved by putting them into benefices, unless they could preach and be really worthy of their cure.[49]

The Universities are in a bad way. He has no specific news of Oxford, but he is in touch with Cambridge, and his sermons echo the complaints of other men of his time (like Roger Ascham, who wrote to Cranmer about his old university[50]). 'There be none now but great men's sons in colleges, and their fathers look not to have them preachers.' This is a new type, and not a welcome one.[51]

Works of charity are diminished. Latimer shares the disappointment of other reformers who hoped that evangelical religion preached from the pulpit would result in the visitation of prisoners and care of the poor. Why should there not be curates attached to the jails?[52] But instead of such holy work, there are carelessness, indifference, and widespread vice. The stews on Bankside in Southwark were certainly put down, but the inhabitants have fanned out elsewhere, and gross immor-

[46] *Sermons*, pp. 190–1.   [47] ibid., p. 196.   [48] ibid., pp. 122, 176, 202.
[49] ibid., p. 124.   [50] cf. Strype, *Memorials of Cranmer*, II.6, p. 75.
[51] *Sermons*, pp. 179, 203.   [52] ibid., p. 180.

ality abounds. So does gambling. It is of little purpose to change the places and continue the vices.[53] Young men should give themselves to manly exercise, and there is nothing better than archery:

There be such dicing houses also, they say, as hath not been wont to be, where young gentlemen dice away their thrift; and where dicing is, there are other follies also. For the love of God let remedy be had, let us wrestle and strive against sin. Men of England, in times past, when they would exercise themselves (for we must needs have some recreation, our bodies cannot endure without some exercise), they were wont to go abroad in the fields a shooting; but now it is turned into glossing, [gluttonous eating], gulling, [guzzling], and whoring within the house. The art of shooting hath been in times past much esteemed in this realm: it is a gift of God that he hath given us to excel all other nations withal: it hath been God's instrument, whereby he hath given us many victories against our enemies; but now we have taken up whoring in towns, instead of shooting in the fields.[54]

There are frequent references to protests that he has received from hearers of his sermons,[55] and particularly resentment against some of his remarks concerning the Lord Admiral's attainder and death.[56] Thomas Seymour was not without supporters in that faction-ridden court, and nothing could be easier than to suggest that getting rid of him by way of attainder was not to give him bare justice. Latimer stood by the government of the day, but what he said in the pulpit was of greater interest to his hearers because the Admiral had himself sent for Latimer. Seymour was no coward, and had come to his death on Tower Hill with such boldness that people not favourable to his brother, the Protector, were quick to assert he must have been innocent. This Latimer would not have, and it is obvious that what he says is not by way of being the mere mouthpiece of the King's uncle. The Admiral represented the very type of the men Latimer saw as the greatest menace to true religion and honest living. What kind of counsel he gave to Seymour a few days before his death we shall never know, but it is certain that he could make no pleas in his defence. The details of this eyewitness amaze us, and it is not surprising that some later editions of Latimer's sermons were shorn of

[53] ibid., pp. 133, 196.
[55] ibid., pp. 140, 141, 154, 194.
[54] ibid., p. 196f.
[56] ibid., pp. 155–64.

them: but they were in the edition of 1549 which was for the generation most concerned, and before either Warwick had brought off his coup against the Protector or it was evident that Edward the Sixth would not live to maturity.

Latimer held back from full reference to the affair until the fourth sermon before the King, on 29th March, nine days after the Admiral's execution. These passages give us our clearest picture of Latimer as he must have been remembered by men who ever heard him speaking in council or preaching on current matters. Latimer certainly would not have subscribed to any theory that Christian preaching should not touch upon controversial politics.

I spake of this gear the last day, and of some I had little thank for my labour. I smelled some folks that were grieved with me for it, because I spake against temerarious judgment. 'What hath he to do with judgment?' say they. I went about to keep you from arrogant judgment. [Well; I could have said more than I did, and I can say much more now. For why? I know more of my lord-admiral's death since that time than I did know before. 'Oh', say they, 'the man died very boldly; he would not have done so had he not been in a just quarrel.'] This is no good argument, my friends: A man seemeth not to fear death, therefore his cause is good. This is a deceivable argument: He went to his death boldly, *ergo*, he standeth in a just quarrel. The Anabaptists that were burnt here in divers towns in England (as I heard of credible men, I saw them not myself,) went to their death even *intrepide*, as ye will say, without any fear in the world, cheerfully. Well, let them go. . . . If I should have said all that I knew, your ears would have irked to have heard it, and now God hath brought more to light. And as touching the kind of his death, whether he be saved or no, I refer that to God only. What God can do, I can tell. I will not deny, but that he may in the twinkling of an eye save a man, and turn his heart. What he did, I cannot tell. And when a man hath two [57] strokes with an axe, who can tell but that between two strokes he doth repent? It is very hard to judge. Well, I will not go so nigh to work; but this I will say, if they ask me what I think of his death, that he died very dangerously, irksomely, horribly. The man being in the Tower wrote certain papers which I saw myself. There were two little ones, one to my lady Mary's grace, and another to my lady Elizabeth's grace, tending to this end, that they should conspire against my lord Protector's grace: surely, so seditiously as could be. Now what a kind of death was this, that when he was ready to lay

---

[57] The headsman botched his work at Seymour's execution.

his head upon the block, he turns me to the Lieutenant's servant, and saith, 'Bid my servant speed the thing that he wots of?' Well, the word was overheard. His servant confessed these two papers, and they were found in a shoe of his: they were sewed between the soles of a velvet shoe. He made his ink so craftily and with such workmanship, as the like hath not been seen. I was prisoner in the Tower myself, and I could never invent to make ink so. It is a wonder to hear of his subtilty. He made his pen of the aglet of a point, that he plucked from his hose, and thus wrote these letters so seditiously, as ye have heard, enforcing many matters against my lord Protector's grace, and so forth. God had left him to himself, he had clean forsaken him. What would he have done, if he had lived still, that went about this gear, when he laid his head on the block at the end of his life? Charity, they say, worketh but godly, and not after this sort. Well; he is gone, he knoweth his fate by this, he is either in joy or in pain. There is but two states, if we be once gone. There is no change. This is the speech of the scripture: *Ubicunque lignum ceciderit, ibi erit, sive in austrum, sive in aquilonem:* 'Wheresoever the tree falleth, either into the south or into the north, there it shall rest.' By the falling of the tree is signified the death of man: if he fall into the south, he shall be saved; for the south is hot, and betokeneth charity or salvation: if he fall in the north, in the cold of infidelity, he shall be damned. There are but two states, the state of salvation and the state of damnation. There is no repentance after this life, but if he die in the state of damnation, he shall rise in the same: yea, though he have a whole monkery to sing for him, he shall have his final sentence when he dieth. And that servant of his that confessed and uttered this gear was an honest man. He did honestly in it. God put it in his heart. And as for the other, whether he be saved, or no, I leave it to God. But surely he was a wicked man: the realm is well rid of him: it hath a treasure that he is gone. He knoweth his fare by this. A terrible example, surely, and to be noted of every man.[58]

Later in the same sermon Latimer said that a woman of loose life who was hanged when he himself was in ward with the Bishop of Chichester (*c.* 1540), cried out on Thomas Seymour, that if he had not first seduced her and discarded her, she would not have come to this end. This might seem a light matter to some of his hearers, but the preacher had also heard that Seymour had denied the immortality of the soul.[59] On Good Friday, he reverted once more to the Admiral and said he would always be Lot's wife to him, for he had heard that

[58] *Sermons*, pp. 160-2.   [59] ibid., pp. 164-5.

when Katherine, his wife, arranged for household prayers
twice daily, 'the admiral gets him out of the way, like a mole
digging in the earth'.[60]

It is scarcely surprising that a preacher who could be roused
to such vehemence was not always listened to with rapt attention. He burst out with this complaint after protesting against
loose living and then lapsing into what was, for him, a dull
passage:

> Surely it is all ill misorder that folk shall be walking up and down in
> the sermon-time, as I have seen in this place this Lent: and there shall
> be such huzzing and buzzing in the preacher's ear, that it maketh
> him oftentimes to forget his matter. O let us consider the king's
> majesty's goodness! This place was prepared for banqueting of the
> body; and his Majesty hath made it a place for the comfort of the
> soul, and to have the word of God preached in it.[61]

The comparative mildness of Somerset's character and policy
(would he, unless pressed, have allowed his brother's execution?) encouraged some people to think they might believe
what they like and proclaim it. This was no part of Cranmer's
conception of reformation, and in April 1549 a commission to
try heretics was set up which included Latimer.[62] He is mentioned as 'Doctor of Divinity' in the Register. There is no
record at Cambridge of his proceeding to that degree, but he is
often referred to by the title even by his servant, Augustine
Bernher. Presumably it was by custom rather than accurate
designation, for when he was tried in Oxford he was consistently
treated as 'Master Latimer' in contrast to Ridley, who was full
Doctor.

The most famous of the heretics convented before the com-
missioners[63] was Joan Bocher—usually known as Joan of Kent.
Her heresy was a denial of the full, orthodox belief in the
Incarnation. Cranmer formally excommunicated her at St
Paul's in the presence of the commissioners. Committed to the
secular arm, in accordance with the medieval procedure,
Cranmer and Ridley sought afterwards to convince her of her
mistakes.[64] Joan's retort to her judges shows her adroitness.
'Not long since you burned Anne Askew for a piece of bread,
and yet came yourselves to believe and profess the same
doctrine for which you burned her. And now, forsooth, you

[60] *Sermons*, p. 228.   [61] ibid., p. 204.   [62] Strype, *Cranmer*, II.92.
[63] Rymer's *Foedera*, XV.181.   [64] Strype, *Cranmer*, II.8. p, 99.

will burn me for a piece of flesh, and in the end you will come
to believe this also, when you have read the Scriptures and
understand them.' [65]

There is some ground for Canon C. H. Smyth's opinion that,
if Edward the Sixth had lived, the Church of England would
have burned two-thirds of those whom Mary burned.[66] Latimer certainly never showed any qualms about the execution
of Anabaptists, and within a few years every conceivable
doctrinal heresy abounded, though one may be a good deal
more charitably disposed towards their unfortunate holders
than were their judges. Joan Bocher was kept in prison for a
full year, and then burned at Smithfield on 2nd May 1550.
Latimer fully concurred in the sentence against her, and made
lengthy reference to her in a sermon preached at Grimsthorpe
on St John the Evangelist's Day, 1552:

Further, I told you that our Saviour Christ was formed and framed
of the most poorest flesh; and he became the natural son of Mary,
and she also was his natural mother. I told you, the last time, of one
Joan of Kent, which was in this foolish opinion, that she should say
our Saviour was not very man, and had not received flesh of his
mother Mary: and yet she could shew no reason why she should
believe so. Her opinion was this, as I told you before. The Son of
God, said she, penetrated through her, as through a glass, taking no
substance of her. But our creed teacheth us contrariwise; for we say,
Natus ex Maria Virgine, 'Born of the Virgin Mary': so this foolish
woman denied the common creed, and said that our Saviour had a
phantastical body; which is most untrue, as it appeareth evidently in
the epistle to the Hebrews, where St Paul plainly saith, that Christ
was made of the woman, that he took his flesh from the woman. And
though Mary had a prerogative, as she had indeed, namely, that
she knew no man, that she was a virgin; yet her prerogative took
not away the very humanity of Christ.[67]

The Prayer Book was published in March 1549 and was to
be universally in use after Whitsuntide. No one could guess
then that its influence was to become, with the Bible, so remarkable wherever the English tongue might be spoken. One
of our finest modern writers has said, 'The miracle of the
Prayer-Book, if allowed to speak in its own order plainly, is
that it speaks both timelessly and to the occasion.' [68] The glory

[65] Gairdner, *History of the English Church*, p. 279.
[66] Vide his *Cranmer and the Reformation*, pp. 3–4.   [67] *Remains*, p. 114.
[68] Charles Morgan, *Reflections in a Mirror: Second Series*, p. 53.

of that ordering is Cranmer's. Following long-established pre-
cedent, by which various morning or evening offices were taken
at one time, Matins and Evensong derived from the older
services. The intention was that, in the future, only two books
would be necessary for all occasions of worship everywhere—
the Book of Common Prayer and the Bible, supplanting the
many missals, breviaries, sacramentaries, and other books. We
have lost much wonderful medieval craftsmanship and art, but
the plan was a good one for uniformity and spiritual usefulness.
The tone of the book was nothing like sufficiently Protestant
for many of Cranmer's friends, especially those who had been
on the Continent, and its intermediate position, with a large
possibility of interpretation as to doctrine, has made it preferred
by Anglo-Catholics to his more definite book of 1552. In
Edward the Sixth's time it completely satisfied nobody. But
its order for Holy Communion ('commonly called the masse')
provided for administration in both kinds, though the wafer
was prescribed, and 'Men must not think less to be received in
part than in the whole, but in each of them the whole body of
our Saviour.'

There was no great mutiny at its introduction except in the
West, and that was put down soon without altering the issue.
But there was widespread restlessness, especially among the
parish priests in the countryside, and Cranmer found it necessary to answer the Fifteen Articles drawn up by the insurgents,
who had proclaimed, 'We will not receive the new service,
because it is but like a Christmas-game.' But there was bitter
social discontent and hardship everywhere, prompting the
masses to rise. Kett's followers in Norfolk put that in the forefront of their complaint rather than religious dissatisfaction.

We have no detailed commentary of Latimer on the Prayer-
Book, but plenty on the social condition, and this no doubt
contributed to his tremendous popularity as a preacher in
London. Few indeed in our days are the preachers who could
be the innocent cause of such entries as that in the Church
Wardens' accounts of St Margaret's, Westminster, in 1549:

Paid to William Curlewe for mending of divers pews that were
broken when Dr Latimer did preach—1/6d.

Latimer's concern for the Universities was made plain in his
court sermons; men who had made abbeys and chantries their

prey would not be likely to spare learned foundations. In May, Ridley, Bishop of Rochester, and the Bishop of Ely, with other commissioners, carried out a visitation at Cambridge, particularly reporting on Latimer's old college, Clare, which was in a sorry state of poverty and deprivation, and in some danger of being merged with her neighbour, Trinity Hall. Ridley evidently considered it worth while to use Latimer's link with Clare as a means of influencing the Protector, and, incidentally, providing us with a contemporary estimate of his worth: [69]

I consider not only what learned men may be brought up there in time to come, but also how many hath been already, some such as I think it is hard for the whole University to match them with the like. I will speak now but of one, I mean Master Latimer, which is, as I do think, a man appointed of God and endued with excellent gifts of grace to set forth God's Word, to whom in my judgment not only the King's Majesty and his honourable Council, but also the whole realm is much bound, not only for his constant maintenance and defence of God's truth, when Papists and persecutions did assault the godly, but also for that now he preacheth the Gospel so purely, and so earnestly and freely rebuketh the worldly of his wickedness. Alexander, if I do rightly remember the history, in the victorious course of the conquest, did spare a city for the memory of the famous poet Homer's sake. Latimer far passeth that poet, and the King's Highness by your grace's advice shall also excell that Gentile Prince in all kind of mercy and clemency.

Warwick, the most unpleasant among the many unpleasing people jockeying for influence with the boy King, successfully brought off his coup against Somerset in the autumn of 1549. It is for the secular historian to attempt the unravelling of the tangle of motives and events which brought the Protector's downfall at his rival's hands. Whatever may have been the Duke of Somerset's failings, he can at least be acquitted of the charges of selfish aggrandisement by any and every means of which his supplanter was guilty.

The fall of the Protector might have slowed up or even stopped completely the work to which Cranmer and his friends had put their hands. Somerset's tolerance could be interpreted as a sign of weakness when tolerance was not, as yet, even a debatable point in most men's conversation. Would Warwick's virility display itself in a reversal of his rival's religious policy?

[69] *State Papers, Domestic*, Ed. VI, II.15, 16.

There were many who attributed the social unrest and western rebellion to the Protestant policy. Cranmer and Latimer must have wondered whether it would be Gardiner's turn now, for Southampton was a Catholic leader among Warwick's supporters. Cranmer would, as it turned out, be able to go ahead with his policy more swiftly than previously. His—as A. W. Pollard remarked [70]—was the initiation, 'and the comparative caution with which the Reformers at first proceeded was as much due to Somerset's restraining influence as the violence of their later course was to the stimulated zeal of Warwick'.

Stimulated or not, there were several significant moves in the early months of 1550, including a campaign against any remaining images, and tendencies to invoke the saints.

John Stumphius, writing to Henry Bullinger from Oxford at the end of February, gave some details of the fears the reformers had of the triumph of the Catholics. He and his friends had been greatly relieved to learn of Somerset's being set free (on 6th February)

for those cruel beasts, the Romanists, with which Oxford abounds, were now beginning to triumph over the downfall of our duke, the overthrow of our gospel now at its last gasp, and the restoration of their darling the mass, as though they had already obtained a complete victory.[71]

Whether he is right or wrong in asserting 'that a bishoprick has been offered to Latimer, the king's preacher, whose place is now occupied by our friend master Hooper', it is quite certain that Latimer did not entertain the idea. Hooper preached on Wednesdays that Lent (Latimer could use his sermons on Jonah as a basis for his own allusions) and Poynet was the Friday preacher; but Latimer was in poor health, and evidently feared that his end had come. But he did preach once at the court—on Monday, 10th March, the sermon being a double-decker, occupying the forenoon and the afternoon. There is much personal allusion in the sermon, references to his recent illness, 'whereof I looked to have died', and to his age,[72] 'for I have not long to live, so that I think I shall never come here into this place again'.

This is to be his last sermon, he feels, before the King, and

[70] *C.M.H.*, II.481.   [71] *Original Letters*, 2, pp. 464–5.
[72] *Sermons*, pp. 243, 244, 246.

he takes full advantage of the occasion to summarize and re-
capitulate what he had said in his series the year before. He
tells the King again that he should beware what kind of
marriage he makes—

for God's love beware where you marry; choose your wife in a
faithful stock. Beware of this worldly policy; marry in God: marry
not for the great respect of alliance, for thereof cometh all these evils
of breaking of wedlock, which is among princes and noblemen.

His theme is covetousness, but covetousness gives him opportunity to speak of the increasing immorality of the realm, the
social unrest ('Covetousness was the cause of rebellion this last
summer'—in the West, and Kett's rising in Norfolk), and en-
closures. He pleads again for consideration of the commons
and peasantry, and for their sufficiency of land to keep stock.
'They in Christ are equal with you. Peers of the realm must
needs be. The poorest ploughman is in Christ equal with the
greatest prince that is.' [73] Current fashions do not escape his
lash, especially prevailing ways of women's hair-dressing and
the noblemen's laziness—'Many complain against you that ye
lie a-bed till eight, or nine, or ten of the clock', and then their
servants tell poor suitors who come asking for help that their
masters have been on the King's business all night. The old
prophet was making the most of what he thought would be his
last chance.

He would like the full powers of the Church's discipline to
be enforced. Immorality should be punished, adultery by
death, [74] though either partner to a marriage might sue for
pardon for the first offence. 'Restore unto the church the discipline of Christ, in excommunicating such as be notable offenders. . . . Bring into the Church of England open discipline of
excommunication, that open sinners may be stricken withal.' [75]
He was thereby expressing what the Bishops had asked for in
the previous November, but Parliament was in no mood to
restore anything like the powers that had belonged formerly to
the Church.

Bribery received his full scorn. Who was the unlucky courtier
who heard his recent transaction described? 'He that took the
silver bason and ewer for a bribe, thinketh that it will never
come out: but he may now know that I know it; and I know it

---

[73] ibid., p. 249.   [74] ibid., p. 244.   [75] ibid. p. 258.

G*

not alone, there be more beside me that know it.' [76] And soldiers, armourers, carpenters, smiths, all in the King's service cannot get their pay—some of them are up to twelve months in arrears.

It was now that he spoke of the secret restitution (Bradford's). The preacher had just paid in £180 to the King's council. [77] But there has been other restitution as well, and he proceeds to clear the name of 'Master Sherington an honest gentleman, and one that God loveth. He openly confessed that he had deceived the king, and he made open restitution.' [78] Latimer thus sought to clear the Vice Treasurer at the Bristol Mint who had enriched himself by bad coinage and had been implicated in dealings with the Lord Admiral, but acknowledged his wrong.

He does not leave his theme until he has once more pleaded for active Bishops, and cites the titular Bishop of Exeter John Voisey as typical of the kind England ought not to have. Voisey preferred living in his native Sutton Coldfield to discharging his duties at Exeter, where Miles Coverdale was his co-adjutor.

Who is bishop of Exeter? Forsooth, Master Coverdale. What, do not all men know who is bishop of Exeter? What? He hath been bishop many years. Well, say I, Master Coverdale is bishop of Exeter: Master Coverdale putteth in execution the bishop's office, and he that doth the office of bishop, he is the bishop indeed. [79]

Voisey (or Vesey), as it has turned out, became a great benefactor to the inhabitants of modern Birmingham by leaving Sutton Park in perpetuity to his fellow-townsmen, and Miles Coverdale—thanks to the pressure of King Christian the Third that Queen Mary should let him go to Denmark—lived to be one of the Bishops assisting at Matthew Parker's consecration. Latimer's pragmatical views would not commend him to some of his successors on the bench of Bishops today. A man's character and work took precedence with him over correctness of procedure in appointment, and apostolical succession was not a living issue for one who attached so much importance to the ecclesiastical authority of the Crown.

In the spring of 1550 new impetus was given to the alterations in religion by the translation of Ridley from his See of

Rochester to that of London on 1st April. (Bonner having been deprived in the previous October.) The short-lived diocese of Westminster was merged with London, Thirlby, its Bishop, going to Norwich. This brought in a most able man, strongly reformed in theology and extremely devout. Only a few weeks passed before he instituted a searching visitation of his diocese. His clergy were closely scrutinized, inquiry was made regarding any private Masses or the survival of any old-time 'superstitious' practices like kissing the altar, 'licking the chalice', elevation, use of candles and bells. Altars were to be removed and 'The Lord's Board' must be 'an honest table decently covered in such place of the choir or chancel as shall be thought most meet by their discretion and agreement, so that the ministers with the communicants may have their place separated from the rest of the people, and to take down and abolish all other by-altars or tables'.[80]

It was now, as we have noted,[81] that the unfortunate Joan Bocher came to her fate at Smithfield.

One of the happiest results of his court preaching for Latimer, personally, must have been the friendship it had started with John Bradford. Bradford was now well established as Fellow of Pembroke, and very much under Ridley's wing. Bradford refers in a letter to his friend, John Traves, to a present of cheese which he has shared with Latimer—'I thank him I am as familiar with him as with you: [82] yea, God so moveth him against me, that his desire is to have me come and dwell with him whensoever I will, and welcome.'

Latimer would see more of Bradford now, for Ridley ordained him deacon at Fulham (10th August 1550), and appointed him as one of his chaplains in his house.

With the increase of Warwick's power and the pressure of what we would today call the left-wing of the reformers, Latimer did not figure so prominently in influential circles. The most conspicuous figure among the English reformers at this time, with an embarrassing degree of nuisance-value to some of his best friends, was Hooper. After his successful preaching at court, he was appointed Bishop of Gloucester, on 15th May 1550,[83] and forthwith there began the famous controversy, the first of those vestiarian disputes which were to be so

[80] Vide Gairdner, *History*, p. 280.   [81] Vide supra, VIII, p. 194 f.
[82] Bradford, *Letters*, p. 34.   [83] *Acts of Privy Council*, III.31.

serious and perturbing in the next hundred years. Hooper, so often called 'the Father of English Nonconformists', jibbed at wearing the full vestments of a Bishop, and was brought before the Council in the following January, being committed to Cranmer's custody. It took a spell in the Fleet as well as much controversy with his best friends to bring him reluctantly to heel, for the Continental visitors Peter Martyr and Bucer [84] did not back his peculiar obstinacy 'to prescribe orders and necessary laws of his head'.

Latimer had never entered deeply into controversies with his brethren who had been much influenced by Swiss Reform, and partly because his interests were so practically English, framed by the conditions of life he had observed, and true to the initial impulses of his conversion, and partly, one feels, because he could leave these matters to younger men, like Ridley, who were more competent theologically. With Hooper's thorough visitation of the diocese of Gloucester, which had once been in his own care before Worcester was divided up, he would be in full sympathy, and especially with his desire to have the Lord's Prayer and simple articles of belief well and truly known. There are no references of real significance to the controversy of his friends with Hooper.

We cannot follow him closely through the last years of Edward the Sixth's reign, but, thanks to the zeal of his servant, Bernher, we have a considerable quantity of the sermons he preached, and these give some clue to his friendships and movements.

In the autumn of 1550 he was in Lincolnshire, preaching at Stamford on 9th November, which was the 23rd Sunday after Trinity. His text is from the Gospel—he usually did preach from the Gospel or Epistle for the day—'Render therefore unto Caesar the things which are Caesar's; and unto God the things that are God's' (Matthew 22 [21]). It is a plain spoken sermon, fit for countrymen's consumption, but lit up as usual with personal reminiscence. The sermon was begun in the morning and completed in the afternoon. The theme was one after Latimer's own heart, and Lincolnshire had been the scene of risings both after the dissolution of the monasteries and, more recently, under Kett. Was Latimer sent there as an official preacher? This could have happened, but there is no positive

[84] *Original Letters*, p. 488.

evidence to prove it. His reputation would bring him no lack of invitations to preach if he were in the neighbourhood. He says he had never been in the county before, except when he was ordained at Lincoln. 'But I dare say, if Lincolnshire be as other places that I know, this text condemneth a great many of Lincolnshire, and driveth them down to hell for breaking of this commandment.' [85]

He was on the borders of his own country. Stamford was only thirty-one miles east of Leicester on the road running through Uppingham, and Grimsthorpe Castle, the home of the dowager Duchess of Suffolk, was a dozen miles to the north-east. Grimsthorpe would see much of him in the future, for the Duchess, a versatile and eager supporter of reform, was to be his hostess and friend. This lady, whose father was Lord Willoughby de Eresby, and whose mother came over with Katherine of Aragon and was one of her maids of honour, had been given in ward to Charles Brandon, Duke of Suffolk, when her father died in 1526. She had succeeded to his fortune and position, and she became the fourth wife of the Duke when sixteen years of age. This, in itself, could illustrate the theme of marriage of alliance so often denounced by Latimer. Left with two sons in 1545, she devoted herself to their care, and then they both died of the sweating sickness on the same day, 16th July 1551. She married Richard Bertie at the end of the next year, 1552.[86] Her enthusiasm for the Edwardian reform put her very much in Gardiner's bad books, and she and her husband escaped overseas, to live a wandering life on the Continent during Queen Mary's reign.

Latimer's arguments could not have pleased his congregation, but they show him as entirely the King's man. The King could, indeed, do wrong; but even so, the subject must willingly endure and pay his taxes, just or unjust. The Lincolnshire landowners and farmers would probably have preferred the consolation of having their own money in their own pocket.

And know this, that whensoever there is any unjust exaction laid upon thee, it is a plague and punishment for thy sin, as all other plagues are; as are hunger, dearth, pestilence and such other.[87]

Similarly, they should pay their tithes. Of little use to say, 'Our curate is naught; an ass-head; a dodipole; a lack-latin,

[85] *Sermons*, p. 298.   [86] *Dictionary of National Biography*.   [87] *Sermons*, p. 300.

and can do nothing.' They may indeed complain to the Bishop, and beyond him to the Council. But beyond that they must betake themselves to prayer—'and He will either turn his heart, and make him better; or remove him from thee, and send a better in his place; or else take him away altogether'.

A postscript to the sermon shows Latimer's practice of ensuring that people know the Lord's Prayer in English. Because, in response to his questioning among the people,

they answer some, 'I can say my Latin *Pater-noster*'; some, 'I can say the old *Pater-noster*, but not the new', Therefore that all that cannot say it may learn, I use before the sermon and after to say it. Wherefore now I beseech you, let us say it together:
'Our Father which art,' &c.[88]

Latimer was back in London during the winter, and was appointed as a member of the Royal Commission which was to inquire into heresies.[89] He was not conspicuous in this work, and it is a fair assumption that he was only rarely in the capital now. The summer of 1551 was notable for the heavy plague of the sweating sickness, and the economic structure revealed its falseness in the swift and alarming rise of food prices. Official religion was approaching its maximum in pressure upon members of the old religion, or fellow-travellers. The Princess Mary was one object of attack, but the most critical opponent is bound to recognize her fine and open loyalty to her faith. For her it would be the Mass, and nothing but the Mass, in her household and life so long as a priest could be found willing to celebrate. Gardiner, in prison, was now deprived of his bishopric. He had been Wolsey's servant once, and Wolsey was a Bishop of Winchester. Cranmer had issued his book on the Lord's Supper, repudiating transubstantiation, and wordy battle was joined with Gardiner. The central doctrinal points might be of interest to thoroughly sincere men on either side; they did not in any way stop the rapicity of Warwick and his gang. A time of theological dispute may offer fine opportunities for plunder, and the Church was rapidly being reduced to poverty by the covetousness of which Latimer had been the boldest denouncer. This in itself could explain his absence from official pulpits. Another Royal Commission was set up in October 1551 for the revision of canon law, and Latimer's

[88] *Sermons*, p. 308.   [89] Rymer's *Foedera*, XV.250.

name appears with Peter Martyr's and A. Lasco's among those of the thirty-two appointed.[90] But he did not serve. Some of those previously named were not thought fit and a new commission was appointed on 9th November of eight men to start the work.[91]

It was on 16th October that Somerset was arrested, and events moved swiftly by which his rival would become Duke of Northumberland, and bring him to the block as a traitor, on Tower Hill on 22nd January 1552. Parliament met the next day, and immediately fell to debating a bill to compel people to go to church! The famous Second Act of Uniformity, which introduced the Second Prayer Book, was passed in April. Cranmer had been subjected to much criticism, and was very ready to consider revision of the earlier book which by no means expressed his full mind. To Martin Bucer's censures, and Peter Martyr's from Oxford, could be added the opinion of Calvin himself. The King, too, under the influence of his teachers, of whom Sir John Cheke was chief, was eager to go forward with revision.

And because there has arisen in the use and exercise of the aforesaid common service (that of the book of 1549) in the church, heretofore set forth, divers doubts for the fashion and manner of the ministration of same, rather by the curiosity of the minister, and mistakers, than of any other worthy cause: Therefore . . . the Lords and Commons in this present Parliament assembled, and by the authority of the same, has caused the aforesaid order of common service, entitled, The Book of Common Prayer, to be faithfully and godly perused, explained and made fully perfect. . . .[92]

The new book was to come into use in the next November, and would mark the farthest point of advance towards a Protestantism which might please the most Continental of the English reformers. Gardiner could bring himself to tolerate the service in the 1549 book; but this book seemed purely Zwinglian. Not only was all reference to traditional vestments, prayers for the departed, invocation of saints omitted; but there was the Black Rubric definitely laying down concerning kneeling to receive the Sacrament,

that it is not meant thereby, that any adoration is done or ought to be done either unto the Sacrament bread or wyne there bodily

---

[90] *Acts of Privy Council*, III.381–2.   [91] ibid., p. 410.
[92] Gee and Hardy, *Documents Illustrative of English Church History*, p. 371.

received or unto any real and essential presence there being of Christ's natural flesh and blood.

The compromises made possible by the emendations in the later Elizabethan revision of the book were, without doubt, nearer the general mind of Englishmen, however unsatisfactory to men of deep conviction in either of the opposed schools of theology.

Latimer had no active part in this work, so far as one can tell. That he was privy to the opinions of Cranmer and Ridley (whose influence was by no means negligible) cannot be doubted.

The priest was converted absolutely into a minister, the altar into a table, the eucharist into a commemoration, and a commemoration only.

This summary of Froude's,[93] sympathetic as he was to the Reformation, warns us of the power of the few who had either been abroad themselves or were foreigners living here. But it is quite true to say that the view thus represented very closely expresses what Latimer finally believed. Doctrinally, what he hoped for had been expressed: his aim was to continue the purifying of religion in its daily practice.

Latimer was busy as a preacher now in the country, and we have substantial records edited by Bernher, of sermons preached in Lincolnshire, at Grimsthorpe and in the neighbourhood. They appear to represent a sequence of seven sermons on the Lord's Prayer, and an almost continuous sequence of sermons on the Epistle or Gospel for the day from the end of October 1552, to the following Sexagesima. This is how they are printed in Corrie's edition. But one cannot rely on the accuracy of Bernher's dates, for there were in fact twenty-four Sundays after Trinity in 1551, but not in 1552; and there were not five Sundays after Epiphany in 1553. If Latimer preached the autumn sermons in 1551 and followed on through Christmas to Sexagesima, 1552, then we can think of him as having been in Lincolnshire for at least five months of continuous residence.[94] But these sermons, first edited by Bernher and pub-

---

[93] Ed. VI, cp. 5.

[94] A letter from the Duchess of Suffolk to Cecil (her neighbour) sending him a buck wishes she had been able to send one for the churching of Latimer's niece (formerly misread as wife). Latimer apparently was no longer at Grimsthorpe. (*State Papers*, *C.S.P.*, *Domestic*, Ed. VI, XIV, June 1552.)

lished in the reign of Queen Elizabeth, cannot be used as more than a rough guide to his movements. Some inaccuracies are conspicuous—like that of attributing to Latimer the ability to preach at Baxterley in Warwickshire on Christmas Day, 1552, and on the next day to preach at Grimsthorpe, and refer to the Christmas Day sermon as having been preached to the same audience as that now listening to the message on St Stephen's Day. Latimer could move pretty fast, in his time, but it would give a modern Bishop with a good car a heavy Christmas Day's duties to preach in both places on the same day, and stay overnight at Grimsthorpe to preach again on 26th December.

These sermons are very different from those which exasperated the courtiers. The majority of the congregation would be people of the farm and household; and while Latimer would not refrain from criticizing people in authority, he did believe so much in preaching to the folk actually before him that he kept close to their daily devotions and duties. Of course, he lit up his sermons with many personal reminiscences. Superstition still holds in the country, and one has known women who would not cross the threshold of a friend's house until they had been churched lest they should bring bad luck. Latimer tilted at that particular survival of medieval superstition with a long anecdote about the woman he and Bilney helped in Cambridge, for whom he obtained a pardon from Henry the Eighth after his first sermon at Windsor.[95]

He had recently been with a sick man, and an old woman came in who at once asked whether they could not get some holy water . . . or there was the matter of ringing bells to scare the devil . . . or lighting candles.

I was once called to one of my kinsfolk (it was at that time when I had taken degree at Cambridge, and was made master of art), I was called, I say, to one of my kinsfolk, which was very sick and died immediately after my coming. Now there was an old cousin of mine, which after the man was dead, gave me a wax candle in my hand, and commanded me to make certain crosses over him that was dead: for she thought the devil would run away by and by. Now I took the candle, but I could not cross him as she would have me to do; for I had never seen it afore. Now she, perceiving that I could not do it, with a great anger took the candle out of my hand, saying, 'It is a pity that thy father spendeth so much money upon

[95] *Sermons*, pp. 334 ff.

thee'. . . This and such like things were nothing but illusions of the devil: yet for all that we put our trust so in them, that we thought we could not be saved without such things. But now, let us give God most hearty thanks, that he hath delivered us from such snares and illusions of the devil; and let us endeavour ourselves most earnestly to hear God's most holy word, and to live after it.[96]

Falsehood and dishonesty were the same whether practised in court or countryside. This preacher could draw rogues to the life as they were to be found in the cattle sales:

I have known some that had a barren cow: they would fain have had a great deal of money for her; therefore they go and take a calf of another cow, and put it to this barren cow, and so come to the market pretending that this cow hath brought that calf; and so they sell their barren cow six or eight shillings dearer than they should have done else. The man which bought the cow cometh home: peradventure he hath a many of children, and hath no more cattle but this cow, and thinketh he shall have some milk for his children. . . .

This last touch shows how close he remained to the needs of the ordinary people.

The other fellow, which sold the cow, thinketh himself a jolly fellow and a wise merchant; and is called one that can make shift for himself. But I tell thee, whosoever thou art, do so if thou lust, thou shalt do it of this price,—thou shalt go to the devil, and there be hanged on the fiery gallows world without end.[97]

It is all of the same texture—homely, direct, forceful. This preaching could be understood by the simplest with its definite guidance in matters of conduct that would keep men wholesome in their neighbourly and business relationships, and with their God.

Apart from his residing as the guest of the Duchess of Suffolk in Lincolnshire, Warwickshire seems to have claimed him most, though his semi-retirement did not mean that he was completely out of touch with Englishmen abroad. A letter written by Augustine Bernher to Henry Bullinger in May 1552, is sent from Baxterley.

My master, doctor Latimer, had intended to write to you, but he has tomorrow to undertake a long and arduous journey, so that the excellent old man and your most loving friend, is unable to send

<hr/>

[96] *Sermons*, p. 499.　　　　　　　　　　[97] ibid., pp. 400–1.

you a letter at this time; but he especially commands me to salute you in his name as honourably and lovingly as possible.[98]

Baxterley Hall was the home of his friend, John Glover, the eldest of three brothers, all of whom were well known for their strict lives of biblical piety. Their family was of some wealth and standing in Warwickshire. When the troubles came in 1555, John and William escaped, but Robert was ill, and arrested in bed. He died at the stake in Coventry on 20th September 1555; [99] but Foxe reckoned all three as being truly martyrs for their beliefs.[100] Latimer seems to have been connected by marriage with Robert, his wife being either his niece or cousin.[101]

Baxterley, now a colliery village, lies some two miles west of the Watling Street with its rush of lorries by day and night. Most of the land round about belongs to the National Coal Board; but where the sandstone church stands apart on its low hill, very weatherbeaten and small, one has an impression still of the deep quietness that must have possessed it when John Glover's new Hall was the great house. Apart from the church and the lodge, no buildings of his time remain; but on that wooded ridge the eye roves to great distances, eastwards to the fields of Leicestershire, westwards over a great tract of his former diocese.

It was in such a place, between haytime and harvest, that Latimer learned the King had died; and he knew what to expect.

[98] *Original Letters*, pp. 361–2.
[100] Foxe, op. cit., VII.384 ff.
[99] Bernher was present to comfort him.
[101] Ridley, *Works*, p. 384.

CHAPTER NINE

'Such a Candle'

NO ONE today doubts Mary's right to the succession, and no one can fail to see how she misjudged the times and the people, throwing away her opportunity. A psychologist has a happy hunting ground here. How much of her later fanaticism was due to thwarted desires in her young womanhood when she saw her mother, to whom she was always deeply attached, shamed by her father? How much was due to her own desertion by her husband? Her father's dominant desire for years was a male heir. An heir was to be her longing, and it was denied her.

Plain in appearance, intense in feeling, half-Spanish in temperament as in blood, she never looked for ideas or inspiration beyond the Catholic world of southern Europe as her mother had known it. She never heeded contemporary opinion which challenged its shaken authority. Deeply religious, and in a world where the most fervent Catholics saw that reform must touch the Papacy or all would be lost, she remained a complete Papalist.

To what extent were her people with her in these matters? Did she confuse their excitement over her accession with an apparent longing for religious changes? If this was her reading of events, it was a sad mistake with tragic consequences.

In his last months Edward the Sixth had been won over by Northumberland to exclude both his sisters from the throne. There never was a more selfish plot or a more innocent victim than Lady Jane Grey. A sense of fair play in the English mind, as well as detestation of Northumberland, prompted the boisterous welcome which Mary received on entering London. A sense of her Tudor blood was aroused by her bravery and astuteness. Her brother had died on 6th July, and she had evaded the trap set for her by moving to Framlingham, a stronghold of the Howards, and in country where Northumberland was particularly execrated. Before the end of the month Queen Jane's father had himself proclaimed Mary on Tower Hill and at Paul's Cross, Ridley was in the Tower, and the way was open. She passed through the City, with Elizabeth beside her, in triumph, on 3rd August. Cranmer conducted Edward the Sixth's funeral service at the Abbey, the last State service of Protestant sort, but Mary also demanded a requiem Mass for him in the chapel at the Tower. She had struck for her rights, and the host of men ready to fight for her gave her proof positive of her good chance of success. That she was of the old religion, everyone recognized. Her loyalty to it had never faltered. But devotion to the Mass might not be synonymous with subjugation to the Pope. They did not yet know that her secret, single-minded policy would be to restore the old religion to its pride of place and prestige as seen in Wolsey's day. That, with all it implied, was her wish—the supremacy, not of the English Crown in affairs of English religion, but the English Crown in devoted service to the Papacy. The liturgy should be as it was when her father and mother were married, and there must be the complete reversal of every act which had altered the laws of England concerning the faith. She purposed ample amendment spiritually and materially, restoring to Rome in repentance for her realm's sin, the authority, the institutions, and the lands (if this were possible) which had been filched away. The bravery of the Tudors and of Aragon met in her. What was lacking was the sure touch on the pulse of the people's life, amounting to a sixth sense, which Henry, even at his worst, possessed, and which her half-sister would show to be her greatest asset. A modern historian has neatly hit off the contrast between Edwardian and Marian policy as, 'Left Incline and Right About Turn'.[1]

All who had initiated or sympathized with the increasing Protestantism of the Edwardian policy knew that Mary's accession might be fatal for them as well as for their religious activities. Mary lost no time in beginning reaction. Her proclamation, issued on 18th August, declared that she 'cannot now hide that religion which God and the world would know she has ever professed from her infancy' and she 'would be glad the same were of all her subjects quietly and charitably embraced'.[2] The Queen did not immediately compel such conformity, but irregular preaching was forbidden and all unlicensed printing.

[1] S. T. Bindoff, *Tudor England*, p. 147.
[2] Gee and Hardy, *Documents Illustrative of English Church History*, p. 373.

Gardiner, released from oblivion, was ready at hand as her servant, and returned to his diocese of Winchester, but in effect to be primate, since it was clear that Cranmer could not expect to continue in active work. Gardiner was appointed Lord High Chancellor on 23rd August, Bonner came back to London, Heath to Latimer's old diocese, which had been Hooper's conjointly with Gloucester, and Day replaced Scory at Chichester, while the aged Cuthbert Tunstal was restored to Durham, which had been suppressed, and its revenues sequestrated, by Northumberland. Gardiner was commanded to choose and authorize preachers throughout the realm, and wherever priests or corporations (like some Oxford colleges) desired, the Mass was at once brought in and the Prayer Book discarded. The Roman service could not be made compulsory everywhere until some rounding-up of prominent persons had been done.

The foreigners went home or to fresh refuge within a few weeks. Cranmer obtained passports for them, and the most notable strangers like Peter Martyr and a Lasco departed with their fellows. The most outstanding English Protestant leaders all stayed and awaited judgement. It is noteworthy that some three hundred people who, with Cranmer, Latimer, Ridley, Hooper, and Bradford, would die at the stake, were almost all from the ranks of the ordinary citizens. Few of the nobility and gentry were sufficiently troubled or convinced to be unable to conform to whatever might be the mode of the Crown in matters religious. The English have never been conspicuously theological; they grow to opinion through established habit, and a Protestant way of life and thought had not been the practice of households and parish churches long enough to provoke immediate opposition to their acknowledged Queen. It would be very different in the middle of the seventeenth century when Puritanism was well established. Some men, in the ranks of the Edwardian clergy, and later to be more conspicuous, hid at home. Matthew Parker did this. Others went abroad, like the apologist Jewell, who was expelled from his fellowship at Oxford, then recanted, but was smitten in conscience, and was assisted by Augustine Bernher to flee overseas, and there repented of his recantation. William Cecil, though undoubtedly Protestant in sympathy, was successful in extricating himself from his Edwardian responsibilities, and acquiesced in the new Queen's demands. Cecil was not the only layman of truly Protestant views found to be indispensable. The Princess Elizabeth conformed to the extent of attending Mass.

Latimer, in Warwickshire, was remote from the swift changes in the capital. On 4th September the Council resolved he should be summoned before them.[3] He could have escaped. Indeed, it would seem as though he was presented with the opportunity to do so; but he was old, and he had made up his mind. Bernher gives an eyewitness's account of what happened. John Careless—a Coventry weaver of strong Protestant convictions, and who himself died later in gaol—came over some six hours before the arrival of the Queen's agent, who had been sent down to call Latimer to the Council. The intention of the Council was shown openly so that his friends could convey him out of the country or into safe hiding. Latimer, however, made himself ready for the journey into captivity, and on the arrival of the pursuivant, greeted him,

My friend, you be a welcome messenger to me; and be it known unto you and to the whole world, that I go as willingly to London at this present, being called by my prince to render a reckoning of my doctrine, as ever I was to any place in the world; and I do not doubt but that God, as he hath made me worthy to preach his word before two excellent princes, so he will able me to witness the same unto the third, either to her comfort, or discomfort eternally.[4]

The officer merely delivered his letters to this latterday Polycarp, and said he was commanded not to wait—a plain hint that escape could be attempted. Latimer's route took him through Smithfield, and looking about him he remarked that the place 'had long groaned for him'.

He came before the Council on 13th September and was sent to the Tower because of his seditious demeanour, 'there to remain a close prisoner, having attending upon him one Austy his servant'.[5] Cranmer followed the next day. The Archbishop had been most anxious to maintain as openly as possible his belief in the correctness of the views expressed in the 1552 Prayer Book, and wanted to have a public disputation, with the help of such distinguished allies as Peter Martyr. But Scory's copy of the manifesto got out, and in no time copies were on sale everywhere in London. This gave immediate

[3] *Acts of the Privy Council*, IV.340.   [4] Bernher's Dedication, *Sermons*, p. 321.
[5] *Acts of the Privy Council*, IV.345–6.

opportunity to the Council, though it was obvious that Cranmer must sooner or later face serious charges. If the net for heresy failed, Mary would find some other means of dealing with the prime agent of the divorce. He was, in fact, committed for treason, and joined Ridley and Latimer in the Tower. The prisoners were in separate cells in the autumn and early winter, and they appear to have experienced harsh treatment at first. It was typical of Latimer that he should get the Lieutenant of the Tower himself to come to his cell by sending the mystifying message that, if the prisoner were not better attended his jailer might be deceived. ' "Yea, master lieutenant, so I said", quod he, "for you look, I think, that I should burn: but except you let me have some fire, I am like to deceive your expectation; for I am like here to starve for cold." ' [6]

Cranmer, as the most important prisoner, received the strictest ward, but all three had personal servants in attendance, and were able to hold a certain amount of correspondence. Ridley was, not surprisingly, the most vigorous in mind, and he lost no opportunity to clarify his own position, whether by speech or writing. He initiated a correspondence with Latimer on the matters which would be likely to arise in any conflict with the religious authorities. The prisoners were completely dependent upon the fidelity of their servants, and Bernher especially associated himself with the 'little treatise which Mr. Latimer and I wrote in the Tower', as Ridley described it in a letter to Cranmer and Latimer when they were again separately lodged at Oxford.[7]

Foxe muddles this important contribution to our knowledge of their minds, but the two 'Godly, Learned and Comfortable Conferences' were safely conveyed overseas. A copy was taken to Gambold, formerly Ridley's chaplain. In 1556 the book was printed, probably at Zurich, the editor being John Olde, Geneva. The Preface comments:

M. Latimer came earlier in the morning, and was the more ancient workman in the Lord's vineyard; who also may very well be called (as divers learned men have termed him) the Apostle of England, as one much more worthy of that name for his true doctrine, and for his sharp reproving of sin and superstition, than was Augustine, bishop of Canterbury, for bringing in the pope's monkery and false

---

[6] *Remains*, p. xxii; Foxe, *Acts and Monuments*, VII. 464–5.
[7] Ridley's *Works* (Parker Soc.), pp. 361 ff.

religion. M. Ridley came later, about the eleventh hour; but no doubt he came when he was effectually called.[8]

There was a threefold value of practical importance in these Conferences. The prisoners, denied the opportunity of conversation or easy access to books, could help one another to a clear view of their true position, especially regarding the Mass, which was necessarily at the centre of the doctrinal trouble to come upon them. They would be fortified in spirit and be enabled to check their personal position in the light of a comrade's conviction. A third possibility was that their friends overseas or in this country might subsequently know what was their precise opinion, if they could put it in writing and smuggle it out—for official accounts of trials might be falsified or not fully reported.

This work could only be done slowly; it would occupy the months of the autumn and early winter of 1553-4.

The first Conference was entirely given up to the consideration of the Mass. Ridley would make a short comment and this would be passed to Latimer for his discussion, and the paper would go back by the hands of a servant. The following extract is typical of the method and manner:

N. Ridley.

The causes that move me to abstain from the mass, be these:

1. It is done in a strange tongue, which the people doth not understand, contrary to the doctrine of the apostle.

H. Latimer.

Where is no understanding, there is neither edifying, nor comfort; for besides that they speak into the air, the mind receiveth no profit; they are one to another as aliens. The parishioners will say, their priests are mad, whereas all things ought to be done so as they may edify. Let every man know, that the things which I write, saith St. Paul, are the commandments of the Lord. Such absurdities are to be eschewed.[9]

This necessity of English comes up repeatedly: it is a cardinal point for the maintenance of their cause. They indulge in a good deal of sarcasm at the expense of the old order:

N.R.

8. The priest turneth himself from the altar, and speaketh unto the people in an unknown tongue, saying, *Dominus vobiscum, orate pro*

[8] ibid., pp. 99–100.　　　　　　　　[9] ibid., pp. 103–4.

me, fratres et sorores &c; that is, the Lord be with you and pray for me, brothers and sisters; and turning from the people, he saith in Latin, 'Let us pray, and the peace of the Lord be always with you.' Also the people, or at least he which supplieth the place of the people, is compelled three times to say, 'Amen', when he hath heard never a word of that the priest hath prayed or spoken, except these few words, *Per omnia secula seculorum.* Whereas to the answering of 'Amen', St Paul willeth the answerer, not only to hear, but also to understand, the things that were spoken.

H.L.

Yea, and *Ite, missa est,* must be sung to them with a great rolling up and down of notes, so bidding them go home fasting, when he hath eaten and drunken up all himself alone. A fellow, once rebuked for going away before mass was ended, answered, that it was not good manners to tarry till he were bidden go. After that he was blamed for not taking holy bread he answered, that he was bidden go away before.[10]

Latimer added several pages in which he wrote in his characteristically free style (one supposes him dictating to Bernher). He gives us a glimpse of the ardour he gave to reading his New Testament—

I have read over of late the New Testament three or four times deliberately; yet can I not find there neither the popish consecration, nor yet their transubstantiation, nor their oblation, nor their adoration, which be the very sinews and marrow-bones of the mass.[11]

As an old campaigner, to whom prison routine and inconvenience were well known, he boldly addressed the younger man:

Fear of death doth most persuade a great number. Be well ware of that argument; for that persuaded Shaxton, as many men thought, after that he had once made a good profession openly before the judgment-seat. . . . Lo! sir, here have I blotted your paper vainly, and played the fool egregiously. But so I thought better, than not to do your request at this time. Pardon me, and pray for me: pray for me, I say, pray for me, I say. For I am sometime so fearful, that I would creep into a mousehole; sometime God doth visit me again with his comfort.[12]

The Second Conferences are longer and range over many matters of churchmanship and doctrine. Ridley imagines the

---

[10] Ridley's *Works* (Parker Soc.), p. 108.　　　　　[11] ibid., p. 112.
[12] ibid., pp. 115–16.

opposition stating the Roman position—'I would have you to think that these darts are cast at my head of some one of Diotrephes' or Antonius' soldiers.'

Once more the question of the language of the various services comes prominently before the reader, as in the discussion on Baptism.

The Thirteenth Objection of the Antonian.

Seeing you are so obstinately set against the mass, that you affirm, because it is done in a tongue not understanded of the people, and for other causes, (I cannot tell what) therefore it is not the true sacrament ordained of Christ, I begin to suspect you, that you think not catholicly of baptism also. Is our baptism, which we do use in a tongue unknown to the people, the true baptism of Christ or not? If it be, then doth not the strange tongue hurt the mass. If it be not the baptism of Christ, tell me how were you baptized? Or whether ye will, (as the Anabaptists do) that all which were baptized in Latin, should be baptized again in the English tongue.

The Answer.

N. Ridley.

Although I would wish baptism to be given in the vulgar tongue, for the people's sake, which are present, that they may the better understand their own profession, and also be more able to teach their children the same; yet, notwithstanding, there is not like necessity of the vulgar tongue in baptism, as in the Lord's supper. Baptism is given to children, who by reason of their age are not able to understand what is spoken unto them, (in) what tongue soever it be. The Lord's supper is and ought to be given to them that are waxen. Moreover, in baptism, which is accustomed to be given to children in the Latin tongue, all the substantial points, (as a man would say) which Christ commanded to be done, are observed. And therefore I judge that baptism to be a perfect and true baptism, and that it is not only not needful, but also not lawful, for any man so christened to be christened again. But yet, notwithstanding, they ought to be taught the catechism of the christian faith when they shall come to years of discretion; which catechism whosoever despiseth, or will not desirously embrace and willingly learn, in my judgment he playeth not the part of a christian man. But in the popish mass are wanting certain substantials, that is to say, things commanded by the word of God to be observed in the ministration of the Lord's supper, of the which there is sufficient declaration made before.

H. Latimer.

Where you say, 'I would wish', surely I would wish that you had spoken more vehemently, and to have said, 'It is of necessity, that all things in the congregation should be done in the vulgar tongue, for the edifying of them that are present'. Notwithstanding that the child itself is sufficiently baptized in the Latin tongue.[13]

It is noticeable how complementary they are to each other. Ridley, inclined to trust to his skill in the schools and sure of his knowledge, yet feels an inner uncertainty. Will he be able to stand in the evil day, especially if his intellectual weapons are knocked out of his hands? Latimer greatly needs a refresher course—he is sure of his faith, but his 'memory is altogether slippery'.[14] If Ridley says much the same thing ('My memory was never good: for help whereof I have used for the most part to gather out notes of my reading')[15] it is obvious that he is far superior to Latimer in nimbleness of mind and ability to base his convictions upon authorities. But he knows Latimer's power of prayer and faith in prayer. So Latimer says:

Nay, I rather thank you, that you have vouchsafed to minister so plentiful armour to me, being otherwise altogether unarmed: saving that he cannot be left destitute of help which rightly trusteth in the help of God. I only learn to die in reading of the New Testament, and am ever now and then praying unto my God, that he will be an helper unto me in time of need.[16]

It is in the conclusion of these Conferences we find Ridley's famous prayer which is often assumed to be connected with the actual martyrdom, whereas it belongs to the period of dread waiting in the Tower almost two years before the last ordeal.

O! heavenly Father, the Father of all wisdom, understanding and true strength, I beseech thee, for thy only Son our Saviour Christ's sake, look mercifully upon me, wretched creature, and send thine Holy Spirit into my breast; that not only I may understand according to thy wisdom, how this pestilent and deadly dart is to be borne off, and with what answer it is to be beaten back; but also, when I must join to fight in the field for the glory of thy name, that then I, being strengthened with the defence of thy right hand, may manfully stand in the confession of thy faith and of thy truth, and continue in the same unto the end of my life, through the same our Lord Jesus Christ—Amen.[17]

---

[13] Ridley's *Works* (Parker Soc.), pp. 140–1.   [14] ibid., p. 128.
[15] ibid., p. 128.   [16] ibid., p. 140.   [17] ibid., p. 142.

Ridley's anxieties were not without cause.

That autumn the Queen sought by every means possible to bring her realm back into complete harmony with Rome by submission. She was crowned by Bishop Gardiner on 1st October, and four days later the First Act of Repeal cancelled the nine acts passed in Edward's reign which affected Church life and faith, so that the *status quo* of the last year of her father's reign was restored. This was merely a temporary basis for her real projects. The reaction of the vast majority of the people about her is revealed in a comment of the Venetian Envoy:

With the exception of a few most pious Catholics, none of whom are under 35 years of age, all the rest make this show of recantation yet do not effectually resume the Catholic faith.

This idea of complete submission to Rome did not commend itself to the people any more than the mooted Spanish Alliance. The Council was willing to approve the Queen's religion; they did not refrain from questioning the wisdom of a Spanish marriage. No one wanted either the restoration of full Papal authority or the interference which that might bring in the ownership of lands formerly belonging to the Church. Parliament was very definite on the latter point. Convocation assembled soon after Parliament met, with Bonner acting as President, since the Archbishop was in the Tower, and was quite ready to bring back the old theological views concerning the Sacraments and worship. But the clergy showed no more eagerness than the members of Parliament, to be subject to the Papal See. The non-committal position, as it was in Henry the Eighth's last days, was quite good enough even in this pro-Catholic assembly.

Far away at Lake Garda, Cardinal Pole was immersed in theological quests and probably never thought of himself as a possible consort for his relative, the Queen. He had been exiled from England for twenty-one years. Truly sincere, a scholar, and eager for the reformation of the Church without any departure from its accepted Catholic structure and dogma, his ideas were closely related to those of Contarini. He had imbibed the humanism of Italy and was by this time out of touch with affairs here. When news came to the monastery that Mary was queen, he promptly wished to volunteer for service in recapturing his native land for the Pope. The Pope had

anticipated him. Julius the Third had already commissioned
him to be the ambassador of this cause. 'We leave everything
to your prudence, your learning, your charity, your zeal for the
restoration and the progress of our religion.' [18]

What had not occurred to Pole did not miss the intelligence
of Englishmen or the Emperor. Charles the Fifth, old in
strategy and experience, was not taking any chances. He succeeded in putting enough hindrances in the Cardinal's way to
prevent his arrival here as legate until the late autumn of 1554,
by which time his son had been safely, if not happily, married
to Mary. The marriage treaty was signed in the New Year,
and London apprentices had some fun in snowballing Imperial
servants. In the West there was rebellion. Sir Peter Carew's
men took Exeter. Then came the much more serious rising of
Sir Thomas Wyatt in Kent. Gairdner has called it 'an heretical
conspiracy with a political pretext',[19] but it nearly succeeded.
Wyatt was held at the City wall, and the noise of fighting and
clamour came to the ears of the prisoners in the Tower. Mary
could no longer risk the living presence of Lady Jane Grey in
her realm, and the unfortunate girl paid the price of others'
rebellion in her own person. In February the Queen was
married by proxy to Philip, and the same month the Tower
was crowded with fresh prisoners from Wyatt's rebellion. In
consequence Cranmer, Ridley, Latimer, and Bradford, his
younger convert, were housed together, and there could be no
let or hindrance to their fellowship. They were together from
the beginning of February until the end of March.

Bradford gives us a glimpse into their life in a letter to his
mother. There is something Pauline in its phrasing. These
men do not concentrate on details of what is physical but accept
their destiny with spiritual grandeur.

You shall know, therefore, good mother, that for my body, though
it be in a house out of the which I cannot come when I will, yet, in
that I have conformed my will to God's will, I find herein Liberty
enough, I thank God; and for my lodging, bedding, meat, drink,
godly and learned company, books and all other necessaries for
mine ease, comfort and commodity, I am in much better case than
I could wish; and God's merciful providence here is far above my
worthiness. Worthiness quoth I? Alas! I am worthy of nothing but

[18] Quoted by Schwenk, *Reginald Pole* (Longmans), p. 124.

[19] J. Gairdner, *History of the English Church in the Sixteenth Century*, p. 330.

damnation. But, besides all this, for my soul I find much more commodity; for God is my Father, I now perceive, through Christ: therefore, in prisoning me for his Gospel, he maketh me like to the image of his Son, Jesus Christ here, that, when he cometh to judgment, I might then be like unto him, as my trust and hope is I shall be. Now he maketh me like to his friends the prophets, apostles, the holy martyrs and confessors. Which of them did not suffer, at the least, imprisonment or banishment for his gospel and word.[20]

Bradford asks that the letter should be burned, 'for if it were known that I have pen and ink and did write, then should I want all the foresaid commodities I have spoken of concerning my body, and be cast into some dungeon in fetters of iron'. It was only by the kindly connivance of servants that a small measure of comfort could be obtained or communication be made with the outside world.

In his written statement, delivered to the Commissioners at Oxford in the spring of that year, Latimer referred to the same experience:

Yet behold! the providence of God, which will have this truth known, (yea, if all men held their tongues, the stones should speak,) did bring this to pass that where these famous men, viz. Mr Cranmer, archbishop of Canterbury, Mr Ridley, bishop of London, that holy man, Mr Bradford, and I, old Hugh Latimer, were imprisoned in the Tower of London for Christ's gospel preaching, and for because we would not go a massing, every one in close prison from other; the same tower being so full of other prisoners, that we four were thrust into one chamber, as men not to be accounted of, (but, God be thanked! to our great joy and comfort,) there did we together read over the new testament with great deliberation and painful study: and I assure you, as I will answer (at) the tribunal throne of God's majesty, we could find in the testament of Christ's body and blood no other presence, but a spiritual presence; nor that the mass was any sacrifice for sins: but in that heavenly book it appeared that the sacrifice which Christ Jesus our Redeemer did upon the cross, was perfect, holy, and good; that God, the heavenly Father, did require none other, nor that never again to be done; but was pacified with that only omnisufficient and most painful sacrifice of that sweet slain Lamb, Christ our Lord, for our sins.[21]

On 8th March the Council made an order that Cranmer, Ridley and Latimer should be taken to Oxford, and the

[20] Bradford's *Letters &c.*, pp. 74 ff. (Parker Society).
[21] *Remains*, p. 258 f.

Lieutenant of the Tower received instructions to hand them over to Sir John Williams for safe conveyance.[22] The journey was broken at Windsor and they arrived at Oxford just before Easter, which in that year was on 25th March. This is Ridley's dating of the journey in a letter to Grindal,[23] as opposed to Foxe's 'about the tenth of April'.[24] Ridley comments that they 'were suffered to have nothing with us, but that we carried upon us'. Ridley's memory may have been at fault, for what is time to a man long in prison? The disputations were not 'about the Whitsuntide following', as he says, but in the middle of April. At Oxford they were lodged in Bocardo, the well-known prison at the North Gate. Only its door now survives in safe keeping in the church of St Magdalene. Bocardo is a term in medieval logic for an awkward syllogism to escape from—a good name for an Oxford prison holding Cambridge men.

Ridley said they were soon denied even the privilege of air and exercise on the wall and their servants' liberty was restricted.[25] The prisoners were called to answer for their faith without long delay. A distinguished company of scholars was appointed by Convocation and the two Universities to try the accused, with Dr Hugh Weston, Dean of Westminster, to preside as Prolocutor. Cambridge, the mother of them all, was instructed to select representatives to join with the Oxford doctors, and their quota included the Vice-Chancellor, John Young, who had succeeded Ridley as Master of Pembroke, and several other heads of houses, William Glynn, the President of Queen's, Richard Atkinson, Provost of King's, and the Masters of Christ's and St. John's, Cuthbert Scott and Thomas Watson. They also had with them the Regius Professor of Divinity, Thomas Sedgwick of Trinity.[26] The Oxford Commissioners also included the Vice-Chancellor, Dr Tresham, who was Rector of Lincoln, and who necessarily acted as host to the visitors from Cambridge when they arrived on Friday, 13th April. They had been two days on the way and came fully armed with the authority of their University, though some of them had omitted to bring their own scarlet and were pro-

---

[22] *Acts of the Privy Council*, IV.406.   [23] Ridley's *Works*, p. 390.
[24] Foxe, Edition of 1563, p. 931, Vol. VI, App. III.
[25] Ridley's *Works*, p. 359. (In a letter to Bradford, now a prisoner of the King's Bench.)
[26] Strype's *Cranmer*, App. 77 and 78.

vided with robes borrowed in Oxford. The older University incorporated the Cambridge men, and admitted them to all the privileges of their proper degrees. Foxe does not fail to point out the number of courtesies shown. They lodged at the Cross Inn 'and, shortly after [their arrival], two of the beadles came from the vice-chancellor of Oxford and presented the vice-chancellor of Cambridge with a dish of apples and a gallon of wine'.[27]

No detail of ceremony or of pageantry was omitted from the ecclesiastical and university proceedings. It was a scene that would have delighted a Hollywood producer—processions, dinners, crowd-scenes, and grave dignity suddenly exchanged for violent exchanges of temper. The processions passed along the narrow streets among the colleges and halls, the spring light falling on the coloured throng of doctors and masters, with the Town well in evidence in its best and its worst demonstrations. The Mayor and the Aldermen were involved—their prison had become 'a college of quondams', as one of the three described Bocardo. It had never happened before, surely it could never happen again that an Archbishop of Canterbury, a Bishop of London, and a former Bishop of Worcester would pass through the streets as prisoners to face their judges on charges of heresy. It might be explained that this was Mother Church taking exquisite care to bring back to her bosom three erring children whose average age was sixty-four; but the crowd knew, and the Commissioners knew, that they were doomed. Even if they should, all three, completely recant their deeds and professions, great and small, what place of rest could be given them on earth?

The three articles with which they would be confronted went straight to the heart of the matter which divided them from their Catholic forebears and present judges, affirming the dogma of transubstantiation and its implications.

Convocation had already expressed its mind with regard to Cranmer's views, but the articles were now to be formally presented so that the heretics might be properly confuted in the eyes of all.

On Saturday, 14th April, there was accordingly a great procession to St Mary's, where the Mass of the Holy Ghost was sung by the choirmen of Christ Church, to which college the

[27] Foxe, op. cit., VI.440.

H

procession returned. Dinner was taken at Lincoln, the Vice-Chancellor's College, and so they went back to St Mary's for the beginning of the real business. The thirty-three Commissioners were seated in the choir before the altar, and the prisoners were brought before them singly.

Cranmer was naturally the first to appear. The Prolocutor spoke a few words of introduction on the necessity of unity, and that it was the Queen's pleasure that the Commissioners should bring him back to his former state; and so they would present to him the articles agreed upon by Convocation. The Notary at once read out the articles. They affirmed:

I.   In the sacrament of the altar, that the words of consecration uttered by a priest, by the divine virtue, is made the very real and natural body born of the Virgin, under the kinds of bread and wyne.
II. After the consecration, the substance of bread and wine do not remain, nor any other substance, but of God and man.
III. In the mass there is a propitiatory and lively sacrifice, for the quick and the dead.

Cranmer read over the articles three or four times and denied them as false. They were against God's Word. He was advised to write out his opinion that night, for he would have to dispute on Monday, the 16th.

Ridley came next. As soon as he had looked over the articles he denounced them. 'They sprang out of a bitter and sour root. His answers were sharp, witty and very learned.' He was quite ready to undertake disputation, but, not unreasonably, wanted access to his books and to have time. He was promised, as Cranmer had been, that he should have what the Commissioners considered sufficient facilities, and must be ready for Tuesday. Ridley showed more eagerness than either of the older men to run a full course of academic disputation. He was ten years younger than the Archbishop, and perhaps had some hopes of success in controversy, though he could have had no expectation of doing more than give a good witness for his cause to the world.

Last of all came in master Latimer in like sort, with a kerchief, and two or three caps on his head, his spectacles hanging by a string at his breast, and a staff in his hand, and was set in a chair; for so was he suffered by the prolocutor. And after his denial of the articles, when he had Wednesday appointed for disputation, he alleged age, sickness, disuse, and lack of books, saying, that he was almost as meet to dispute as to be a captain of Calais: but he would, he said, declare his mind either by writing or word, and would stand to all they would lay upon his back: complaining moreover, that he was permitted to have neither pen nor ink, nor yet any book but only the New Testament there in his hand, which, he said, he had read over seven times deliberately, and yet could not find the mass in it, neither the marrow bones nor sinews of the same. At which words the commissioners were not a little offended; and Dr Weston said, that he would make him grant that it had both marrow-bones and sinews in the New Testament. To whom master Latimer said again, 'That you will never do, master doctor.' [28]

The prisoners were sent back, to be separated for the rest of their days, Cranmer to Bocardo, Ridley to the Sheriff's house, Alderman Irish, whose wife seems to have been an added penalty,[29] and Latimer to the Bailiff's. Thus there was no opportunity for fellowship or consultation between these 'partners in distress'.

On Monday the 16th the disputation was held in the Divinity Schools, and for six hours Cranmer maintained his point of view against the questionings and disputing of his adversaries. The place was crowded with members of the University and Town. The proceedings often lacked the decorum of academic debate, though it is not surprising that feeling ran high. Interruptions and clapping did not alter Cranmer's demeanour, and although his opinions were anathematized, his personal bearing won him praise.

Ridley endured the same ordeal on the next day. Foxe's eyewitness, 'A Scholar of the University', remarks, 'He shewed himself to be learned, and a great scholer: they could bring nothing, but he knew it as well as they.' But such proceedings were likely to have evil consequences for any Protestant in either University. The Cambridge representatives had brought with them the subscription of their scholars, and now in Oxford, 'Here is suche subscribing as never hath been sene afore. . . . All oure house have subscribed, saving I and my chamberfelowe, and we looke every houre when we shall not onely loose our

[28] *Remains*, pp. 250 ff.
[29] Ridley's *Works*, p. 392. 'I have never myself had a wife, yet from my daily association with this couple I seem in some measure to understand how great an evil and intolerable a yoke it is to be joined in wedlock with a bad woman.'

colledge, but also goe to prison, which maister Doctor Weston threateneth sore.' [30]

Latimer came on Wednesday at the same time, eight o'clock in the morning; but he was obviously in no state to sustain argument at length, and with him the proceedings were finished in less than three hours. He handed in his written protestation, saying that he had prepared this, but he was not permitted to read it. All the signs of age and illness were on him, his voice low, his condition such that he dared not drink for fear of vomiting. As compared with his words spoken in earlier debatings, there seems sometimes to be a note of querulousness; he is very conscious of his age. He wished to speak in English, not Latin—'I have not these twenty years much used the Latin tongue. . . . Let me here protest my faith, for I am not able to dispute; and afterwards do your pleasure with me.' [31]

One can scarcely blame the Prolocutor for forbidding Latimer to read his statement. It was the nearest approach possible to preaching his faith, and it did not attempt to follow the path of scholastic disputation. His memory was weak, but his faith was strong; and faith can be most infectious. There were people present like Foxe's 'scholar' who could be roused or stimulated. But his age and sorry plight did not save him from the mockery of his enemies. And even this is understandable, for when Cranmer's policy had been in operation throughout Edward the Sixth's reign, some of these champions of Catholicism had known personal loss and discomfort, including the man now presiding over the examination.

Part of Latimer's written statement was read—sufficient, no doubt, to make it quite clear to the hearers that he had completely rejected the idea of submission. He makes his comments at once on the three articles.

I say, That there is none other presence of Christ required than a spiritual presence; and this presence is sufficient for a christian man, as the presence by the which we both abide in Christ, and Christ in us, to the obtaining of eternal life, if we persevere [in his true gospel.] And the same presence may be called a real presence, [because to the faithful believer there is the real, or spiritual body of Christ:] which thing I here rehearse, least some sycophant or scorner should suppose me, with the anabaptist, to make nothing else of the sacrament but a bare and naked sign.

[30] Foxe, 1563 Edition, pp. 931–6. Vol. VI, App. III.   [31] *Remains*, p. 251.

It is noteworthy that he thus does not take the Zwinglian view with which the English reformers are too often credited. Weston pinned him down presently to his position, which was Cranmer's, for the Prolocutor insisted upon questioning him, and called upon Dr Smith to dispute, though Weston himself did much more talking than Smith, and at times three or four people were jostling one another with questions and comments. Latimer had submitted his statement, and was challenged by the Prolocutor to subscribe or dispute.

Smith. Because I perceive that this charge is laid upon my neck to dispute with you, to the end that the same may go forward after a right manner and order, I will propose three questions, so as they are put forth unto me. And first, I ask this question of you, although the same ought not to be called in question: but such is the condition of the church, that it is always vexed of the wicked sort. I ask, I say, whether Christ's body be really in the sacrament?

Latimer. I trust I have obtained of Mr Prolocutor, that no man shall exact that thing of me which is not in me. And I am sorry that this worshipful audience should be deceived of their expectation for my sake. I have given up my mind in writing to Mr Prolocutor.

Smith. Whatsoever ye have given up, it shall be registered among the acts.

Latimer. Disputation requireth a good memory. *Ast abolita est mihi memoria.* My memory is clean gone, and marvellously weakened, and never better, I wis, for the prison.

Weston. How long have ye been in prison?

Latimer. These three quarters of this year.

Weston. And I was in prison six years.

Latimer. The more pity, sir.

Weston. How long have you been of this opinion?

Latimer. It is not long, sir, that I have been of this opinion.

Weston. The time hath been when you said mass full devoutly.

Latimer. Yea, I cry God mercy heartily for it.

Weston. Where learned you this newfangleness?

(Foxe here interjects the remark—'Then they hissed and clapped their hands at him.')

Latimer. I have long sought for the truth in this matter of the sacrament, and have not been of this mind past seven years: and my lord of Canterbury's book hath especially confirmed my judgment herein. If I could remember all therein contained, I would not fear to answer any man in this matter.

Tresham [the Vice-Chancellor of Oxford]. There are in that book six hundred errors.

Weston. You were once a Lutheran.

Latimer. No. I was a papist: for I never could perceive how Luther could defend his opinion without transubstantiation. The Tigurines once did write a book against Luther, and I oft desired God that he might live so long to make them answer.

Weston. Luther, in his book *De Privata Missa*, said, that the devil reasoned with him, and persuaded him that the mass was not good, fol. 14. *Contigit me, &c.* Whereof it may appear, that Luther said mass, and the devil dissuaded him from it.

Latimer. I do not take in hand here to defend Luther's sayings or doings. If he were here, he would defend himself well enough, I trow. I told you before, that I am not meet for disputations. I pray you, read mine answer, wherein I have declared my faith.

Weston. Do you believe this, as you have written?

Latimer. Yea, sir.

Weston. Then have you no faith.

Latimer. Then would I be sorry, sir.

Tresham. It is written, (John vi.) 'Except ye shall eat the flesh of the Son of man, and drink his blood, ye shall have no life in you'; which, when the Capernaites and many of Christ's disciples heard, they said, 'This is a hard saying' &c. Now, that the truth may the better appear, here I ask of you whether Christ, speaking these words, did mean of his flesh to be eaten with the mouth, or of the spiritual eating of the same?

Latimer. I answer, (as Augustine understandeth,) that Christ meant of the spiritual eating of his flesh.

Tresham. Of what flesh meant Christ? His true flesh, or no?

Latimer. Of his true flesh, spiritually to be eaten, in the supper, by faith, and not corporally.

Tresham. Of what flesh mean the Capernaites?

Latimer. Of his true flesh also; but to be eaten with the mouth.

Tresham. They, as ye confess, did mean his true flesh to be eaten with the mouth. And Christ also, as I shall prove, did speak of the receiving of his flesh with the mouth. *Ergo*, they both did understand it of the eating of one thing, which is done by the mouth of the body.

Latimer. I say, Christ understood it not of the bodily mouth, but of the mouth of the spirit, mind, and heart.[32]

Tresham pressed him hard, reminding him of his earlier assertions:

To be short, I myself have heard you preaching at Greenwich before

[32] *Remains*, pp. 264–7.

King Henry the Eighth, where you did openly affirm, that no christian man ought to doubt of the true and real presence of Christ's body in the sacrament, forasmuch as he had the word of scripture on his side; *videlicet, Hoc est corpus meum,* 'This is my body': whereby he might be confirmed. But now there is the same truth; the word of scripture hath the selfsame thing, which it then had. Therefore why do you deny at this present that, whereof it was not lawful once to doubt before when you taught it? [33]

Tresham had spoken in Latin, and Latimer replied mostly in the same language, though protesting, 'I cannot speak Latin so long and so largely.' The argument then swung away to the meaning of the cup, and Latimer insisted on his view:

We drink blood sacramentally: he gave us his blood to drink spiritually: he went about to shew, that as certain as we drink wine, so certainly we drink his blood spiritually.[34]

There are not many flashes of Latimer's old form, though he never wavered in his declaration of his faith. It was galling to find Weston putting up against him a former Protestant, Nicholas Cartwright, who had been an ally of Peter Martyr in Oxford a few years earlier. Cartwright acknowledged that he had himself been in error. Latimer was not likely to be convinced by such a man, and retorted:

Will you give me leave to tell what hath caused Mr Doctor to recant here? It is *pœna legis* the pain of the law, which hath brought you back, and converted you and many more: the which letteth many to confess God. And this is a great argument, there are few here can dissolve it.[35]

A gibe of that sort was not likely to mollify the Commissioners. Weston closed the disputation with words of vehemence. One can understand the satisfaction with which he saw an old adversary caught in the meshes of the law, and no one could then see how short-lived the triumph of Papal power was to be. If the words he used hurt the Protestant reader, vulgar and blasphemous as they are, one must recall that toleration was as yet in no man's mind—the Protestant saw in the Mass a foul hyprocrisy, just as the Catholic did not come within a thousand miles of comprehending that there was deep devotion and reverence in the Communion.

[33] ibid., p. 268.   [34] ibid., p. 270.   [35] ibid., p. 272.

The summing up was in these words:

Well, Master Latimer, this is our intent, to will you well, and to exhort you to come to yourself, and remember that without Noe's ark, there is no health. Remember what they have been that were the beginners of your doctrine; none but a few flying apostates, running out of Germany for fear of the fagot. Remember what they have been, which have set forth the same in this realm. A sort of fling-brains and light heads, which were never constant in any one thing; as it was to be seen in the turning of the table, where, like a sort of apes, they could not tell which way to turn their tails, looking one day west, and another day east, one that way and another this way. They will be like, they say, to the apostles, they will have no churches. A hovel is good enough for them. They come to the communion with no reverence. They get them a tankard, and one saith, I drink and I am thankful. The more joy of thee, saith another. And in them was it true that Hilary saith, *Annuas et menstruas de Deo fides facimus*; that is, 'We make every year and every month a faith.' A runagate Scot did take away [36] the adoration or worshipping of Christ in the sacrament; by whose procurement that heresy was put into the last Communion Book; so much prevailed that one man's authority at that time. You never agreed with the Tigurines,[37] or Germans, or with the church or with yourself. Your stubbornness cometh of a vain glory, which is to no purpose; for it will do you no good when a fagot is in your beard. And we see all by your own confession, how little cause you have to be stubborn, for your learning is in feoffer's hold. The queen's grace is merciful, if ye will turn.

Latimer. You shall have no hope in me to turn. I pray for the queen daily, even from the bottom of my heart, that she may turn from this religion.

Weston. Here you all see the weakness of heresy against the truth: he denieth all truth, and all the old fathers.

On Friday, the 20th, the prisoners came for the last time before the Commissioners in St Mary's to hear judgement against them. Weston made the usual formal attempt to dissuade them, and Cranmer tried to speak in protest against the statement that he had been overcome in argument. But everyone knew that they were there to hear a verdict. Ridley and Latimer in their turn said that they would hold to what they

---

[36] Weston's allusion is probably to Alexander Aless, of Edinburgh. He helped to translate the 1549 Prayer Book into Latin. (*Liturgy and Worship*, p. 813.)
[37] i.e. Zurich.

had already stated and the way was open for Weston to pronounce sentence.

They were 'no members of the Church' and, with their associates would be condemned as heretics unless, at this last moment, they would turn. They would not turn; and after being sentenced, they spoke as follows:

Cranmer. From this your judgment and sentence, I appeal to the just judgment of God Almighty; trusting to be present with Him in heaven, for whose presence in the altar I am thus condemned.

Ridley. Although I be not of your company, yet doubt I not but my name is written in another place, whither this sentence will send us sooner, than we should by the course of nature have come.

Latimer. I thank God most heartily, that he hath prolonged my life to this end, that I may in this case glorify God by that kind of death.

Weston retorted swiftly, 'If you go to heaven in this faith, then I will never come thither, as I am thus persuaded.'

The prisoners were carried back to their previous quarters—Cranmer to Bocardo, Ridley to the Sheriff's house, and Latimer to the Bailiff's.

On the next day there was a solemn Mass and procession, and it was arranged that the three heretics should see in it their own defeat symbolized. Cranmer watched the procession from Bocardo, with Weston himself carrying the Sacrament, four doctors bearing the canopy over him; Ridley was at the Sheriff's, and Latimer was brought out into the street. He thought the summons was for his burning, and called out to a stander-by, Augustine Cooper, a catchpole, to make a quick fire. At Carfax, however, he saw what was afoot, and promptly got as fast as he could into a shop, refusing to look.

Latimer accepted his condemnation. Cranmer and Ridley both wrote letters of protest against the misordering of the disputation, but it was not likely that the authorities would take any notice.

The Council determined on 3rd May that they should seek opinion as to what 'in lawe hir Heighness may doo touching the caases of the said Cranmer, Rydley and Latymer, being all redye by bothe the Universities of Oxforde and Cambridge judged to be obstinate heretikes'.[38] The Mayor of Oxford was to submit his bill for expenses incurred. But the gap between

---

[38] *Acts of Privy Council*, V.17.

H*

undertaking and performance would prove to be not less in Mary's time than in that of some other monarchs. The city fathers of Oxford would have to wait twenty months before a resolution would be taken on 2nd February 1556 that three pounds a week should be allowed for the keeping of their prisoners and servants. Ten years later the bill was still unsettled.[39]

It was impossible for the three friends to know one another's answers, as they had been examined separately, and some of their difficulties are revealed in a letter from Ridley to Cranmer, written very soon after the trial:

I trust, the day of our delivery out of all miseries, and of our entrance into perpetual rest, and unto perpetual joy and felicity, draweth nigh. The Lord strengthen us with His mighty Spirit of grace! If you have not what to write with, you must make your man your friend. And this bearer deserveth to be rewarded, so he may and will do your pleasure. My man is trusty; but it grieveth both him and me, that when I send him with any thing to you, your man will not let him come up to see you, as he may to Master Latimer, and yours to me. I have a promise to see how my answers were written in the schools, but as yet I cannot come by it. Pray for me, I beseech you, and so shall I for you. The Lord have mercy of his church, and lighten the eyes of the magistrates, that God's extreme plagues light not on this realm of England! TURN OR BURN.[40]

For understanding the conditions of the prisoners we are more indebted to Ridley's correspondence with the outside world than to Latimer. The older man clearly recognized that, quite apart from his sentence, he would not have long to live. He was rapidly declining in health, and, even in the best comfort of a friend's home, he would not be well. In addition to the constant pain of his injured back, and a complaint which

[39] Strype, *Cranmer*, III.21. Winkle and Wells, the Oxford bailiffs, petitioned Archbishop Parker in 1566 for the balance due to them—£43 10s. 2d. All they had received in Mary's reign was £20, though apparently some embezzlement had occurred, money to the tune of £40 for Cranmer having been misappropriated, as well as sums for Ridley and Latimer. Accounts were kept in detail. For instance, although the prisoners were separated, they were occasionally allowed a meal together. On 1st October their dinner consisted of:
Bread and ale, 2d.; oysters, 1d.; butter, 2d.; eggs, 2d.; ling, 8d.; a piece of fresh salmon, 10d.; wine, 3d.; cheese and pears, 2d.: 2s. 6d. in all. They always ended dinner and supper with cheese and pears, and took wine (but not costing more than 3d.). Prices of provisions are interesting, and tantalizing—a goose 1s. 2d., a pig 1s., two chickens 6d., six larks 3d., a breast of veal 11d., roast beef, 1s. But these prices were dear.
[40] Ridley's *Works*, p. 363.

seems to have been of an acute catarrhal nature, his eyesight had greatly failed, and his mental state gave cause for anxiety to his friends. Ridley speaks of him once as having been 'crazed', though happily now recovered.

Their friends did not desert them. Bernher, to his own peril, hovered about, when he could not actually be with his old master, doing whatever service he could, and Ridley's friends and relatives were able to send gifts of food, clothes, or money. In all this Bernher was a most astute messenger, for Latimer and Ridley were not allowed to keep their own trusted servants.[41] The prisoners shared what was given to them. Mrs Wilkinson, of Soper Lane, London, the friendly nurse of former days, was a benefactress continually, and Latimer's only letter addressed to an individual by name is to her, presumably in the summer of 1555, when she was staying at the manor of English, Oxfordshire.

If the gift of a pot of water shall not be in oblivion with God, how can God forget your manifold and bountiful gifts, when he shall say unto you, 'I was in prison, and you visited me?'

God grant us all to do and suffer while we be here as may be his will and pleasure! Amen.

Yours in Bocardo

Hugh Latimer.[42]

Latimer was now over seventy years of age, and the rigours of confinement were telling heavily against him. The poverty of his appearance was very possibly not due simply to his want, for Ridley was well groomed at his appearances before his judges, and at the end. Old men are often neglectful of such matters, and Latimer was never slow to dramatize situations: his threadbare gown could stand in as good evidence of other-worldliness and sincerity as Fisher's or More's hair shirts. His only study was the New Testament, and his time was given chiefly to prayer, 'wherein oftentimes so long he continued kneeling, that he was not able to rise without help'. Bernher, for he was the eyewitness, recorded that there were three matters to which he gave himself passionately:

First, that as God had appointed him to be a preacher of his word, so also he would give him grace to stand to his doctrine until his death, that he might give his heart-blood for the same.

[41] ibid., p. 390.   [42] *Remains*, p. 444.

Secondly, that God of his mercy would restore his gospel to England once again; and these words 'once again, once again' he did so inculcate and beat into the ears of the Lord God, as though he had seen God before him, and spoken to him face to face.

The third matter was, to pray for the preservation of the queen's majesty that now is; [Elizabeth], whom in his prayer he was wont accustomably to name, and even with tears desired God to make her a comfort to his comfortless realm of England.[43]

Two long letters written during his imprisonment show better than anything else the steadfastness and sincerity of Latimer's spirit. The first [44] is written '*To One in Prison for the Profession of the Gospel*', and cannot be dated with certainty as belonging to the earlier or later period of his own imprisonment.

The friend he is writing to has sought advice. Should he buy himself out of prison?

But I understand by your letters, that he which tempteth and envieth you this glory, ceaseth not to lay stumblingblocks before you, to bereave you of that crown of immortality which is now ready to be put on your head: persuading that you may for money be redeemed out of a glorious captivity into a servile liberty.

One feels this to be a different tone from that of the younger Latimer who, having just escaped by compromising himself before Warham's Court in 1531, then boldly counselled Bainham not to fear death or be anxious about his widow. Calm certainty, the fruit of absolute conviction, and maturity gained in the vicissitudes of his long life, are plainly to be seen. He is now completely reliant on the Word of God as he finds it in the New Testament.

The wise men of the world can find shifts to avoid the cross; and the unstable in faith can set themselves to rest with the world: but the simple servant of Christ doth look for no other but oppression in the world. And then is it their most glory, when they be under the cross of their master Christ; which he did bear, not only for our redemption, but also for an example to us, that we should follow his steps in suffering, that we might be partakers of his glorious resurrection. . . .

I cannot see how we might go about to deliver ourselves from the death we are called unto for money. . . .

He cites the Scriptures at length, beginning with the Gospels and working through to the Apocalypse.

[43] *Remains*, pp. xxiii ff.   [44] ibid., pp. 429 ff.

Be these undoubted scriptures? We may be sufficiently taught that that here is no means for us to fly, that are caught under the cross, to any such worldly means as the flesh can devise. Again, we were created to set forth God's glory all the days of our life; which we, as unthankful sinners, have forgotten to do, as we ought, all our days hitherto. And now God by affliction doth offer us good occasion to perform, one day of our life, our duty. And shall we go about to chop away this good occasion, which God offereth us for our honour and eternal rest. . . .

For as long as we are in the body, we are strangers to God, and far from our native country, which is in heaven, where our ever-lasting day is. We are now more near to God than ever we were, yea, we are at the gate of heaven; and we are a joyful spectacle because, in this our captivity, to God, to the angels, and to all his saints, who look that we should end our course with glory. We have found the precious stone of the gospel; for the which we ought to sell all that we have in the world. . . . The martyrs in the old time were racked, as St Paul testifieth, and would not be delivered, that they might have a better resurrection.

Let us follow them, and leave the pope's market, who buyeth and selleth the bodies and souls of men, to Balaam and his false prophets, 'who love the reward of iniquity'.

If any man perceive his faith (not) to abide the fire, let such an one with weeping buy his liberty, until he hath obtained more strength; lest the gospel by him sustain an offence of some shameful recantation. . . . Embrace Christ's cross, and Christ shall embrace you. The peace of God be with you for ever, and with all them that live in captivity with you in Christ!

The modern reader, with the perspective of four hundred years to give objectivity to such writing, discerns here not only a letter to a fellow-captive but a summary of the arguments of his faith addressed to Latimer by himself.

The second letter is more vivid in its imagery, characteristic of his preaching style, not intended for one reader but many. It exhorts all men and women of his persuasion to a readiness for death in persecution,[45] giving, in addition to the general argument for fidelity from the scriptures, and examples of patriarchs, saints and martyrs, some special warnings applicable to people caught in the peculiar circumstances of their own time.

For he that hath played the wise builder, and laid his foundation on a rock, will not be afraid that every drizzling rain or mist shall

[45] ibid., pp. 435–44.

hurt his buildings, but will stand, although a great tempest do come, and drops of rain as big as fir-fagots. But they that have builded upon a sand will be afraid, though they see but a cloud arise a little black, and no rain or wind doth once touch them; no, not so much as to lie one week in prison, to trust God with their lives which gave them. . . .

And forasmuch, my dearly beloved brethren and sisters in the Lord, as I am persuaded of you that you be in the number of the wise builders, which have made their foundation sure by faith upon the infallible word of God's truth, and will now bring forth the fruits to God's glory after your vocation, as occasion shall be offered, although the sun burn never so hot, nor the weather be never so foul: wherefore I cannot but signify unto every of you to go forward accordingly after your master Christ; not sticking at the foul way and stormy weather: which you are come unto, or are like to come.

He recalls the names of many in the scriptural roll of heroes, and the enormous number of Christians in the primitive Church who must have found the warnings of their Lord literally fulfilled. They need not therefore fear loneliness in their hard vocation.

But if none of these were, if you had no company to go with you, yet have you me your poorest brother and bondsman in the Lord, with many other, I trust in God. But if ye had none of the fathers, patriarchs, good kings, prophets, apostles, evangelists, martyrs, holy saints, and children of God, which in their journey to heaven found that you are like to find, (if you go forwards, as I trust you will,) yet you have your general captain and master, Christ Jesus, the dear darling and only-begotten and beloved Son of God, in whom was all the Father's joy and delectation; ye have him to go before you: no fairer was his way than ours, but much worse and fouler, towards his city of the heavenly Jerusalem. Let us remember what manner of way Christ found: begin at his birth, and go forth until ye come at his burial; and you shall find that every step of his journey was a thousand times worse than yours is. . . .

Now the devil and his ostlers and tapsters stand in every inn-door in city and country of this world, crying unto us, 'Come in and lodge here; for here is Christ, and there is Christ; therefore tarry with us until the storm be overpast.' Not that they would not have us wet to the skin, but that the time might be overpast, to our utter destruction.

Latimer drew particular attention to the temptation of what would later be called 'occasional conformity'. The way was made easy for Protestants to mingle with the vast crowd of those whose religion would always be that dictated by the government.

And let men beware that they play not wilily, beguiling themselves, as I fear me they do, that go to mass. And because they worship not, nor kneel not down, as others do, but sit still in their pews, therefore they think rather to do good to others than hurt. But, alas! if such men would look on their own consciences, there they shall see if they be very dissimulers; and seeking to deceive others, they deceive themselves. For by this means the magistrates think them to be of their sort. They think that at the elevation time all men's eyes are set on them, to mark how they do; they think that others, hearing of such men's going to mass, do see or inquire of their behaviour there; and thus they play wilily, beguiling themselves.

Towards the end of the letter he asks for their prayers, and gives what was to be his last written exhortation:

Read the tenth Psalm; and pray for me your poor brother and fellow-sufferer for God's sake: his name therefore be praised! And let us pray to God that he of his mercy will vouchsafe to make both you and me meet to suffer with good consciences for his name's sake. Die once we must; how and where, we know not. Happy are they whom God giveth to pay nature's debt (I mean to die) for his sake. Here is not our home; let us therefore accordingly consider things, having always before our eyes that heavenly Jerusalem, and the way thereto in persecution.

This letter was dated the 15th May 1555. Precisely five months later he would endure the flames and show all those qualities which he coveted for himself and for all who professed a similar faith.

Philip left England on 28th August 1555, and his inconsolable Queen was left to pursue the policy, from which she had never swerved, of eliminating heresy from her unhappy realm. It was well known that there could now be no heir born of her marriage, and Protestant hopes could fasten upon the future. The present was dark indeed.

At Oxford the three Bishops were called again before commissioners, appointed now under the legate, Cardinal Pole, as the direct representatives of the Pope. They would be condemned judicially in ratification of the sentences of heresy already passed against them by the earlier commission over which Weston had presided in the spring of the previous year.

Cranmer accordingly was brought to St Mary's on 12th September, and Ridley and Latimer at the end of the month. They all maintained their previous positions, but Cranmer, as a Metropolitan, was granted the legal fiction of being cited to appear at Rome within eighty days. Just how he was to get from Bocardo, where he was again committed, to the Pope's presence, was not apparently anybody's concern. The others could be dealt with—and were—more summarily.

Thus once more they came to the Divinity Schools. The Commission sat at eight o'clock in the morning on 30th September, in the persons of White, Bishop of Lincoln, Brooks of Gloucester, and Holyman of Bristol. The procedure was similar to that of the earlier trial, Ridley coming first, and Latimer second, but each alone.

There was a long hold-up of the proceedings when Ridley demonstrated his refusal to acknowledge the commissioners' and the Pope's authority. He was meticulous to bow his knee and remove his cap at mention of the Queen's name, and willing to pay to Pole personally the homage he would accord to any man of blood royal, but he differentiated between the cardinal's family and office.

As touching that you said, my lord, that you of your own persons desire ne cap ne knee, but only require the same, in consideration that you represent the cardinal's grace's person, I do you to wit, and thereupon make my protestation, that I did put on my cap at the naming of the cardinal's grace, neither for any contumacy that I bear towards your own persons, neither for any derogation of honour to the lord cardinal's grace: for I know him to be a man worthy of all humility, reverence, and honour, in that he came of the most regal blood, and in that he is a man endued with manifold graces of learning and virtue. And as touching these virtues and points, I, with all humility (therewith he put off his cap, and bowed his knee) and obeisance that I may, will reverence and honour his grace: but in that he is legate to the bishop of Rome (and therewith he put on his cap) whose usurped supremacy, and abused authority, I utterly refuse and renounce, I may in no wise give any obeisance or honour unto him, lest that my so doing and behaviour might be prejudicial to mine oath, and a derogation to the verity of God's word.[46]

After the Bishop of Lincoln had formally admonished him three times, he told the beadle to take off Ridley's cap, and

[46] Foxe, op. cit., VII.519.

'Master Ridley, bowing his head to the officer, gently permitted him to take away his cap'.

What sometimes seems to the modern reader artificial or melodramatic would possess full significance for the bystanders. Our unceremonious age has long forgotten the realities of loyalties implied in Tudor deportment. But such a preliminary was not likely to lead to the submission for which the Bishop now pleaded, and so the articles and the condemnation made by Weston's commission were brought forward, the prisoner being offered the choice of direct affirmation or denial. But here Ridley showed once more his magnificent ability, and threw his judges into some sort of embarrassment with reference to the Real Presence:

If you take *really* for *vere*, for spiritually, by grace and efficacy, then it is true that the natural body and blood of Christ is in the sacrament *vere et realiter*, indeed and really; but if you take these terms so grossly that you would conclude thereby a natural body having motion, to be contained under the forms of bread and wine, *vere et realiter*, then really is not the body and blood of Christ in the sacrament, no more than the Holy Ghost is in the element of water at our baptism.[47]

The notaries were puzzled whether to put this down as affirmatively or negatively, and this gave opportunity for further development by Ridley of his view, that in the Sacrament was a change, the bread after consecration not being a mere figure, 'but effectuously represented his body, that even as the mortal body was nourished by that visible bread, so is the internal soul fed with the heavenly food'. Such change could not be made by any man, 'but only that omnipotency of Christ's word'.

This examination was no more than a brief résumé of the matters at issue, and having promised that he should have ink and paper to write an answer to the first article, Ridley was handed over to the mayor until the next morning, when he was to appear at St Mary's.

Latimer was then brought in. He had been waiting during Ridley's examination, and at once protested for consideration of his age and weakness:

My lords, if I appear again, I pray you not to send for me until you

[47] ibid., p. 527.

be ready; for I am an old man, and it is great hurt to mine old age to tarry so long gazing upon the cold walls.

The Bishop of Lincoln replied, not unkindly, that it was the bailiff's fault, and it would not happen again. The figure before him was in pathetic contrast with what he had been. This old, faltering man, his head muffled with nightcaps and a kerchief, to protect him from the draughts that were so fearsome in unheated medieval buildings, was shabbily dressed in a worn gown. It was tied round with 'a penny leather girdle, at the which hanged by a long string of leather his Testament, and his spectacles without case, depending about his neck upon his breast'. The voice that had been as a trumpet sounding the assault had shrunk to this complaining, the stalwart son of a yeoman with the countryman's talk and robust manner had become 'a withered and crooked silly old man'.

The President then rehearsed how, in returning to full obedience to the Roman Pontiff he would be coming home, where he had once been content, and would be acknowledging error which had already been confessed by the whole realm.

But if you shall stubbornly persevere in your blindness; if you will not acknowledge your errors; if you, as you now stand alone, will be singular in your opinions; if by schism and heresy you will divide yourself from your church, then must we proceed to the second part of the commission, which we would be loth to do; that is, not to condemn you, for that we cannot do, (that the temporal sword of the realm, and not we, will do,) but to separate you from us, acknowledge you to be none of us; to renounce you as no member of the church; to declare that you are *filius perditionis*, a lost child; and, as you are a rotten member of the church, so to cut you off from the church, and so to commit you to the temporal judges, permitting them to proceed against you according to the tenor of their laws. . . . Let not vain-glory have the upper hand; humilitate yourself; captivate your understanding; subdue your reason; submit yourself to the determination of the church; do not force us to do all that we may do; let us rest in that part which we most heartily desire and I for my part (then the bishop put off his cap) again with all my heart exhort you.[48]

This is not lacking either in dignity or sincerity, and there was other pleading, appealing to Latimer to remember his past, but especially his 'soul's health'. It would have been a

[48] *Remains*, pp. 280–1.

notable victory if either Ridley or Latimer could have been brought to submission; but there was no likelihood of it. Words that once would have struck home, as they did when he was first accused before Warham, could not touch him now. He was allowed to sit and speak for a few minutes; but Latimer was still the kind of preacher whose words had barbs. He referred to a sermon on the authority of the priesthood, preached by Brookes, Bishop of Gloucester, on 12th November 1553 at Paul's Cross, 'a large authority, I assure you. What gelding of scripture is this! What clipping of God's coin!'

He had roused his audience, as he knew he would, for Brookes was there, and now stood up to acknowledge his book.

Was it yours, my lord? Indeed I know not your lordship, neither ever did I see you before, neither yet see you now through the brightness of the sun shining betwixt you and me.

The burst of laughter which greeted this strictly unnecessary sally, caused the old man to round upon them:

Why, my masters, this is no laughing matter. I answer upon life and death. *Væ vobis qui ridetis nunc, quoniam flebitis!*

Lincoln appealed for silence, but Gloucester could not resist the taunt, 'Master Latimer, hereby every man may see what learning you have.' This stirred Latimer to speech in his best style:

Lo, you look for learning at my hands, which have gone so long to the school of oblivion, making the bare walls my library; keeping me so long in prison, without book, or pen and ink; and now you let me loose to come and answer to articles. You deal with me as though two were appointed to fight for life and death, and over night the one, through friends and favour, is cherished, and hath good counsel given him how to encounter with his enemy: the other, for envy, or lack of friends, all the whole night is set in the stocks. In the morning, when they shall meet, the one is in strength and lusty, the other is stark of his limbs, and almost dead for feebleness. Think you, that to run through this man with a spear is not a goodly victory? [49]

The President brought back the proceedings to order by insisting they were not there to dispute but to require Latimer's answer, 'Yes' or 'No', to the articles which had already been

presented to Ridley, and were exactly similar in theological
content to those he had confronted in 1554.

Latimer made a similar protest to Ridley's, that whatever
he said, he wished the notaries to register that he did not acknowledge the Pope's authority in any matter; he was the subject of the Crown only. As to the Sacrament, 'every man, by
receiving bodily that bread and wine, spiritually receiveth the
body and blood of Christ, and is made partaker thereby of the
merits of Christ's passion. But I deny that the body and blood
of Christ is in such sort in the sacrament, as you would have it.'

He again affirmed that the change in the bread and wine
was such 'as no power but the omnipotency of God can make,
in that that which before was bread should now have the dignity
to exhibit Christ's body; and yet the bread is still bread, and
the wine still wine'. Like Ridley, he affirmed that after consecration the elements were not bare signs but effective to
represent Christ's body. He would have nothing to do with the
Mass as a propitiatory sacrifice.

The proceedings ended at one o'clock. Latimer pleaded
that he might be released from any further appearance, but
was told he must come tomorrow to St Mary's.

Town and gown were there in full force at eight o'clock on
that morning of 1st October. As at the beginning of their trial
before Weston and the earlier commissioners, so now before
the three Bishops representing the regained power of the Pope,
no touch of colour or ceremony was omitted. It was ecclesiastical procedure, but in an academic setting. In every generation St Mary's adds notably to its unique fame in English
religion. Did the shade of Wyclif come to see this further
consequence of what he had begun two hundred years before?

Ridley, accorded the full etiquette of his degree as doctor,
sat at a table covered with a silken carpet—a term usually
applied then to table-coverings. High up, on a throne decked
with silks, sat the commissioners, the Bishop of Lincoln presiding, and near the prisoner were chairs occupied by heads of
houses, other representatives of the University and local
magnates.

Once more Ridley contested, as in the schools, disputing with
the President as far as he was able, holding that St Augustine's
famous sentence 'totus mundus Christianus Romanae sub-
jectus est' applied only to Europe. Presently he was taunted

with having taken down the altars in his former diocese, to which he replied,

> Neither was the supper of the Lord at any time better ministered, more duly received, than in these latter days when all things were brought to the rites and usage of the primitive church.

Lincoln. A goodly receiving, I promise you, to set an oyster table instead of an altar, and to come from puddings at Westminster, to receive: and yet, when your table was constituted, you could never be content, in placing the same now east, now north, now one way, now another, until it pleased God of his goodness to place it clean out of the church.

Ridley. Your lordship's unreverent terms do not elevate the thing. Perhaps some men came more devoutly from puddings, than other men do now from other things.[50]

This kind of talk could have no effect except to quicken tempers. Ridley had prepared a written answer to the first article, but it was wrested from him, and excerpts only were read by Lincoln: he said it would be blasphemous to read the whole.

The Bishop of Gloucester then took up the tale and exhorted Ridley to forsake his heresy:

> If you would once empty your stomach, captivate your senses, subdue your reason, and together with us consider what a feeble ground of your religion you have, I do not doubt but you might easily be perduced to acknowledge one church with us, to confess one faith with us, and to believe one religion with us. For what a weak and feeble stay in religion is this I pray you? Latimer leaneth to Cranmer, Cranmer to Ridley, and Ridley to the singularity of his own wit: so that if you overthrew the singularity of Ridley's wit, then must needs the religion of Cranmer and Latimer fall also.[51]

The President wanted to conclude the trial, and himself pleaded once more with Ridley that he would turn. He showed more patience and sorrow than some of the audience, especially Dr Weston, who protested that Ridley had been promised he might speak forty words as to why he would not acknowledge the Pope's authority, but had spoken four hundred.

The Bishop of Lincoln, determined to fulfil his promise to the letter, said Ridley might speak forty words, and the doctors counted him out after that precise number. So he was sentenced, condemned as a heretic, to be degraded from all his

[50] Foxe, op. cit., VII.536.   [51] ibid., p. 538.

orders, handed over to the temporal powers and excommunicated. Ridley was led away as the mayor's prisoner, the cloth
was removed from the table and Latimer, who was not evidently
officially ranked as doctor, though often called by the title,
came in. Standing there, with his old felt hat under his arm,
he at once complained of his treatment. The crowd had jostled
him and hurt his sore back. Lincoln promised that he should
have better attention at his exit, and Latimer curtsied low.

He had not long to wait. The previous day's proceedings
were referred to:[52]

We have called you here before us, to hear whether you are content
to revoke your heretical assertions and submit yourself to the
determination of the church . . . or to know whether you persevere
still the man that you were, for the which we would be sorry.

The Bishop would have gone further, but Latimer, obviously
anxious to be finished with the matter, interrupted:

Your lordship often doth repeat the catholic church, as though I
should deny the same. No, my lord, I confess there is a catholic
church, to the determination of which I will stand; but not the
church which you call catholic, which sooner might be termed
diabolic. And whereas you join together the Romish and catholic
church, stay there, I pray you. For it is one thing to say Romish
church, and another thing to say catholic church.

Latimer would have compared himself to Cyprian, but the
Bishop brushed the comparison aside. Cyprian had suffered
persecution for Christ's sake, Latimer was on trial because of
'false assertions contrary to the word of God and the received
truth of the church'. He had been given respite for consideration—what was his answer? The Bishop read the first article.

The old warrior repeated his protestation that he did not
recognize the commissioners because they were there as the
Pope's representatives. With regard to the first article,[53]

I answer now, as I did yesterday, that in the sacrament the worthy
receiver receiveth the very body of Christ, and drinketh his blood
by the Spirit and grace: but, after that corporal being which the
Romish church prescribeth, Christ's body and blood is not in the
sacrament under the forms of bread and wine.

This was final enough. As to the second article, 'That in the
sacrament of the altar remaineth still the substance of bread

    [52] *Remains*, pp. 289-90.   [53] ibid., p. 292.

and wine', Latimer referred to the answers he had already given. But the Bishop of Lincoln pressed him for a definite statement on the third article regarding the Mass as an offering of sacrifice, and Latimer replied:

Christ made one oblation and sacrifice for the sins of the whole world, and that a perfect sacrifice; neither needeth there to be any other, neither can there be any other, propitiatory sacrifice.

After an exhortation to recant, similar to that spoken to Ridley, Latimer was condemned. He asked for permission to state why he had refused the Pope's authority, and on being denied opportunity, asked whether any appeal might be made against the findings of the court. To whom? 'To the next general council which shall be truly called in God's name.'

His long course was almost finished. The Bishop of Lincoln handed him over to the mayor's keeping, and ended the assembly; but he was as good as his word in allowing Latimer to wait until the crowd had dispersed.

There was little more than a fortnight before the last ordeal. On the 15th the Bishop of Gloucester, the Vice-Chancellor, and other University officials came to Irish's house, where Ridley was still lodged, to degrade him. He resisted as well as he could, but force was used to put on him the vestments whose significance he had denied, and to thrust into his hand the chalice, while Brookes went through the absurd ritual of degrading a man so obviously his superior in Christian achievement.

Nothing of that sort was deemed necessary for Latimer, who had long been, in his own phrase, 'a quondam'.

The contrast between Ridley and Latimer continued in the last scenes. On the night of the 15th Ridley prepared himself meticulously for his appearance at the stake, had his beard washed, and his legs, and made supper a party. His brother-in-law, who had continually been in Oxford since the imprisonment began, was there, and even Mrs Irish was moved to tears. 'Tomorrow I must be married', he said, as he invited all present to share the evening with him. His brother-in-law, Shipside, wanted to watch all night with him. 'No, no, that you shall not. For I mind (God willing) to go to bed, and to sleep as quietly tonight as ever I did in my life.' Of Latimer's preparation we know nothing.

They were to die outside the north wall in the ditch opposite Balliol, now Broad Street. Steps were taken to have sufficient men at hand to prevent anything in the nature of a rescue or even protest. The town officials brought out their prisoners, Ridley well dressed in black, his gown ornamented with fur, wearing a velvet tippet trimmed with fur, a velvet nightcap, and a cornered cap, his feet in slippers. The former Bishop of London was determined to go in as full dignity and style as he was allowed to 'his marriage'. Poor man, he little knew how the fire would be boggled and keep him in torment. The mayor was on one side, and an alderman on the other. Latimer was in his poor Bristol frieze, with a big buttoned cap and kerchief, the only new garment being a shroud which was draped over him. Bocardo stood where modern traffic is at its noisiest and most congested near the junction of Cornmarket and the Broad. The little procession passed by, but there was no sight of Cranmer. He was being interviewed by the friar, De Soto. A backward glance by Ridley showed old Latimer hobbling along. 'Oh, be ye there?' 'Yea, have after as fast as I can follow.'

Latimer was in good fettle, undismayed by the prospect of the fire. They embraced each other—they had been long separated, and now were to be joined indissolubly in death and victory. They knelt down by the stake, Ridley kissing it, and were able to speak together for a little time. The usual procedure was followed: it was familiar to the condemned men, for Latimer had preached on such an occasion as Smith, his opponent at Weston's examination, was to do now. The sun was shining, and some folk moved into the shade. Smith's sermon had one merit—it lasted only fifteen minutes, a description of their dangerous heresy; but even now they might return to Mother Church and be saved. It was not likely that such a plea from the lips of a man who had changed sides twice already would sway these two. They kneeled down to Lord Williams [54] of Thame, the Vice-Chancellor, and other members of the commission, and asked for permission to speak. This was refused unless they would recant. 'Well', said Ridley, 'so long as the breath is in my body, I will never deny my lord Christ, and his known truth: God's will be done in me.'

They were told to get ready. Ridley handed his gown and

[54] Who, as Sir John Williams, had brought them to Oxford.

tippet to his brother-in-law and gave little keepsakes to gentlemen with Lord Williams, napkins, nutmegs, ginger, his dial, and a new groat to Sir Henry Lea. Onlookers were greatly moved. This kind of thing did not commend itself to Englishmen: it was no common hanging of a desperado. Latimer had nothing to give. His keeper took off his hose and garments, and now in his shroud he surprised men as not being so shrunken as they supposed. Ridley wore a truss, but being advised that it would increase his pain, and that it might serve some poor man, he unlaced it. The attendant blacksmith chained them together. 'Good fellow', Ridley said to him, 'knock it in hard, for the flesh will have his course.'

Shipside had provided bags of gunpowder, and these were tied around their necks in the hope that death would be more speedy and merciful. And so, after Ridley had asked Lord Williams to use his influence to see that certain leases and bequests he had made when Bishop of London should be carried out, a lighted faggot was put to the pyre.

'Be of good comfort, master Ridley, and play the man. We shall this day light such a candle, by God's grace, in England, as I trust shall never be put out.'

The words of Latimer's greatest exhortation and prophesy were spoken. Side by side they committed themselves to God's keeping. The flame flared up about Latimer, who was crying, 'O Father of heaven, receive my soul.' He stood in a wave of fire, seeming to bathe himself in it; his end was swift and, for such a death, comparatively painless.

For Ridley it was long-drawn-out torture. The fire was burning underneath. His well-meaning brother-in-law put on more faggots as he leaped up and down in anguish. This only served to slow down the fire, until to his cry, 'Let the fire come unto me, I cannot burn', someone with a bill moved the faggots. The flame shot up; he turned into it; the gunpowder exploded, and he fell at Latimer's feet.

CHAPTER TEN

Conclusion

IMPRISONMENTS and martyrdoms, the noblest and the least, are reflected in matter-of-fact terms belonging to daily work and expense. One supposes that even the sacred events on Calvary, apart from which Latimer would never have come to the Town Ditch in Oxford, were once itemized in duty rosters and a centurion's report. This usually misses our attention.

Among the last details of the disbursements [1] of Winkle and Wells, the Oxford bailiffs, appears this melancholy list:

For three loads of wood fagots to burn Ridley and Latimer	12. 0.
Item, one load of furs fagots	3. 4.
For the carriage of these four loads	2. 0.
Item, a post	1. 4.
Item, two chains	3. 4.
Item, two staples	0. 6.
Item, four labourers	2. 8.

It is strange to think that the man these officers had to petition for tardy payments of their bill (25s. 2d.) eleven years after the burning, was Archbishop Matthew Parker, chief author of the Elizabethan Settlement that would have suited Latimer so well. The prayer he had prayed so passionately in the Tower and at Oxford, beating his breast and imploring that the Gospel might be restored to England 'once again, once again', had been answered. Anne Boleyn's daughter—and Henry's—was safe on the throne and in her people's hearts.

Today the Reformation in England is often tacitly regretted as an unfortunate incident which had as its chief result the splitting of the Church in our midst into irreconcilable sects. Latimer and his fellow martyrs are neglected or disparaged by silence. We have been for so long a time a people enriched by free access to the English Bible, and under no fear of priestly domination, that we are prone to forget how terrible might

Strype, *Cranmer*, III.21.

have been our plight had the Marian ideals been realized. We are continually in debt to the bravery and faith of the men who were willing to be sacrificed, encouraged as they were by the example of Luther and others on the Continent. They would have been the first to admit they were not faultless. Latimer's sense of humour would probably have got the better of him, if he had read many of the pages in Foxe's *Acts and Monuments*. A hagiography, in which he and his friends claimed men's memories (though not their prayers) as true saints might have earned his bitterest scorn—the setting up of a new veneration of mortal men and sinners in place of images and relics. But in the New Testament sense of the word, he was a saint— a man glad to be reckoned among the members and ministers of 'Christ's Church militant here in earth'. It is in this way we regard Latimer as a man who maintained his ministry with increasing consistency.

There were many matters on which he only came to conclusions slowly—most notably his arrival, thanks to Cranmer, at a sure conviction regarding the true nature of the Sacrament. He was not latterly, if he ever was, an astute or deeply learned theologian; but he was a good scholar, and in his earlier manhood an effective member of his University. In later life, in the practical work of the ministry, he was like many sound pastors and preachers, his heart was often convinced before his mind had completely articulated his views. He had begun as a passionate defender of the old order; its defence was the aim of his B.D. oration. He ended with a calm certainty of the personal relationship between himself and his Saviour which put him far beyond the possibility of being swung back to a profession of loyalty to Rome. The change, which came into his life through Bilney's insistent quest of him, stands true to the classic type of evangelical conversion. If any man, humanly speaking, ever owes his soul to another, Latimer owed his to little Bilney; but speedily the convert grew greater than the master. Together they perceived a contrast between what they found in the pages of the New Testament, and what they saw around them as the common practice and life of the Church.

The intensity and reality of that personal religion which he gained awakened Latimer to clear sight of the abuses which imprisoned his neighbours in a system at variance with what he had discovered in the Bible and the Early Church. It was

the Bible that spoke to him first of all as God's Word; and therefore his life must be given to proclamation of what could there
be discerned to help other men. He was no sectary. He
believed in a holy, catholic, and apostolic church; but the
Church he saw most plainly about him was by no means holy,
and for most of its humble people its rites were meaningless in
a foreign tongue. If England was to be saved, her people must
worship God in the speech they understood: about that single
theme all his various activities were joined. The need was
therefore for preachers. How else could men hear, or, hearing,
understand? The experience as parish priest at West Kington,
and later as Bishop of Worcester, confirmed him in this belief,
all the more so as he discerned the lamentable ignorance of
the people of the countryside, overlaid with gross superstition.
If it is true that the chief glory of his life's work was the series
of sermons preached before Edward the Sixth and his court,
we should be careful not to forget that these are but a few of
hundreds of sermons he preached to men who would remember
and discuss what they had heard so impressively. In addition,
there was the intimate advice given in pastoral conversation.
By every means he sought to proclaim personal and national
religion of biblical kind, and, as he would contend, of the first
disciples of Christ. Statues of saints might be defended as
'laymen's books', but the Church had too long been content
with a low valuation of the ordinary man's place and responsibility. He saw the spiritual need that could only be satisfied
by the Book itself expounded in such a context of English
liturgy as Cranmer had provided in the Prayer Book.

   Latimer founded no school. He left no declared disciples,
though hosts of men cherished his memory and phrases. His
influence was direct, challenging, daring, to the men of his
own generation, which is a preacher's true province. No
English preacher has ever spoken more boldly than he, more
unperturbed in the presence of men great in station or powerful
in influence. If he was the greatest of our Reformation
preachers in England, it was because he knew how to reach
home to the minds and consciences of men in terse, picturesque
speech related to themes of immediate interest in home, market,
or court, but of eternal consequence. He brought the Gospel
as God's message to men whose days were fraught with peril
from hard circumstance and their own sin. Long before

Richard Baxter's time, he anticipated his saying and 'preached as dying man to dying men'. The enforced silence of the last few years of Henry the Eighth's reign sufficed to guarantee that he would not waver again, if he were given another chance to witness to his faith. That witness he bore in the toil of his preaching during Edward the Sixth's reign, and in his imprisonment and death.

Like every true preacher, Latimer was continually at his task. When the usual hour of rising was four or five o'clock he began his daily work at two. His energy, discipline, and economy would have satisfied Wesley's standards—and there are none more exacting. No slovenly courtier could ever taunt him as an idle cleric or as one who served for gold. He enjoyed friendship with men and women, but there was no whisper against him in matters of morality. What he most detested was sloth in the lives of men who were professedly the ministers of Christ's Church.

Religion and doctrine were to be wrought into life. He was no overturner of the customary Tudor social order; indeed, he was well content with it. The King and the nobility were of the essence of national stability; but he emphasized the precept of Scripture which reminds us that most is required from those who have received most. One of his marked disappointments was that the free passage of the Scriptures into men's homes did not immediately bring greater charity, concern for the poor and for the care of education. Perhaps, like many other ardent reformers, he expected the same loyalty to spiritual perception as he demanded from himself. The later days of Henry, and the whole reign of his son, gave opportunity to selfishness and material aggrandizement on an unparalleled scale. If it should be said that this was an argument for the retention of the old ecclesiastical order, the answer can be stated very shortly. So far as the Church was concerned all the errors and abuses were naked to the eye and calling for attention. No effective attention was given. For one Dean Colet or John Fisher, a hundred little Wolseys could be found, men ready to turn the most sacred office that came their way into a means for selfish material advancement.

Latimer's plea, then, was for religion freed from superstition, where the means of grace would be accessible 'without money and without price'. No willing destroyer of Church order, he would yet become increasingly sure that there is an effective 'priesthood of all believers'. Above all, religion must be expressed in the tongue of the people by whom it must be practised. If households in farm or city were to reflect the beauty of holiness, that holiness must be made apparent to them in their own idiom, sustained by constant prayer. This would require diligent pastors in every parish, men of the people's homes, capable of teaching them from God's Word, and themselves living lives that would clearly proclaim their doctrine.

This was the candle of which he spoke; and its light was already in himself.

Select Bibliography

ALLEN, P. S., *The Age of Erasmus* (Oxford, 1914).

BASKERVILLE, G., *English Monks and the Suppression of the Monasteries* (Cape, 1937).

BECON, *Works* (Parker Society).

BINDOFF, S. T., *Tudor England* (Penguin Books, 1950).

BINNS, L. E., *The Reformation in England* (Duckworth, 1937).

BRADFORD, J., *Writings* (P.S., 1948).

BRIGHTMAN, F. E., *The English Rite*, 2 vols. (Rivingtons, 1905).

BURCKHARDT, J., *The Civilisation of the Renaissance in Italy* (Phaidon Press, ed. 1944).

BURNET, G., *History of the Reformation*, 7 vols., ed. Pocock (Oxford, 1865).

Cambridge Modern History.

CAMDEN SOCIETY, *Narratives of the Reformation* (Nichols); *Suppression of the Monasteries* (Wright); *Wriothesley's Chronicles.*

CARLYLE, R. M. and A. J., *Latimer* (Methuen, 1899).

Catholic Encyclopaedia.

CHAMBERS, R. W., *Thomas More* (Cape, 1935).

CLARKE, W. K. L. (ed.), *Liturgy and Worship* (S.P.C.K., 1932).

COMMONS, HOUSE OF, *Journal.*

COULTON, C. G., *Five Centuries of Religion*, 3 vols. (C.U.P., 1923–36); *Ten Medieval Studies* (C.U.P., 1930); *Medieval Panorama* (C.U.P., 1938).

CRANMER, T., *Works; On the Lord's Supper* (P.S., 1844); *Remains; Letters &c.* (P.S., 1846).

DEANESLY, M., *The Lollard Bible* (C.U.P., 1920).

DEMAUS, R., *Hugh Latimer* (R.T.S., 1869, 1881).

Dictionary of National Biography.

DIXON, R. W., *History of the English Church from the Abolition of the Roman Jurisdiction*, 6 vols. (Clarendon Press, 1895–1902).

FISHER, J., *English Works* (E.E.T.S.).

FOXE, J., *Acts and Monuments*, 8 vols., ed. J. Pratt (R.T.S., 1877).

FROUDE, J. A., *History of England*, 'Henry VIII', 'Edward VI', 'Mary Tudor' (Longmans, & Everyman); *Short Studies* (Longmans, & Everyman); *Life and Letters of Erasmus* (Longmans).

FULLER, T., *History of Cambridge*, 1840 ed.

GAIRDNER, Jas., *Lollardy and the Reformation in England*, 4 vols. (Macmillan, 1908–13); *History of the English Church in the Sixteenth Century* (Macmillan, 1904).

GEE and HARDY, *Documents Illustrative of English Church History* (Macmillan).

GREENSLADE, S. L., *The Works of Wm. Tyndale* (Blackie, 1938).

Homilies, Book of

HOSKYNS, E., *Cambridge Sermons* (S.P.C.K., 1938).

HUTCHINSON, F. E., *Cranmer and the English Reformation* (E.U.P., 1951).

KIDD, B. J., *Documents of the Continental Reformation* (Clarendon Press).

LATIMER, Hugh, *Sermons* (P.S., 1844); *Remains* (P.S., 1845).

LEACH, A. F., *The Schools of Medieval England* (Methuen, 1916).

LEVER, Thos., *Sermons*.

LINDSAY, T. M., *History of the Reformation*, 2 vols. (Clark, 1907).

MORE, Sir Thomas, *English Works*.

MOZLEY, J. F., *William Tyndale* (S.P.C.K., 1937).

MULLINGER, J. B., *History of the University of Cambridge*.

Original Letters relating to the English Reformation, 1537–1558. 2 vols. (P.S., 1846–7).

PARKER SOCIETY, *Works of the English Reformers*.

PARKER, T. M., *The English Reformation to 1558* (O.U.P., 1950).

POLLARD, A. F., *Henry VIII* (Longmans, 1934 ed.); *Wolsey* (Longmans, 1929); *Cranmer* (Putnams, 1904); *C.M.H.*; *History of England from Accession of Edward VI to the Death of Elizabeth*, 2 vols. (Longmans, 1906).

POWICKE, F. M., *The Reformation in England* (O.U.P., 1941).

PRIVY COUNCIL, THE, *Acts of the Privy Council*.

PROCTOR, F., and W. H. FRERE, *History of the Book of Common Prayer* (Macmillan, 1914 ed.).

RASHDALL, H. (ed.) POWICKE and EMDEN, *Universities of Europe in the Middle Ages* (O.U.P., 1936).

RIDLEY, N., *Works* (P.S., 1843).

RUPP, E. G., *English Protestant Tradition* (C.U.P., 1947).

RYMER'S *Foedera*.

SCHWENK, W., *Reginald Pole* (Longmans, 1950).

SEEBOHM, F., *The Oxford Reformers* (Longmans, 1896, & Everyman).

SMITH, H. M., *Pre-Reformation England* (Macmillan, 1938); *Henry VIII and the Reformation* (Macmillan, 1948).

SMYTH, C. H., *Cranmer and the Reformation* (C.U.P., 1926).

SORLEY, J. C., *Kings' Daughters* (C.U.P., 1937).

State Papers: Letters and Papers, Foreign and Domestic, of the Reign of Henry VIII (L. & P.); Calendar of State Papers, Edward VI and Mary (C.S.P.); *Calendar of Venetian State Papers*.

STENTON, F. M., *Anglo-Saxon England* (O.U.P., 1943).

STOW'S *Chronicles and Annals*.

STRYPE, J., *Ecclesiastical Memorials*, 6 vols. (Clarendon Press, 1822); *Memorials of Archbishop Cranmer*, 4 vols. (Oxford, 1854).

TREVELYAN, G. M., *English Social History* (Longmans, 1944); *History of England* (Longmans, 1926); *England in the Age of Wycliffe* (Longmans, ed. 1929).

TYNDALE, W., *Works* (P.S.).

VENN, J. A., *Alumni Cantabrigienses*.

Victoria County History, Worcestershire (*V.C.H.*).

WHITNEY, J. P., *History of the Reformation* (1940 ed.).

WILKINS' *Concilia*.

WOOD, A. à, *Athenae Oxonienses*.

WORCESTERSHIRE HIST. SOCIETY, *Journal of Prior More*.

WORDSWORTH, C., *Ecclesiastical Biography* (Rivingtons, 1853 ed.).

I

INDEX

Made in the USA
Las Vegas, NV
10 December 2020

12568637R00148